THE GENTRY OF
SOUTH-WEST WALES,

1540-1640

THE GENTRY OF SOUTH-WEST WALES,

1540-1640

by

HOWELL A. LLOYD

UNIVERSITY OF WALES PRESS

CARDIFF

1968

TO

MY MOTHER AND FATHER

Contents

Preface

This book has several aims. It relates to the "debate over the gentry" that has exercised many English historians, and still continues. It examines a significant section of Welsh society during a particularly important and difficult period in the country's history. It attempts a critical analysis of evidence which, though often suspect and disappointing, must form the basis of any such examination, once essayed. Above all, it seeks to discover the attitude of mind during that period of the men who constitute its subject.

I have sought to treat this subject as comprehensively as possible. In doing so I have from time to time ventured opinions upon matters with which I feel poorly equipped to deal. To trespass in the fields of specialists is undoubtedly indiscreet, perhaps rash. But it is my belief that in social portraiture to avoid any aspect, within the limits of practicability and of evidence, is to court distortion. Sadly, awareness of what ought to be done is no guarantee of its successful accomplishment.

In writing this book I have incurred many obligations. Professor David Williams, whose beneficence towards me as an undergraduate I am glad to record, first suggested the subject to me. Professor Hugh Trevor-Roper supervised my researches at Oxford and has shown me many kindnesses. Professor H. J. Habakkuk and Professor Glanmor Williams gave me the benefit of their comments. Professor J. P. Kenyon encouraged me to publish my work.

The following were good enough to send me useful replies to queries on matters of law: Professor T. G. Barnes, Dr. Eric Ives, Professor W. J. Jones, Professor A. F. R. Kiralfy, Dr. T. Ellis Lewis and Mr. A. W. B. Simpson. Mr. D. J. Bowen saved me from much folly in contending with sixteenth-century Welsh poetry. Mr. Elwyn Evans gave me assistance in translating passages therefrom. Dr. Joan Thirsk allowed me to see proofs of *The Agrarian History of England and Wales*, vol. iv (1500-1640), published after my own work had reached the printers' hands; my final typescript being already complete, I was unable to take advantage of her kindness as I should have liked.

I am very grateful to the following for their generosity in making available to me the pioneer work contained in their unpublished theses: Dr. J. T. Cliffe, Mr. B. E. Howells, Miss Carys E. Hughes,

Mr. E. G. Jones, Miss M. E. Jones, Mr. T. I. J. Jones, Miss Helen Miller and Dr. G. Dyfnallt Owen. I would also pay tribute to those whose care and expertise in compiling Calendars, of documents in the National Library of Wales and especially of lawsuits in the courts of Exchequer and Star Chamber, greatly eased my path.

It gives me pleasure to express my thanks to my colleague, Dr. Gordon Connell-Smith, who read my manuscript and offered many valuable suggestions for its improvement. My colleague, Dr. K. R. Andrews, read my book in proof and made several useful observations. I would also thank the officers of the University of Wales Press Board, and its reader, for their helpfulness.

Whatever qualities this book may possess it owes in great measure to these. Whatever defects it retains are entirely my own responsibility.

The dedication marks a debt of love and duty that I can neither adequately record nor ever repay. My wife, Gaynor, has typed no manuscript, read no proofs and prepared no index; rather, she has incomparably created for me the circumstances in which this book could be written—and given me so much more.

University of Hull,   H. A. Ll.
Oak-apple Day, 1967.

Abbreviations

A.P.C.	*Acts of the Privy Council*, 1542-1630, 45 vols., London, 1890-1960.
Add. MSS.	British Museum: Additional Manuscripts.
Agr. Hist. Rev.	*The Agricultural History Review*, published by the British Agricultural History Society, London, 1953-.
Arch. Camb.	*Archaeologia Cambrensis*, published by the Cambrian Association, London, 1846-.
B.M.	The British Museum.
B.B.C.S.	*The Bulletin of the Board of Celtic Studies*, published by the University of Wales, Cardiff, 1921-.
Cal. Comm. Comp.	*Calendar of the Proceedings of the Committee for Compounding, etc.*, 1643-1659, 4 vols., London, 1890-1892.
C.P.R.	*Calendar of Patent Rolls*, 1547-1566, 12 vols., London, 1924-1960.
Cal. Portland MSS.	Historical Manuscripts Commission: *The Manuscripts of His Grace the Duke of Portland, preserved at Welbeck Abbey*, 10 vols., London, 1891-1931.
Cal. Salis. MSS.	Historical Manuscripts Commission: *The Manuscripts of the Marquis of Salisbury, preserved at Hatfield House*, 18 vols., London, 1883-1932.
C.S.P. Dom.	*Calendar of State Papers (Domestic Series)*, 1547-1649, 34 vols., London, 1856-1897.
C.R.O.	Carmarthen Record Office (Cawdor Collection and Museum Collection).
Ceredigion	*The Transactions of the Cardiganshire Antiquarian Society*, 1950-.
C 1.	Public Record Office: Early Chancery Proceedings.
C 3	*Ibid.*: Chancery Proceedings, Series II.
C 66	*Ibid.*: Chancery Enrolments; Patent Rolls.
C 142	*Ibid.*: Chancery Inquisitions; Inquisitions *Post Mortem*, Series II.
C.J.	*Journals of the House of Commons*, vol. i (1547-1628), London, 1803.
D'Ewes	D'Ewes, Sir Simonds, *The Journals of all the Parliaments during the Reign of Queen Elizabeth*, London, 1682.
D.N.B.	*The Dictionary of National Biography*, 22 vols., London, 1908-1909.
D.L. 42.	Public Record Office: Duchy of Lancaster; Administrative, Financial, *etc.*—Miscellaneous Books.

Econ. H.R.	*The Economic History Review*, published by the Economic History Society, London, 1927-.
Egerton	British Museum: Egerton Manuscripts.
E.H.R.	*The English Historical Review*, London, 1886-.
E 101.	Public Record Office: Exchequer; The King's Remembrancer—Various Accounts.
E 112	*Ibid.*—Bills, Answers, *etc.*
E 113.	*Ibid.*—Bills and Answers against Defaulting Accountants.
E 123.	*Ibid.*—Entry Books of Decrees and Orders, Series I.
E 124.	*Ibid.*, Series II.
E 134.	*Ibid.*—Depositions taken by Commission.
E 150.	*Ibid.*—Inquisitions *Post Mortem*, Series II.
E 159.	*Ibid.*—Memoranda Rolls.
E 178.	*Ibid.*—Special Commissions of Inquiry.
E 179.	*Ibid.*—Subsidy Rolls, *etc.*
E 199.	*Ibid.*—Sheriffs' Accounts, *etc.*
E 210.	*Ibid.*—Ancient Deeds (Series D).
E 315.	*Ibid.*; The Augmentations Office—Miscellaneous Books.
E 376	*Ibid.*; Lord Treasurer's Remembrancer, Pipe Office—Recusant Rolls, Chancellor's Series (Controller of the Pipe).
E 377.	*Ibid.*, Pipe Office Series (Clerk of the Pipe).
Harleian	British Museum: Harley Manuscripts.
H.M.C.	The Historical Manuscripts Commission.
L.R. 2.	Public Record Office: Exchequer; Land Revenue—Miscellaneous Books.
Lambeth	Lambeth Palace Library: MS. 905 (Survey of the Rectory or Parsonage of Carew, 1647); MS. 915 (Inquisition of Church Lands, Impropriations, Preaching, *etc.*, in Pembrokeshire, 1650).
Lansdowne	British Museum: Lansdowne Manuscripts.
L.P.H. VIII.	*Letters and Papers (Foreign and Domestic) of Henry VIII*, vols. viii-xxi (1535-1546), London, 1885-1932.
L.J.	*Journals of the House of Lords*, vol. iv (1628-1642), n.d.
N.L.W.	The National Library of Wales.
P.C.C.	Somerset House: Wills proved in the Prerogative Court of Canterbury.
P.R.O.	The Public Record Office.
S.C. 11.	Public Record Office: Special Collections; Rentals and Surveys—General Series (Rolls).
S.C. 12.	*Ibid.* (Portfolios).

St. Ch. 2.	*Ibid.:* Star Chamber Proceedings (Henry VIII).
St. Ch. 5.	*Ibid.* (Elizabeth).
St. Ch. 6.	*Ibid.,* Supplementary.
St. Ch. 8.	*Ibid.* (James 1).
S.P. 12.	*Ibid.:* State Papers (Elizabeth).
S.P. 14.	*Ibid.* (James I).
S.P. 16.	*Ibid.* (Charles I).
Stowe	British Museum: Stowe Manuscripts.
Trans. Carms. Antiq. Soc.	The *Transactions of the Carmarthenshire Antiquarian Society and Field Club,* 1905-.
T.H.C.S.	The *Transactions of the Honourable Society of Cymmrodorion,* 1893-.
T.R.H.S.	The *Transactions of the Royal Historical Society,* 1872-.
V.C.H.	The *Victoria History of the Counties of England.*
Wales 7.	National Library of Wales: Great Sessions Records; Calendar Rolls.
Wales 18.	*Ibid.;* Plea Rolls (County Cardigan).
Wales 19.	*Ibid.* (County Carmarthen).
Wales 25.	*Ibid.* (County Pembroke).
Wales 28.	*Ibid.;* Miscellanea (County Pembroke).
Wards 5.	Public Record Office: The Court of Wards and Liveries; Valuation Documents—Feodaries' Surveys.
Wards 7.	*Ibid.;* Inquisitions *Post Mortem.*
Wards 9.	*Ibid.;* Miscellaneous Books.
Welsh MSS.	Historical Manuscripts Commission: *Report on Manuscripts in the Welsh Language,* 2 vols., London, 1898-1902.

Spelling, punctuation and capitalisation have been modernised in all quotations, but not in the titles of books. Dates are Old Style, with the year beginning on 1 January.

Introduction

1. PERIOD

In the view of a perceptive contemporary observer, the century between the Dissolution of the Monasteries and the outbreak of the Civil War produced in England a social re-distribution of the main sources of economic power, with significant political effects. [1] In the last quarter-century, several distinguished modern historians have arrived at conflicting interpretations of these developments, in a debate of which "it is safe to say that no historical controversy in the last fifty years has attracted so much attention". [2] During this debate the delimiting dates "1540-1640" have come, with slight variations, to be regarded as standard. For Wales they are peculiarly relevant. The years 1536 and 1543 saw the passing of the Acts of Union with England and the emancipation of Welshmen into "all and singular freedoms, liberties, rights, privileges and laws within this realm and other the King's dominions as other the King's subjects naturally born within the same have, enjoy and inherit". [3] However far adherents to a later political attitude may bemoan this event, it has an obvious significance as a historical watershed. But one reservation must be made. Political decisions taken at the centre of government do not immediately transform society. These dates are convenient, in some respects illuminating, but they are not exclusive. To consider a section of society prior to the Civil War without some consideration of the attitudes of its representatives in the war itself would be as unrewarding as to discourse upon that community during the preceding century without reference to that society's earlier form.

---

(1) "Coraunus [*i.e.*, Henry VIII] . . . dissolving the abbeys, brought, with the declining state of the nobility, so vast a prey to the industry of the people, that the balance of the commonwealth was too apparently in the popular party to be unseen by the wise council of Queen Parthenia [*i.e.*, Elizabeth], who, converting her reign through the perpetual love-tricks that passed between her and her people into a kind of romance, wholly neglected the nobility. And by these degrees came the house of commons to raise that head, which since has been so high and formidable to their princes that they have looked pale upon those assemblies" (James Harrington, *The Commonwealth of Oceana*, p.60).

(2) L. Stone, *Social Change and Revolution in England, 1540-1640*, p.xiv. For the leading contributions to the debate, *vide infra*, Bibliography.

(3) 27 Henry VIII, c.26: "An Act for Law and Justice to be ministered in Wales in like form as it is in this Realm".

2. REGION

Geographically, the three shires of Carmarthen, Cardigan and Pembroke present three major types of relief. There is the hill country, with summits rising to between one and two thousand feet, reaching their highest elevation in north Cardiganshire. Upland conditions of climate and vegetation obtain in the higher levels of the moorland plateaux of Prescelly in Pembrokeshire and in north Carmarthenshire, which in turn form extensive tracts, in altitude over six hundred feet. Thirdly, there are the lowlands, best developed in the broad alluvial plain of the Vale of Towy, in the south Pembrokeshire coastal plain, and, to a lesser degree, in the lower vale of Teifi in Cardiganshire.

The region has, in some measure, a tradition of political and administrative homogeneity. Camden cited Ptolemy, Gildas and Nennius to show that these three shires covered the area that was once the kingdom of the Demetae.[1] Ceredigion, Ystrad Tywi and the old kingdom of Dyfed formed, with Brycheiniog, the medieval kingdom of Deheubarth. Deheubarth, "in the stricter sense",[2] was both the scene of the resistance of the sons of Gruffydd ap Rhys ap Tewdwr to the Normans in the twelfth century, and the basis of the authority in south Wales of one of their number, the Lord Rhys, in his years of friendlier relationship with Henry II. The extension of foreign control in the thirteenth century, and the developing administrative and judicial arrangements of Henry III and Edward I, suggest some further consolidation within these southern confines of the Principality. By the Act of Union the three shires were grouped together to form one of the circuits of the courts of Great Sessions.

But more significant than this appearance of unity is the influence of historical forces making for disharmony and disintegration within the region. If modern Cardiganshire retains the borders of ancient Ceredigion, it "alone among Welsh shires . . . can trace back its history to the primitive states of Wales".[3] The Dyfed of the ninth century included, in addition to modern Pembrokeshire, the cantrefs of Emlyn and Cantref Gwarthaf, most of which are now in Carmarthenshire. From the end of the eleventh century, the extension, from the base at Pembroke, of Norman forms of organisation on

(1) William Camden, *Britannia*, vol. ii, p.504.
(2) J. E. Lloyd, *A History of Wales from the earliest times to the Edwardian conquest*, vol. ii, p.501.
(3) T. F. Tout, "The Welsh Shires", *Collected Papers*, vol. ii, p.13.

shire lines over the cantrefs of Rhos, Penfro and Daugleddau, together with the Flemish settlement of *circa* 1108, endowed this locality with a distinct character which it still, in certain particulars, retains.[1] Elsewhere in the region, the spread of foreign institutions during the reigns of the first two Henrys, though seemingly interrupted by the ascendancy of Rhys ap Gruffydd ap Rhys, represented a persistent if uneven encroachment upon native forms, never offset by a revival comparable with that of Gwynedd and dispiriting in its political effects. In the early thirteenth century, the divisions among the leaders of Deheubarth provided John with rare successes in Wales; the rallying of the princes of all Wales[2] to Llywelyn ap Gruffydd in 1258 was marred by the treachery of Maredudd ap Rhys of Dryslwyn; and Llywelyn in his later years was better rewarded in the north and east than in this region with its petty leaders, its uncertain loyalties and its mongrel character.

For well before the culmination of the conquest of Wales the south-west revealed an organisation and a composition, administrative, social and economic, in notable contrast to the "unified Celtic state"[3] evolved by the princes of Gwynedd. Apart from the county palatine of Pembroke, itself much smaller than the modern county,[4] the royal lands had developed at least from 1241 as the counties of Carmarthen and Cardigan, each composed of several stewardships associated with a county nucleus of a single commote.[5] This compromise between English administrative forms and a basic Welsh commote structure is reflected both in judicial arrangements and in the social and economic spheres, with the division within lordships between lowland Englishry and upland Welshry, the former geared to manorial forms grounded upon individual tenure, the latter to the Welsh tribal structure founded on collective rights. Whereas the Welsh structure, already in process of modification, disintegrated further under both internal and external pressures in the post-conquest period, its surviving features, coupled with the legal and administrative complexity, were potent enough to achieve violent expression in the fifteenth century in the Glyndwr revolt: an out-

---

(1) Sir Frederick Rees has written of "that sense of the line between . . . the Englishry and the Welshry which outsiders seem never quite able to acquire" (*Studies in Welsh History*, p.83).
(2) Except, of course, Gruffydd ap Gwenwynwyn of Upper Powys.
(3) William Rees, *South Wales and the March*, p.31.
(4) Tout, *op cit.*, p.6.
(5) J. Goronwy Edwards, "The Early History of the Counties of Carmarthen and Cardigan", *E.H.R.*, vol. xxxi (1916), pp.90-98.

burst born less of aspiration than of distress and discord.

Sixteenth-century observers held divergent views of the region, its inhabitants and its economic potential. To Camden, "the county of Maridunum, called by the English Carmarthenshire, produces plenty of corn, abounds with flocks, and yields tolerable quantity of coal. It is bounded . . . on the South by the Ocean, which forms so great a bay inland that this county seems to have withdrawn itself for fear of it."[1] George Owen thought Carmarthenshire "a great shire, much good land", and its inhabitants tall and personable men, but unruly, with a tendency towards frequent brawls and other disorders.[2] Thomas Phaer produced a less genial picture. "All this country", he wrote, "is very bare of corn and [men] be not able to live of their own provision, for the most part of their tillage is oats, and are served of wheat and malt out of the Forest of Dean and other parts."[3] John Ogilby, a century on, considered Carmarthen town to be "large, well-built, and well-inhabited, seated on the navigable Towy".[4] The other towns were less prosperous. Leland describes Kidwelly as being "near all desolated . . since the haven of Gwendraeth Fychan decayed".[5] The general impression, Phaer excepted, suggests at least latent natural wealth.

Appraisals of Pembrokeshire were more conflicting. For a native of the county George Owen was surprisingly scathing in his comments, declaring it to have little good land and consisting largely of meanly-inhabited champion country, with the men who lived there "the worst of Wales" for military purposes. Haverfordwest was "a good town, wealthy and well-governed", and Tenby "a little town lying by the sea, good for the quantity", but the other towns were poor and decayed, with Pembroke itself extremely ruinous.[6] Camden, however, described Pembrokeshire as "a good corn country, well-stocked with cattle and furnished with marl and such kind of manure, as also with pit-coal . . . 'a wheat country, plentifully supplied with sea-fish, wines imported, and which is best of all its nearness to Ireland makes the air extremely healthy'". He eulogised the harbour of Milford, "the noblest and safest in Europe for its many creeks and good anchorages which cleave the banks like so

---

(1) Camden, *loc. cit.*
(2) George Owen, *The Description of Penbrokshire*, vol. iv, p.401.
(3) Thomas Phaer, *Anglia Wallia*, p.426.
(4) John Ogilby, *Britannia*, p.168.
(5) John Leland, *Itinerary*, vol. iii, p.59. *Cf. infra*, p. 153.
(6) Owen, *op. cit.*, vol. iii, p.359.

many fibres".[1] But for Phaer the county was rather patchy; around Tenby he found the country very "barren and little good store of victualling"; around Pembroke and Haverfordwest it was "fruitful of corn and all good provision as England"; whereas the Newport area was "bare of corn but plenty enough of cattle". He was nevertheless much impressed by Milford Haven, remarking on its possibilities for trade "without controllment, for men may do what they will ere they be spied by the officer and pass where they please by reason of the haven being so large and secret".[2]

On Cardiganshire most commentators were agreed. Owen described it as "barren and champion" land, its inhabitants being "tall men and serviceable, quiet in government but abounding in theft". All the towns were ruinous, poor and decayed.[3] Camden had little to say concerning it, apart from its being "champion country" to west and south, and "on the east and north where it joins to Brecknock and Montgomery shires is a long chain of mountains yielding plenty of grass, at the foot of which are scattered several lakes".[4] So great were the pastures of the mountains, in Leland's view, that "the hundredth part of it rots on the ground"; but the beef, according to the later writer Gough, "is greatly inferior to that of Monmouthshire . . . Coals and fuel are very scarce". He added that the wealth of the county "lies in its mines and scarce shews itself above ground".[5] Phaer provided a final dismal note: "Cardigan [is] a barred haven, nothing worth but for a 'pytkarde' . . . Aberystwyth, from Cardigan 23 miles, a barred haven of no value . . . All this is a very bare country and mountainous . . . All along the coast is no trade of merchandise but all full of rocks and dangers".[6]

3. GENTRY

A fundamental source of disagreement in the debate over the gentry lies in the problem of deciding who should be included within and who excluded from that category. Social class is both an unmistakable historical reality and equally "evades analysis if we at-

(1) Camden, *op. cit.*, p. 513.
(2) Phaer, *op. cit.*, pp.426-428.
(3) Owen, *op. cit.*, vol. iv, p.479.
(4) Camden, *op. cit.*, p.524.
(5) Richard Gough, "Additions" to *Camden's Britannia*, p.526.
(6) Phaer, *op. cit.*, p.429. In order to avoid false impressions of economic change, the foregoing comments have been deliberately cited out of their chronological order.

tempt to stop it dead at any given moment and anatomise its structure".[1] To some extent aware of this difficulty, Tawney recognised the gentry as a class which "varied widely in wealth" and was "ragged at its edges":[2] a qualification considered too mild by his leading critic,[3] himself held culpable, amongst and by others, for employing excessively broad categories and for premature generalisation.[4] More meaningful units for investigation have accordingly been sought, notably "some other group within the gentry, defined by status", such as "those knighted, or more plausibly those families that provided sheriffs or justices of the peace".[5] It has been reasonably suggested that the term "gentry" might be taken to cover baronets, knights and all esquires and gentlemen recognised by the College of Arms as having the right to bear arms.[6] But the present Garter King of Arms considers, on the basis of the records of the High Court of Chivalry, that "where the plaintiff must establish that he was a gentleman . . . the simple proof by establishing a right to arms is rare. Though only a gentleman could bear arms by right, a man with no right to arms could still be a gentleman".[7] Miss Joyce Mousley has restricted her attention "to the ranks of important holders of office in the county, namely of the positions of deputy lieutenant, county member of parliament, sheriff or justice of the peace".[8] But the Somerset Herald in 1580 allowed the title of esquire to "such who are so *Virtute Officii* . . . as the high-Sheriff of a County, and a Justice of Peace, during their being in office or Commission":[9] thereby placing them on a par with the younger sons of noblemen and above "gentlemen only" in the social hierarchy. Moreover, since the numbers, as well as the duties, of justices

---

(1) E.P. Thompson, *The Making of the English Working Class*, p.9.
(2) R. H. Tawney, "The Rise of the Gentry, 1558-1640", *Econ. H.R.*, vol. xi (1941), p.4.
(3) "The distinction between aristocracy and gentry, as if they were separate social classes, is an arbitrary distinction" (H. R. Trevor-Roper, *The Gentry, 1540-1640, Econ. H.R. Supplement*, i (1953), p.1.
(4) "Their answers are muddied by the excessive breadth of their categories, which obscure possibly important differences" (D. Underdown, "The Independents Reconsidered", *Journal of British Studies*, vol. iii (1964), p.82); "We should stop generalising about 'the gentry'" (C. Hill, *Puritanism and Revolution*, p.27.).
(5) J.P.Cooper, "The Counting of Manors", *Econ.H.R.*, ser. 2, vol, viii (1956), p.381.
(6) J. T. Cliffe, "The Yorkshire Gentry on the Eve of the Civil War", University of London unpublished Ph.D. thesis (1960), p.5.
(7) A. R. Wagner, *English Genealogy*, p. 113.
(8) J. E. Mousley, "The Fortunes of some Gentry Families of Elizabethan Sussex", *Econ. H. R.*, ser. 2, vol, xi (1959), p.467.
(9) Quoted in Wagner, *op. cit.*, p.105.

of the peace tended to increase significantly in this period,[1] this category expands of its own accord to give more and more gentry the appearance of rising.

Alternatively, persistence with the broad category has been urged, on the grounds that "contemporaries seem to have had little difficulty in deciding who was and who was not a gentleman. If we try hard enough we may yet discover that secret".[2] Contemporaries, however, were generally concerned more with expressing personal prejudice and with social *mores* than with social analysis. For this purpose, neither Sir Thomas Smith's ambiguous "who can live idly and without manual labour",[3] nor Burghley's self-denying "Gentility is nothing else but ancient riches",[4] is any more useful as a yardstick than the opinion of William Vaughan of Golden Grove in Carmarthenshire that "the means to discern a gentleman be these. First, he must be affable and courteous in speech and behaviour. Secondly, he must have an adventurous heart to fight, and that but for very just quarrels. Thirdly, he must be endowed with mercy to forgive the trespasses of his friends and servants. Fourthly, he must stretch his purse to give liberally unto soldiers and unto them that have need; for a niggard is not worthy to be called a gentleman. These be the properties of a gentleman, which whosoever lacketh deserveth but the title of a clown or of a country boor".[5] Even with his more scientific purpose, Harrington, as a rule much concerned with definitions, was careless of over-nice distinctions between "nobility" and "gentry" in his affirmation that "where there is not a nobility to hearten the people, they are slothful, regardless of the world, and of the public interest of liberty, as even those of Rome had been without their gentry; wherefore let the people embrace the gentry in peace, as the light of their eyes; and in war, as the trophy of their arms"[6].

No examination of the gentry can ignore the enormous variation of this class in time, in place and in circumstance. Such attempts as

(1) "Numbers rose from less than ten to an average of forty or fifty to a shire" (G. R. Elton, *The Tudor Constitution*, p.453).
(2) I. Roots, "Gentlemen and Others", *History*, vol. xlvii (1962), p.236. *Cf.* R. Kelso, *The Doctrine of the English Gentleman in the Sixteenth Century*, p.18: "The sixteenth century was no more successful than its predecessors in arriving at a complete, unambiguous and generally acceptable definition".
(3) Sir Thomas Smith, *De Republica Anglorum*, pp.39-41.
(4) Quoted in A. L. Rowse, *The England of Elizabeth*, p.244.
(5) William Vaughan, *The Golden-grove*, vol. iii, cap. 16.
(6) Harrington, *op. cit.*, p.43.

the statute of 1363[1] to arrive at some common measure of knights, esquires, gentlemen, merchants, citizens, craftsmen and labourers, can only have been applicable in the broadest possible sense. Esquires with lands or rents worth £200 a year were in this placed below the poorer knights and on a level with merchants and burgesses possessing goods worth £1,000. Below them came esquires and gentlemen worth under £100; below these, craftsmen and yeomen; and so on. Thomas Wilson in 1600 considered that "especially about London and the counties adjoining, he is not counted of any great reckoning unless he be betwixt 1,000 marks or £1,000, but northward and far off a gentleman of good reputation may be content with 300 and 400 yearly".[2] A comparison with Wales is almost painful. Mr. Ogwen Williams has attempted to define a yeoman's land at twenty to forty shillings a year, a gentleman's at between £3 and £10, and an esquire's at £20 to £40.[3] A list in 1593 of gentlemen of property and ability in each shire fit to serve the Queen in some capacity or another gave half a dozen names for nearly every English county but only six for the whole of Wales.[4] The prodigality of the early Stuarts in the distribution of honours, with its damaging effects upon the stability of social groupings,[5] drew a disappointing response from south-west Wales. Under Charles I 36 esquires were believed to reside in Pembrokeshire, 20 in Carmarthenshire and 16 in Cardiganshire;[6] from the last of these came protests from at least ten so described that they had far from sufficient wealth to qualify for the honour of knighthood;[7] from Carmarthenshire about fifty gentlemen made excuses on similar lines.[8]

---

(1) 37 Edward III: "Statute concerning Diet and Apparel" (*Statutes of the Realm*, vol. i, pp. 378-383).
(2) Thomas Wilson, "The State of England, Anno Dom. 1600", *Camden Miscellany*, vol. xvi (1936), p.24.
(3) W. Ogwen Williams, *Calendar of the Caernarvonshire Quarter Sessions Records*, p.lxix.
(4) P.R.O. S.P. 12/244/17. Sir Richard Bulkeley, for Anglesey, was separately entered.
(5) *Vide* L. Stone, *The Crisis of the Aristocracy, 1558-1641*, esp. pp.66-82.
(6) B. M. Harleian 6804, f.181. *The Complete Baronetage* (ed. G. E. Cokayne, vols. 1-2) includes five creations of English baronets from south-west Wales for this period. One, Sackville Crowe of Laugharne, Carmarthenshire, came originally from Kent and was Treasurer of the Fleet. Sir John Stepney of Prendergast (cr. 24 November 1621) and Francis Mansell of Muddlescombe (cr. 14 January 1622) were related by marriage. The others were Richard Rudd of Aberglasney and John Phillips of Picton.
(7) P.R.O. E178/5938.
(8) P.R.O. E178/5901. (This document is badly mutilated).

But if this variable social category defies hard economic definition in constant statistical terms, there can still be little doubt that gentility usually involved a degree of economic superiority. However unreliable their actual cash valuations,[1] the subsidy rolls reflect this at least. In Surrey in 1577 the average individual assessment was 5 shillings; the average assessment for those described as gentlemen was 25 shillings.[2] In Rutland in 1572 the average assessment *per head* was 9s. 4d., each gentleman on the average being assessed at 40 shillings, or roughly four times the overall mean.[3] In Carmarthenshire in 1575 the average assessment was 4s. 9d. for each individual, 14 shillings for each gentleman.[4] The difference was not always so pronounced. In Pembrokeshire in 1582 individuals were assessed at an average of 7 shillings, gentlemen at 12s. 6d.;[5] yet even here in 1595 the 8 shillings average assessment was, for gentlemen, 18s. 2d.[6] In Cardiganshire, again, a distinction emerges in 1577 of 9 shillings as opposed to 5 shillings.[7]

Even so, the difference between the gentry and the class below them, the yeomen, remains "one of status and way of life rather than of wealth".[8] Intermarriage between the two groups was common; a yeoman might, indeed, be materially better off than his "gentle" neighbour, with whom he might live almost on terms of social equality; and yet the difference in rank would be apparent enough *to those involved*. In their own "country", "mere" gentlemen, nonentities in the company of their "court" counterparts, would stand out as powerful and influential. The definitive emphasis should therefore fall on the initial part of Serjeant Doderidge's paraphrase of Sir Thomas Smith and others in 1588: that "in these days he is a gentleman who is so commonly taken and reputed".[9] One can in practice do no other than accept as gentlemen all those who claimed to be such, on the grounds that those who adopted this description

(1) *Vide infra*, pp. 25-26.
(2) P.R.O. E179/257/19.
(3) P.R.O. E179/165/154.
(4) P.R.O. E179/220/113.
(5) P.R.O. E179/223/494.
(6) P.R.O. E179/223/500.
(7) P.R.O. E179/263/37.
(8) Wagner, *op. cit.*, p.111. It seems questionable how far "status" in Wales depended in practice upon the distinction between "common persons" who "are not really *bonheddig* but are so called or termed for fashion's sake by reason of their wealth, offices or behaviour", and the "*gwr bonheddig*" who "paternally descendeth from the Kings and Princes of this land of Britain"—advocated with an eye to "the stipend paid by them to the bards" for their genealogical services (*vide* D. J. Bowen's transcript from N.L.W. Llanstephan 144, in *A Book of Wales* (ed. D. M. and E. M. Lloyd), pp.106-107; and *infra*, p.202).
(9) *Ibid.*, p. 112.

thereby recorded a claim to a position in society and, above all, an
attitude of mind far more significant than any other evaluation which
it is now reasonable to make. In doing this one is, admittedly, left
in many instances with the merest of "mere" gentry. In south-west
Wales this is inescapable. The number of individuals who could in
the loosest sense be termed "court" gentry was minimal; resident
members of the aristocracy were almost entirely lacking.

This survey makes no attempt to estimate the total number of
gentry at any given moment, to deal separately with different gentry-
types, nor, for additional reasons which will hereafter be stated, to
consider how many rose and how many declined during this period.
Its purpose is simply to discover the characteristics and the outlook
of the men who regarded themselves as being in the forefront of
their community and their influence in several spheres upon it. To
introduce at the outset alternative criteria, themselves unsatisfactory,
with a view to supposedly greater precision in classification would
be immediately to unbalance this portrait. Conversely, to re-
emphasise at every juncture the important variations in social and
economic circumstances of different localities within this region
would be burdensome. The selection of viable units for historical
analysis necessarily involves some attribution of homogeneity to
what is essentially heterogeneous. This consideration, together with
the implications of the foregoing definitions of terms, must qualify
any general conclusions that will ultimately be drawn.

In Chapter One, after a critical analysis of some evidence relating
to the values of estates, the implications of local participation in the
market for monastic property are discussed, followed by an examination of the process by which land was accumulated and of factors
affecting estate-consolidation. Next (Chapter Two) comes a statement of some economic circumstances and views of the period; there
follows a discussion of rents, fines, leases, the survival of customary
dues and services, and aspects of agrarian practice, notably enclosures,
with some consideration of the exploitation of mineral deposits; and
the chapter closes with an examination of local trade by sea. In
Chapter Three, the activities in Parliament of members for this
region are assessed; the participation of the locality particularly in
the Essex Revolt and the Civil War considered; and the nature of
local politics examined. There follows in Chapter Four a discussion
of the instruments of local government and the attitudes and
efficiency of officials, illustrated by an account of piracy in the region,

and leading to some observations upon litigation and law. Chapter Five is concerned, first with lay attitudes towards the English Church and lay responsibility for its condition; secondly, with the extent to which the gentry sought education at the Universities and the Inns of Court, and sponsored it in this community; thirdly, with cultural developments, particularly as regards literature; and finally, with three aspects of social life and attitudes. In the Conclusion, there is a brief re-assessment in general terms of the problem under consideration; and two explanations are offered for the conclusion reached.

CHAPTER ONE

Estates

1. EVIDENCE

An effective inquiry into the economic rise or decline of the gentry as a class should be conducted on the basis of comparisons between the values of a representative sample of individual estates at the opening and at the close of a significant period supported by analysis of common factors accounting for change, if any. These values may be ascertained if there are available adequate series of estate-accounts compiled by landlords or their agents for their own information. But for relatively few families do such sources exist. Historians consequently are often driven, like Samuel Butler, to "the art of drawing sufficient conclusions from insufficient premises". Alternative materials, with their attendant disadvantages, may be summarised as follows:

INQUISITIONS POST MORTEM.

Miss Helen Miller has shown how the overall efficiency of this method of assessing the value of a deceased Crown tenant's property for the purpose of securing payment of feudal dues by his heir, is immediately put in question by the apparent failure of commissioners to make returns to the Chancery after letters patent for the taking of inquisitions had been issued.[1] As to those returns that were made, the ability of jurors to make accurate statements has been questioned by Mr. Crump,[2] who goes on to emphasise the responsibility of the escheators. He seems prepared to accept that "it is at least a possible hypothesis and almost a necessary one that there must have been a permanent site for the [escheator's] office, where the growing mass of records could accumulate in safety", whilst admitting that "it is not possible to raise these conjectures above the rank of conjectures, because the wasting influence of time has destroyed these archives beyond hope of discovery".[3] The need for such a site is no proof of its ever having existed; at least an equal

---

(1) Helen Miller, "The Early Tudor Peerage, 1485-1547", University of London unpublished M.A. thesis (1950), p.111.
(2) C. G. Crump, "A Note on the Criticism of Sources", *Bulletin of the John Rylands Library*, vol. viii (1924), p.141.
(3) *Ibid.*, p.142.

possibility is that the records, however thorough they may or may not have been, were treated with scant delicacy and little care, and that the obligation of furnishing plausible details for the inquisition fell on the heir of the deceased or his representative.

In such circumstances nothing but deliberate inaccuracy could have resulted. Seven possibilities for fraud in the inquisitions are listed by Mr. Bell.[1] Ample illustration of their operation and of the inherent limitations of inquisitions can be found by checking them against each other or against private surveys and wills. The total value *per annum* of the Carmarthenshire lands of Sir Thomas Jones of Abermarlais, according to his inquisition taken 25 September 1605, was £80 0s. 4d.[2] This is inconsistent with the fourteenth clause of his will, dated 7 March 1604, which gives instructions that if the Carmarthenshire properties bequeathed to the testator's second son, Thomas, do not amount to the value of £100 a year, then after three years the testator's son, Sir Henry, must add to them further land to make up this sum.[3] William Owen of Pembrokeshire held, according to his inquisition, property in the town of Newport to the value of 40 shillings *per annum*.[4] At this time his son, George Owen, estimated his income from Newport town at £18 18s. a year.[5] In Cardiganshire in 1610 John Stedman was declared to have derived £20 5s. a year from 73 messuages, the site of the monastery of Strata Florida and some additional land.[6] In 1619 James Stedman held the same messuages and site and a significantly increased quantity of land, but the value of the estate had fallen to £15 3s. 10d. *per annum*.[7] On the other hand, Hugh Harris of Haverfordwest seems to have created a false impression of wealth in the minds of the jurors at his inqusition. They believed him to be the holder of eleven messuages in Haverfordwest,[8] whereas he himself noted only six.[9] Examples from each shire are plentiful.

(1) H.E. Bell, *An Introduction to the History of the Court of Wards and Liveries*, pp.50-53.
(2) P.R.O. Wards 7/28/14. (For fuller discussion of feodaries' surveys, *vide infra*, pp. 26-29).
(3) P.C.C. 54 Harte.   (4) P.R.O. C142/222/15.
(5) N.L.W. Bronwydd 3 (*The Vairdre Book*), f.260.
(6) P.R.O. C142/309/175.
(7) P.R.O. C142/369/157. The escheator in this instance was Henry Stedman, esquire.
(8) P.R.O. C142/274/122.
(9) P.C.C. 9 Holney. Harris's will is exceptional in that it appears to state the whole of the testator's landed possessions which pass to his son and heir, Thomas, the widow and executrix receiving the personal estate.

It would be unreasonable to expect otherwise when, on a more important occasion than the taking of a routine inquisition, George Owen felt it necessary to observe in a memorandum before the survey of the lands of Sir John Perrot on his attainder, "that touching the quantity of ground in each tenant's hands and the several kinds thereof, the same is laid down by the examination of the tenants themselves without oath, their neighbours adjoining so near the truth as they could guess or esteem and not by the oath of the jury or by measuring of the land, for that the time would not serve to perform the same."[1] Here is hinted some realization that the Crown would take steps to ensure greater accuracy than was supplied it by the normal methods of inquisition, and that local officials must therefore cover themselves against the probable exposure of the common erroneousness of their declarations.

If, in view of this and of the essential limitations of these inquisitions, the cash values stated therein cannot be used to establish absolute or comparative values of gentry estates, the recorded extents of individual pieces of land are no more reliable for this purpose. Enough has already been written on the "incommensurate units of ownership"[2] which manors undoubtedly are.[3] The same arguments apply to smaller units. Messuages, tenements, tofts, granges, gardens: as standard terms for definite blocks of property they have little meaning. In the same inquisition, taken 4 October 1592, Griffith Dawes was said to have held one tenement and one carucate at Ilande, Pembrokeshire, valued at 20 shillings *per annum*, and three tenements and three carucates in Castlemartin, also valued at 20 shillings.[4] It is obvious enough that all tenements are not equal. The usefulness of inquisitions *post mortem* does not, therefore, extend beyond their indication of the location of estates and some incidental information such as, possibly, the balance between arable and pastoral farming in these localities. Little reliance may be placed upon the valuations they contain.

---

(1) N.L.W. Bronwydd 3 (*The Vairdre Book*), f.137.
(2) J. H. Hexter, *Reappraisals in History*, p.128.
(3) Contemporaries evidently encountered difficulties of a similar nature. George Barlow's misunderstandings with his tenants in Canaston, Wilfrey, Robeston and Newton turned on their refusal "to acknowledge your petitioner [Barlow] to be their landlord, to pay him rent or to do him service of the lands they hold of him", claiming that the said manors be not manors "but riveships and members of the lordship of Narberth" (N.L.W. Slebech 3196). Also *cf. infra*, p.78, for confusion of "lordship" with "manor" and "commote"
(4) P.R.O. C142/232/26.

SUBSIDY ROLLS.

In the parliament of 1601 Sir Walter Ralegh, supporting the
Queen's urgent demand for a subsidy, argued forcefully that it
should fall equally upon every class. He exclaimed against the system
of assessment whereby "a poor man pays as much as a rich, and per-
adventure his estate is no better than it is set at, while our estates are
£3 or £4 in the Queen's books, and it is not the hundredth part
of our wealth."[1] Recently Miss Mousley has analysed at some
length the possible uses and more probable defects of the records of
this unequal levy.[2] She recognises that as time went on the assessments became increasingly nominal, with commissioners, themselves
local gentlemen, tending not only to ignore rising fortunes but even
to reduce the general liability to taxation. If this was so for Sussex,
the problem can scarcely have been less in the remote corners of
Wales. It is not surprising to find the land of Sir Thomas Jones in
Llansadwrn, valued in his inquisition in 1583 at £36. 3s. 9d. *per
annum*,[3] falling in the subsidy of 1593 to £20.[4] In Cardiganshire,
John Price of Gogerddan's extensive properties in and around
Llanbadarn Fawr, valued in his inquisition of 1586 at £18 a year,[5]
fell in the subsidy of 1577 to the value of £10.[6] In his inquisition
of 1581 the late John Wogan was stated to have settled his manor of
Wiston, valued at £20 *per annum*, upon his wife at the time of their
marriage.[7] In the subsidy of 1582 Mrs. Cicill Wogan, widow, was
assessed on lands at Wiston valued at £5.[8] So much for sixteenth-
century methods of tax-evasion. Yet in the same subsidy roll Francis
Laugharne's capital messuage of St. Bride's with its eight appurtenant
messuages were valued at £10,[9] which relatively is not too great
a deviation from the valuation of £9 10s. entered in his inquisition
of 1584;[10] and Richard Nash of Great Nash was assessed in the
same subsidy on £4 in land at Llangwm,[11] 4s. 7d. more than the
total annual value of land attributed to him in his inquisition of

(1) W. Stebbing, *Sir Walter Ralegh*, p.159.
(2) Mousley, "Gentry Families of Elizabethan Sussex", *op cit.*, pp. 467 *et seq.*
(3) P.R.O. C142/198/12.
(4) P.R.O. E179/220/116.
(5) P.R.O. C142/208/242.
(6) P.R.O. E179/263/37.
(7) P.R.O. C142/191/68.
(8) P.R.O. E179/223/494.
(9) *Ibid., loc. cit.*
(10) P.R.O. E150/1217/7.
(11) P.R.O. E179/223/494.

1583.[1]

Valuations in the subsidy rolls are thus neither reliable in themselves nor capable of convenient correction calculated on the basis of a standard deviation from alternative evidence originally compiled for taxation purposes. Further, interpretation of the subsidy rolls encounters, in addition to the obvious motives for deception affecting them, the difficulty of determining, as Miss Mousley has observed, whether "the only assessments to be noted are those for the head of each family or family branch or whether the assessments of relatives are also to be taken into account, and, if so, what degrees of kinship should be allowed for."[2] Problems of identification here become acute, especially in Welsh areas not remarkable for variety in nomenclature. Miss Mousley has herself wisely refrained from using evidence relating to persons whose identity cannot be precisely ascertained; from adopting two scales of values when, as often happens, assessments are on goods in one year and on land in another; and from expecting uniformity in the attitudes of commissioners towards different families. Her own device, of examining the relationship between the assessment on the land of each individual family and the mean assessment on land for all families studied, compared over a period of years in order to determine each family's rise or decline in relation to the average, surmounts only the obstacle of the overall decline in subsidy assessments during this period. All the other foregoing objections apply again with as much force. Moreover, such a method tends in practice excessively to disguise particular factors governing human fortunes, be they demographic as indicated by Mr. Cooper,[3] personal as in the case of the Earl of Cleveland, political as with the attainted Rhys ap Griffith or Sir John Perrot, or any of so many other possibilities. Statistical contrivances do not offset fundamental deficiencies of evidence; they are often disadvantageous in themselves. The assessments given in the subsidy rolls cannot be used to establish the values of gentry estates.

FEODARIES' SURVEYS AND CERTIFICATES

In order to try to overcome the striking deficiencies of established methods of estate-valuation for revenue purposes, feodaries were instructed in 1599-1600 "to certify lands at no lower values than

(1) P.R.O. E150/1217/6.
(2) Mousley, *op. cit.*, p.469.
(3) J.P. Cooper, *op. cit.*, pp.377 *et seq.*

appeared in Elizabeth's reign, in 1606 at values not less than the best since the erection of the Court"[1] of Wards. The result, as embodied in feodaries' certificates[2] of the values of the freehold lands of minors declared in ward to the Crown, has been held to represent, on the whole, a level of accuracy exceptional in the sphere of taxation.[3] But it remains true that "comparison of values found in feodaries' surveys of the early seventeenth century with those submitted to the Committee for Compounding, or found in rentals and estate accounts, shows that the feodary's fractional value for the manors of one estate might be anything between a third and a thirtieth of the true value".[4] This unpredictable variation is both an obstacle to the discovery of true values and a reflection upon the reliability of feodaries themselves. There is little reason to suppose feodaries to have been necessarily more dependable than escheators. In south-west Wales, as elsewhere in England, the respective duties of these officials overlapped.[5] Out of a sample of 67 inquisitions *post mortem* taken between 1540 and 1625, 49% were conducted principally by escheators and 41% by feodaries; in the rest they acted jointly. The results of the one are generally no less questionable than those of the other; and the taking in 1623 of the inquisition of Roland Walter of Roch in Pembrokeshire before the Great Sessions justices[6] is symptomatic of the authorities' despair of both. Feodaries known to have been undependable in one kind of investigation should scarcely be expected to have proved less so in another.

It may be accepted that pressure from a government driven by financial need tended, if laboriously, to extract greater efficiency. When in 1633 Bridget, wife of Richard, Lord Vaughan, and sister of John Lloyd of Cardiganshire, esquire, came to sue out livery as Lloyd's heir, although "the office[7] is returned and transcribed and

---

(1) H. E. Bell, *op. cit.*, p.55.
(2) Heirs of full age inheriting lands in chief were required to "sue out livery", assessments of which were based on feodaries' surveys; in the case of minors feodaries certified their valuations.
(3) J. T. Cliffe, *op. cit.*, p.82.
(4) Mousley, *op. cit.*, p.473.
(5) "Reflecting its diminishing confidence in the authority and reliability of the escheator, the crown increasingly associated him with a commission of three or four men. Of this commission the feodary was invariably a member" (J. Hurstfield, *The Queen's Wards*, p.47).
(6) P.R.O. C142/393/163.
(7) *I.e.*, inquest of office, being an inquiry conducted by jury before the appropriate Crown official. Sir Edward Coke argued, typically, that, by the statute 32 Henry VIII c. 46 erecting the Court of the King's Wards, what the Crown was "entitled to have . . . is by Office to be found" (*Fourth Institutes*, cap. 35).

the schedule drawn up for passing the same" the Court of Wards issued emergency instructions to the feodary of Brecon, as those of Carmarthen and Cardigan were not immediately available, to make a survey of Lloyd's estate[1] This awareness of the inevitable discrepancy between returns "by the office" and "improved values" was wholly justifiable. In 1622 the escheator valued William Scourfield of New Moat's estate at £21 7s.[2] Thomas Canon, Pembrokeshire feodary, promptly certified this same estate at £136 5s. 8d. a year and attributed to Scourfield a personal estate worth £503 10s. 3d.[3] In 1636 the same official certified the estate of John Scourfield, deceased son and heir of the late William, at £16 12s. a year by the office and £109 5s. improved value.[4] This indicates a notable advance over the earlier dubious handling of Hugh Butler's Pembrokeshire estate, valued according to the office in 1604 at £28 10s. 4d.[5] and in 1606 in a survey by feodary Canon at £24 17s. 8d.[6] But the impressive corrective measures which later came to be applied are still not entirely convincing. In a note to the survey of "all and singular the manors, messuages, lands, tenements and hereditaments lately of George Owen, Esquire" in 1623[7] Canon was at pains to point out: "Touching the yearly value of the lands in this *infra*[8] as it is found by the office . . . it is found so low as unless I should wholly neglect his Majesty's instructions I must be forced to value the same in a reasonable manner, answerable to the same instructions, seeing there is so extreme a disproportion between this value in the office and the improved value".[9] He accordingly valued Owen's estate at £100 3s. 4d.; but Owen's own last available

---

(1) P.R.O. Wards 5/51. (The documents in this box are not individually numbered).
(2) P.R.O. C142/393/161.
(3) P.R.O. Wards 5/51.
(4) *Ibid.*
(5) *Ibid.* This document carries a note: "Sold to Sir James Perrot and Elizabeth Butler, the mother, 7 July 1604 for £100", and is intriguingly endorsed by a clerk, "I have added the mother's name by my lord [Robert Cecil]'s especial direction at the request of Sir James Perrot".
(6) *Ibid.*
(7) *Ibid.* Canon adds a note: "I have made this survey as well *ex officio* as by an order dated 30 November 20 Jas. I wherein I am required to express in this survey the true tenures of the lands before mentioned".
(8) *I.e.*, the second item in the survey.
(9) The note continues, revealingly enough: "And under reformation I cannot but remember hereupon the inconvenience that when the warning was given to the feodary, being his Majesty's sworn minister, is omitted, as it was in this case, these undervalues and diminutions of his Majesty's profit do pass thereby which breedeth the feodary when he cometh to his survey a distraction how to serve his Majesty justly and on the other part to avoid clamour and evil will".

valuation gave it at £251 4s. 1d.[1]

Subject as they are to variations in standards of assessment and to the limitations of their original purpose, the accounts of feodaries cannot, any more than other returns for taxation purposes, be used to establish either absolute or relative values of gentry estates, at least over a period sufficient to indicate overall economic trends.

WILLS, MARRIAGE SETTLEMENTS, DEEDS, LAWSUITS.

Documents where the interest of all the parties involved lies in accurate representation of fact are not subject to the main objection which applies to revenue records. Useful evidence is contained in wills as to the identity of holders of individual items of property at particular times. Testators often provide quite detailed statements of possessions, especially when, in cases of division of the inheritance, the possibility of disputes between heirs was anticipated. But rarely do they set out estates in their entirety; and the general usefulness of wills further extends only to their indications of family relationships, of local social and economic circumstances particularly in instances where inventories are appended, or of the charitable inclinations of individual testators. Records of estates beginning as a nucleus embodied in a marriage settlement and built up through a process of exchange by deed and release extant in an unbroken series, would go far to compensate for an absence of private rentals and surveys. Reality provides only fugitive documentation of occasional transactions: valuable glimpses, perhaps, of general processes of estate-growth, of land-use and development, of circumstances encountered by landlords at different times, but uncommunicative as regards the extent and value of any one estate at a single moment. The motives underlying declarations of the values of the possessions of individuals arising from their involvement in lawsuits render these immediately open to question.

In short, where rent-rolls or surveys compiled by landowners for their private information do not survive, or except in quite unusual circumstances, it is impossible to ascertain within an acceptable degree of accuracy the values of individual gentry estates in this period, or even to determine in cash or acreage terms the economic distinction between greater and lesser gentry. Only in one or two instances do such sources exist for south-west Wales. George Owen may confi-

---

(1) N.L.W. Bronwydd 3 (*The Vairdre Book*), f.210.

dently be said to have had in 1583 £160 a year in land.[1] Sir John
Perrot's annual income from land was[2] in the region of £850.[3]
But the materials discussed above do contain useful indications of
the significance of land in the fortunes of the gentry and the means
and methods by which they set about its accumulation and exploitation. Where the evidence does not permit a comparative study
based upon statistics, alternative methods of interpretation must be
applied.

2. MONASTIC LANDS.

The quantity of litigation involving land conducted by Welshmen
from the south-west in the courts of Westminster, Ludlow and elsewhere suggests, at first sight, a high degree of acquisitiveness on their
part. Involvement in such proceedings was by no means confined to
gentlemen; disputes of this kind brought men from all social classes
into conflict with each other, often estranging kinsman from kinsman. Sir Henry Jones of Abermarlais showed himself prepared to
fabricate excuses and prevarications by the dozen, to antagonise his
mother and to drive his stepfather, Sir William Maurice, to distraction, in order to avoid parting with property for the purpose of
paying to the former the bequest to which, under the will of his
deceased father, her former husband, she was entitled.[4] In a similar
spirit the descendants of Sir John Perrot invoked the aid of the most
influential in the land in the course of endeavours to establish their
claims to the estate of their attainted father.[5] Nor was actual
litigation, expensive and arduous as it frequently proved, restricted
to large or valuable pieces of property. In 1624 David Philip Powell
of Llanbadarn Fawr, gentleman, claimed that his brother, Morgan,
had been plagued for fifteen years by Sir Richard Price of Gogerddan
with Exchequer suits over a six-acre close in Perfedd; and that when
the property came to him on his brother's death Price's widow,
apparently abandoning hope of victory by this procedure, falsified
the deeds of ownership and then sued Powell in the Office of Pleas

---

(1) *Ibid.*, f.260.
(2) Within the limits discussed *supra*, p.15.
(3) P.R.O. L.R. 2/260.
(4) T. Jones Pierce (ed.), *Clenennau Letters*, nos 223, 229, 448-450.
(5) H.M.C. *Cal. Salis. MSS.*, vol. vii, p.249; B.M. Harleian 6995, f.141. Both
    Thomas and James Perrot sought the assistance of Essex, who wrote on behalf
    of the latter to Cecil, 9 June 1597.

for trespass.[1] That land was a symbol of the social significance of
its possessor is beyond question. That action at law was frequently
the consequence of motives on the part of the litigant other than
concern for his economic welfare as directly dependent upon the
disputed property, is also very likely. But persistent and determined
wrangling would also suggest that possession of land was viewed
as desirable in itself for the economic benefits it offered immediately.

These reasons alone, as distinct from any prophetic expectation of
rising returns from agriculture or the seeking of land as a buffer
against coming inflation,[2] would prompt one to expect from local
men strenuous competition for the property which came on to the
market at the time of the Dissolution of the Monasteries. The
religious houses of south-west Wales may not have been outstand-
ingly wealthy in comparison with those of England, but their
incomes were by no means negligible. Although in each instance,
according to one valuation at the time of the Dissolution, [3] the
greater proportion of it was derived from spiritualities, the annual
income of the Augustinian Canons of £133 11s. 1d. at Haverfordwest and of £164 4s. at Carmarthen, the £136 9s. 7d. of the Pre-
monstratensians at Talley, or the £135 3s. 6d. of the Cistercians at
Whitland, may be counted sufficient attraction for men anxious to
increase their own.

Yet there are to be found on their part few efforts comparable
with those of John Bradshaw of Radnorshire: who, having in-
gratiated himself with Bishop Rowland Lee, President of the Council
in the Marches, acted as his "alliesman"[4] in his operations and
married his son to the Bishop's niece,[5] persuaded him to intercede
with Cromwell on his behalf for extensive properties in the counties
of Pembroke and Radnor, and eventually secured them by a grant
in fee for £512 2s. 10½d.,[6] upon which foundations his family's

(1) P.R.O. E112/145/88. So apparently insignificant a piece of property produced
    great manoeuvrings in the lawcourts. Lady Price brought a counter-action in
    common law, and Powell strove, without lasting success, to have her committed
    for contempt of the Exchequer (P.R.O. E124/35/172, 207): a litigious enthusiasm
    arising, it would seem, either out of the disproportionate value of the land in
    dispute, or from a more deep-seated hostility between the parties than this issue
    alone would warrant.
(2) Possibilities suggested by Professor Habakkuk ("The Market for Monastic
    Property, 1539-1603", *Econ. H.R.*, ser. 2, vol. x (1958), p.373).
(3) P.R.O. S.C. 12/4/35.
(4) *L.P.H. VIII*, vol xiv, pt. ii (1539), no. 384.
(5) *Ibid.*, vol. xiv, pt. i (1539), no. 1289.
(6) *Ibid.*, vol. xviii, pt. ii (1543), no. 449 (26).

fortunes thereafter flourished. If in the county of Devon 92 separate instances during the reign of Henry VIII are recorded of the Crown's alienating by grant of previously monastic property, most of the purchasers being men "sprung from the ranks of the old-established local gentry",[1] in south-west Wales such men simply did not purchase. Setting aside for the moment the activities of the five most prominent families in this sphere,[2] one finds local men restricting themselves to the leasing of one or two rectories or one or two granges. Hugh Mansell of Whitewell in Pembrokeshire acquired in 1538 a lease of Llanybyther rectory.[3] Griffith Tucker of Carmarthen, merchant, went into partnership with John ap Rice, stated as being of London, for a lease of the rectory of Llanfihangel Rhosycorn.[4] Arnold Butler of Johnston, a former sheriff of Pembrokeshire, secured in 1542 a lease of Camrose rectory;[5] in 1564, in company with Rice Vaughan, he leased a tenement and land in Whitland.[6] These were very modest ventures; more ambitious men often found that they had attempted too much. David ap Henry of Carmarthenshire was granted in 1537 a lease of the rectory of the parish church of Abergwili with the chapels of Llanllawddog and Llanpumpsaint,[7] only to have to surrender them and see them leased again, in 1542, to Dr. Griffith Leyson;[8] the property was ulitmately granted to the Dean and canons of the royal free chapel of St. George the Martyr in Berkshire.[9] If ap Henry was rash Richard Vaughan of Whitland was reckless. He partnered William Games of Aberbrân in county Brecknock in attempting to purchase the site and various appurtenant lands of Whitland Abbey, but on 3 May 1569 they had to admit before the Barons of the Exchequer that they owed the Crown £2,600 for these, and so the property was seized from them by the sheriff.[10]

Dr. G. D. Owen has listed a great many of the leases of the

(1) Joyce A. Youings, "The Terms of the Disposal of the Devon Monastic Lands, 1536-1558", *E.H.R.*, vol. lxix (1954), pp.29-31.
(2) Devereux, Barlow, Jones, Perrot and Lloyd of Llanllyr, *q.v. infra*, pp.33-37.
(3) P.R.O. E315/209/82.
(4) *Ibid.*, /209/49b.
(5) *Ibid.*, /216/8b.
(6) G.D. Owen, "Agrarian Conditions and Changes in West Wales in the Sixteenth Century", University of Wales Ph.D. thesis (1935), p.383.
(7) P.R.O. E315/209/41b-42.
(8) *Ibid.*, /215/41b.
(9) *C.P.R.* (Edward VI), vol. i (1547-1548), p.149.
(10) E.A. Lewis and J. C. Davies (eds.), *Records of the Court of Augmentations relating to Wales and Monmouthshire*, pp.258-259. The property was leased in 1581 to John Morgan Wolfe of Whitland.

monastic lands of west Wales.[1] From these it appears that these lands tended to change hands frequently in the course of the sixteenth century. The lands of Kidwelly Priory, leased in 1543 to George Asshe and Robert Merricke, passed in 1566 to Owen Gwynne, and ultimately to John Parkington. The grange of Ystlwyf, parcel of Whitland Abbey, was leased by Richard Devereux in 1538. In 1540 it was leased by John Vaughan; in 1582 by John Morgan; in 1590 jointly by Gilbert Wakering and Robert Petre; and in 1594 by Thomas Knyvett. In each instance except the first the term of the lease is stated by Dr. Owen to be 21 years. The picture, repeated elsewhere, is confused; it can only suggest that those who did negotiate such leases were often disappointed in their expectations and often surrendered their leases prematurely. It may be that immediately prior to the Dissolution the monks had leased away much of their lands for long terms at large fines, both lessors and lessees hoping "to reap the maximum benefit in the brief space which they had at their disposal"[2]—though the Dissolution Act had made some provision against this very circumstance.[3] Alternatively, it frequently appears that the rents demanded by the Crown were, in relation to valuations at the time of the Dissolution, discouragingly high. The grange of Cokey, parcel of Haverfordwest Priory, and valued at £2 6s. 8d. *per annum*, was leased in 1544 to Henry Jones at £2 10s. Pencothi grange, parcel of Talley Abbey, and valued at 30 shillings *per annum*, was leased in 1536 by William Morgan and James Cole at a rent of exactly that sum. Unless the income from these properties could be speedily improved, such leases were, on the face of it, not attractive.

Lessees who attempted immediate improvement of rents often encountered difficulties. In 1538 John Henry ap Rhydderch of Kidwelly leased the demesne land and all other property of Llanllyr Nunnery. He promptly sought to put up the tenants' rents. There ensued much litigation in the court of Augmentations and elsewhere, in which the tenants either produced old leases granted by the prioress before the Dissolution or pleaded their rights as copyholders.[4] Ap Rhydderch surrendered his lease prematurely, and in

(1) Except where otherwise stated, I am indebted for the factual material in this paragraph, apart from valuations, to G.D. Owen, *op. cit.*, pp.366-388.
(2) Glanmor Williams, *The Welsh Church from Conquest to Reformation*, p.362.
(3) 27 Henry VIII, c.28 (section iv).
(4) T. I. Davies, "The Vale of Aeron in the Making", *Ceredigion*, vol. iii, pt. iii (1958), p.203.

1553 the site, lands and profits of Llanllyr formed part of a Crown sale to William Sackville of the Household and John Dudley, for nearly £2,000, of a considerable quantity of lands and tenements scattered over several counties of England and Wales.[1] It may be that this Sackville had some connection with the then Chancellor of Augmentations, the grasping Sir Richard Sackville. Whether his general intention was one of re-sale at a profit in the manner of a speculator, of agent, or of investment in real property as a source of private income,[2] Sackville seems in this instance to have assigned his interest in Llanllyr to Hugh Llewelyn Lloyd, third son of Castell Hywel.[3] Where ap Rhydderch had failed, Lloyd certainly prospered. His offspring distinguished themselves in the academic, ecclesiastical and judicial spheres;[4] and Llanllyr remained the seat of this prominent family. This suggests either that Lloyd secured the property on unusually favourable terms; or that monastic land in general proved more profitable later in the century than in the years immediately following the Dissolution.

Four more families were significantly involved in land transactions occurring around the time of the Dissolution and having some connection with it; and in each instance one detects, as with Lloyd, particular circumstances. In 1546 Roger Barlow, having amassed a considerable fortune as a merchant in Bristol, and numbering among his kinsmen the influential and redoubtable Bishop of St. David's, was partnered by his brother, Thomas, in obtaining a grant in fee, for £705 6s. 3d., of the lordship, rectory and manor of Slebech in Pembrokeshire, with five messuages there, and divers other lands, the advowson of Martletwy vicarage, the lordship, manor and rectory of Minwear with lands therein, all of which were formerly the property of the commandery of St. John of Jerusalem; the site of Pill Priory, with lands in Pill; the site of Haverfordwest monastery, with rents and lands in Haverfordwest, including the chapel of Cresswell; and the house and site and all the possessions of the late

---

(1) *C.P.R.* (Edward VI), vol. v (1553), pp.286-288.
(2) For some general discussion of these alternatives, *vide* David Knowles, *The Religious Orders in England*, vol. iii, pp.398-399. The exact function in the land market of men who purchased such curious job-lots of property remains a matter of debate. They may have disposed promptly of that which they knew to be unpromising, whilst retaining the exploitable residue.
(3) T. I. Davies, *loc. cit.*
(4) His second son became Principal of Jesus College, Oxford; his third son, chancellor of St. David's; and his grandson, a judge in the Council in the Marches.

Friars Minors of Haverfordwest.[1] To these he added in 1552 a lease of various messuages in Tenby, formerly held by the free chapel of St. John.[2] In 1585 Stephen Barlow obtained a lease of the rectory of Staynton, with lands in South Hook, St. Botolph's, Liddeston and Great Pill, all formerly possessed by Pill Priory:[3] thus rounding off considerable gains for a family later suspected of recusancy.

The Barlows were not a local family.[4] They were exceptional both in their resources and in establishing themselves and their later importance in this region actually through their ability to acquire land that became available through and at the time of the Dissolution. Exceptional in a different sense were the Joneses of Abermarlais, who also figure prominently in the records of the disposal of these monastic lands. In 1545 Henry Jones leased the house and site of the priory of Haverfordwest, with appurtenant lands and three rectories.[5] Two years previously Sir Thomas Jones had leased the site and demesne lands of Talley Abbey, with several rectories and granges;[6] and the latter lease was renewed by successive members of the family in turn during the later years of the century.[7] But the backbone of Sir Thomas Jones's Carmarthenshire estate, and the incentive for his removal there from Haroldston in Pembrokeshire, was provided not by these but rather by lands formerly of the attainted Rhys ap Griffith. In 1545 Jones was granted in fee, for £737 9s. 10d., the lordship and manor of Llansadwrn with all ap Griffith's property in Manordeilo, the capital messuage of Abermarlais, and divers other lands in Llansadwrn and Llandeilo Fawr: and only the advowson of the vicarage of Llansadwrn, valued at £6 13s. 4d. *per annum*, gave an ecclesiastical flavour to that

---

(1) *L.P.H.VIII*, vol. xxi, pt. i (1546), no. 1166(61). The Receiver's account for the year of the Dissolution shows Barlow already holding a lease of the estate of Slebech at an annual rent of £125 15s. 10½d.
(2) Lewis and Davies, *op. cit.*, p.473.
(3) *Ibid.*, p.496.
(4) According to Francis Green ("The Barlows of Slebech", *West Wales Historical Records*, vol. iii (1912-1913), pp.117-122), Roger Barlow was the son of John Barlow of Essex connections, possibly from a younger branch of Lancashire Barlows, and Christian, daughter of Edward Barley of Hertfordshire. But in his will made in Seville before the 1526 expedition to La Plata (*q.v. infra*, p. 204, note 1), Barlow described himself as "Rojel Barlo mercader yngles fijo de Roberto Barlo e de Ana Barlo se muger vesynos que fueron de Solchestre en el reyno de Ynglaterra difuntos" (G. Connell-Smith, "'English Merchants trading to the New World in the early Sixteenth Century", *Bulletin of the Institute of Historical Research*, vol. xxiii, no. 67 (1950), p.66).
(5) P.R.O. E315/216/171b.
(6) *L.P.H. VIII*, vol. xviii, pt. i (1543), no. 982: Augm. Bk. 215, ff. 53-54.
(7) G. D. Owen, *op. cit.*, p. 379.

grant.[1] Further, Henry Jones, lessee in the first of the aforemention-
ed instances, was therein described as being "of the King's Household"; Sir Thomas Jones was described by George Owen as being
at the time of the Act of Union already "a gentleman of worship in
Carmarthenshire, but then dwelling in Pembrokeshire";[2] and, as
an additional asset, his wife, Mary Berkeley, was reputedly a former
mistress of Henry VIII and mother of his supposed bastard, John Perrot.

Beginning in the early fourteenth century, good marriages into
the leading families of the locality had set the Perrot bandwagon
rolling in Pembrokeshire, alliances being formed with the Chastels of
Castleton, the Joneses of Prendergast, the Harolds of Haroldston St.
Issell's, the Wogans of Wiston, and others: a process culminating
in Thomas Perrot's marriage with Mary Berkeley, who later married Sir Thomas Jones.[3] All these roads to conjugal bliss being paved
with property and reinforced by influence in high circles, the Perrots
were by the time of the Dissolution well placed to derive advantage
from it. The indications that they did so are ambiguous. In 1556
Sir John Perrot paid £355 into the Exchequer and was granted in
fee, "in consideration of his service", an extremely scattered selection
of properties in the counties of Warwick, Lincoln, Derby, Chester,
Leicester, York, Salop and Northampton.[4] In July of the same year
he obtained in like form an even more disunited group in nine
English counties;[5] and in May 1557 a payment of £184 15s.
earned him a grant of various lands and rights in Pembrokeshire,
Denbighshire and eight English counties—lands stated to have been
concealed.[6] In 1561 certain lands in Haverfordwest, lately the
Duke of Bedford's, were leased by him,[7] together with several
parcels of the manor of Carew, formerly Rhys ap Griffith's.[8]
This process of gradual accumulation continued over the next ten
years in the form of further leases,[9] supplemented by only one

(1) *L.P.H. VIII*, vol. xx, pt. i (1545), no. 1081(13).
(2) George Owen, *op cit.*, vol. iii, p. 104.
(3) For the Perrot genealogy, *vide* Lewis Dwnn, *Heraldic Visitations of Wales and
    Monmouthshire* (ed. Sir Samuel Rush Meyrick), vol. i, pp.89, 133. The undoubted
    imperfections of Meyrick's edition (*vide* F. Jones, "An Approach to Welsh
    Genealogy", *T.H.C.S.* (1948), p.376) do not obviate its usefulness for general
    purposes.
(4) *C.P.R.* (Philip and Mary), vol. iii (1555-1557), p.192.
(5) *Ibid.*, p.270.
(6) *Ibid.*, pp.297-300.
(7) Lewis and Davies, *op.cit.*, p.479.
(8) *Ibid.*, p.488.
(9) *Ibid.*, pp.481, 483, 503; *C.P.R.* (Elizabeth), vol. ii, p. 222.

major item of previously monastic property in the form of six rectories and four chapels in Pembrokeshire, leased in 1563 by Perrot in partnership with Edward Carye at a fine of £200.[1] In 1584 he leased the grange of Cokey, formerly parcel of Haverfordwest Priory and earlier leased by Henry Jones.[2] This history gives rise to two comments. First, Perrot's acquisitions in Pembrokeshire derived as much from other Crown lands as from previously monastic property. Secondly, it is noteworthy that whereas Perrot appears to have made large and extensive purchases in England, with one exception he only negotiated leases of lands in south-west Wales. It seems possible that whereas in that locality he was operating on his own account, elsewhere he may have been acting as an agent. Viewed in this light, his actual territorial gains consequent upon the Dissolution were scarcely remarkable.

From 1538 the representatives of the house of Devereux set about leasing sizeable blocks of monastic lands in Cardiganshire and Carmarthenshire. The granges of Hafodwen, Penardd, Cwmystwyth, Blaenaeron, Mefenydd, Anhuniog, Morfa Mawr, Ystlwyf, Iscoed, Castell Cossan, Cwrtmaenorforion, Cilfargen, Llwynyrebol, and several rectories: all these passed into their tenure at various times, and many of their leases were renewed by themselves or by their agents to their use well into Elizabeth's reign.[3] This family had succeeded Sir Rhys ap Thomas in domination of this region. Holding the stewardships of six monastic houses before the Dissolution,[4] Devereux held unrivalled advantages over their neighbours and made some profit by them.[5] Their post-Dissolution gains represent an extension of a position already won; certainly the Earl of Essex in 1576 did not consider that these contributed greatly to his economic well-being.[6]

Apart from these, families which were later prominent in this locality figure in these records only incidentally if at all. Appointment to Court office,[7] and especially Hugh Vaughan's position as ad-

---

(1) *C.P.R.* (Elizabeth), vol. ii, p.608.
(2) G. D. Owen, *loc. cit.*
(3) *Ibid., loc. cit.*   (4) Glanmor Williams, *op. cit.*, p.367.
(5) *Vide infra*, pp.112-113
(6) H.M.C. *Cal. Salis. MSS.*, vol. ii, pp. 134-135. Essex complained of the long-term leases granted by the Abbot of Whitland before the Dissolution. *Cf. infra*, p.41.
(7) Hugh Vaughan of Kidwelly, first of the Vaughans to be associated with Golden Grove, should be distinguished from his namesake, who was Governor of Jersey about 1507 (D. Lleufer Thomas, "Iscennen and Golden Grove", *T.H.C.S.* (1940), p.118; *cf.* F. Jones, "The Vaughans of Golden Grove", *T.H.C.S.* (1963), pp. 137-139).

ministrator of the lands of the attainted Rhys ap Griffith, furnished the Vaughans of Golden Grove with exceptional facilities for expanding their estates. They were not slow to exploit them, their acquisitions of Crown property being again very largely in the form of leases and drawn only slightly from formerly monastic lands.[1] John Wogan in 1538 leased the site and much of the lands of Pill Priory, with the rectory of Staynton;[2] in 1546 Hugh Profett, a yeoman of the guard, secured a thirty years' lease on the premises from the expiry of Wogan's lease;[3] and in 1585 the rectory passed into the hands of Stephen Barlow.[4] Not until 1576 does John Stedman appear to have begun, with a lease of a parcel of the grange of Hafodwen,[5] to build up out of the lands of the abbey of Strata Florida[6] the estate which established his in the forefront of Cardiganshire families. If the Stepney family long enjoyed influence in Pembrokeshire, it was the marriage of Alban Stepney in 1565 to Margaret, daughter of Thomas Catharne, that brought them their initial property in the shire: property which, though it contained Prendergast manor and a great deal of land,[7] had been augmented at the time of the Dissolution only by a lease of the rectory of St. Martin of Haverford.[8] Conversely, whereas Sir William Thomas of Llangathen in Carmarthenshire acquired in 1537 a lease of Carmarthen Priory, with the rectory of Llanlluy and the chapel of Llanfihangel Rhosycorn at a rent of £43 0s. 4d.,[9] he does not seem to have effected any spectacular rise in the family's fortunes.[10]

---

(1) F. Jones, *op cit.*, pp.99 *et seq.*
(2) P.R.O. E315/209/109b.
(3) *L.P.H.VIII*, vol. xxi, pt. i (1546), no. 1538: Augm. Bk. 236, f. 189b.
(4) Lewis and Davies, *op cit.*, p.496.
(5) *Ibid.*, p. 236.
(6) The Strata Florida lands were originally leased to Richard Devereux (*ibid.*, p.225).
(7) F. Green, "The Stepneys of Prendergast", *West Wales Historical Records*, vol. vii (1917-18), p.118.
(8) P.R.O. E315/217/126b. This lease was renewed by Catharne in 1565, and again by Stepney in 1579 (Lewis and Davies, *op. cit.*, pp.483, 501).
(9) P.R.O. E315/209/83b.
(10) He left bequests to his three daughters of £30, £20, and £20 respectively, and to his wife £30 a year during the remaining term of his lease on Carmarthen Priory, and £10 a year thereafter (P.C.C. 17 Spert). He himself was sheriff of Carmarthenshire once, in 1542, as was his son in 1565 (*Trans. Carms. Antiq. Soc.*, vol. iii, pp.29, 33); and by 1555 the priory of Carmarthen was held by Dr. Griffith Leyson, sometime Principal of St. Edward's Hall, Oxford (W. Spurrell, *Carmarthen and its Neighbourhood*, p.114). *Cf.* Roger Barlow's bequest in 1554 to his wife, Julayane: £200, the parsonage of Martletwy, the mansion-house of Slebech and the dairy-house of Minwear, with large and valuable quantities of goods (P.C.C. 3 More).

If William Warren of Trewern leased in 1551 chantry lands worth ten shillings a year,[1] most of the dealings of the families of south-west Wales with the court of Augmentations did not occur until some time after that Office was absorbed into the Exchequer. Even then these transactions were both modest and occasional, extending over a considerable period of time, and taking the form not of purchases but of leases.[2] In 1564 Owen Gwynne of Kidwelly leased the site of Kidwelly Priory;[3] in 1577 he added that establishment's demesne lands to what he already held.[4] Not until 1584 did William Walter, in company with his sons and Sir John Perrot, lease two rectories, a grange and some lands, formerly of the priory of Haverfordwest,[5] adding to these in 1593 with a lease of several messuages and lands in and around Staynton and Rosemarket, lately those of the chantries.[6] In 1583 Maurice Scourfield took over a lease of the rectory of New Moat,[7] the name of which thereafter lent that of his family an air of domiciliary distinction. And the early 1590s saw a little burst of activity in Pembrokeshire on the part of Barretts, Powells, Bradshaws, Bowens and Butlers, assigning, renewing and confirming various leases of here a rectory, there a mill or a grange.[8] In Cardiganshire there was far less general participation. The agents of the Earl of Essex[9] encountered little effective competition from the local men, apart from Edward Powell's accumulation over an extended period of several tenements, formerly chantry lands, by virtue of his office as Receiver and Collector of chantry property in that shire.[10]

It would be rash to affirm from this that the Crown was reluctant to alienate the monastic lands of south-west Wales. It is true that there is little indication of their having been given away to local men; and if any were offered at bargain prices, potential local purchasers seem to have been extremely slow to fasten upon them. Their ability to do so is in any case doubtful. If, as recent research

---

(1) Lewis and Davies, *op. cit.*, p.473.
(2) In some instances lessees may, of course, have been concerned in earlier arrangements with monastic landlords.
(3) *Ibid.*, p.264.
(4) *Ibid.*, p.259.
(5) *Ibid.*, p.499.
(6) *Ibid.*, p.490.
(7) *Ibid.*, p.498. The lease was renewed by John Scourfield in 1597 (*ibid.*, p. 489).
(8) *Ibid.*, pp.492-494.
(9) *Ibid.*, p.232. Broughton, Newport and Barroll leased in 1577 various valuable granges, late of the abbey of Strata Florida, for Essex.
(10) G. D. Owen, *op. cit.*, pp.390-391.

suggests, the authorities persisted in asking the normal market price for these lands, apart from a few families in exceptional circumstances men from this region were in no position to compete for them. Would-be participants in this market would have needed an appropriate amount of capital in order to make significant purchases at the standard rating of twenty years' purchase of the estimated income of the property concerned.[1] If there had been in England before the Dissolution regions where there existed some "frustrated demand for land"[2] on the part of people who possessed the resources and the appetite without the opportunity to acquire it, in Wales, while the desire may have been equally strong, the means to satisfy it were lacking. In any case poorer than many regions of England, its evolution of a capitalist economy was much less far advanced and the financial strength of its gentry greatly inferior.[3] It is not surprising that these records of the disposal of monastic property reveal an absence of south-west Welshmen comparable with, for instance, the English Henry Audley or John Cordall, who, were their function that of agent, speculator or private investor, seem to have been able to summon up sufficient capital to make purchases of striking dimensions.[4] Nor is it surprising that, in the alternative sphere of leasing, the Crown required in the way of fines for leases on its property in Wales not the four, five or six years' purchase of the rent which seems to have come to apply most frequently throughout England, but the more modest sum of two years' purchase.[5]

It was not by large *coups* but by a process of gradual acquisition based on transactions amongst themselves and dictated by their existing financial resources that the gentry of south-west Wales set about the business of estate-building.

3. ACCUMULATION.

In 1547 one Richard ap Moris Vaughan settled the "place at Trawsgoed" and the "messuage of David Benlloid" in Cardigan-

---

(1) H. J. Habakkuk, *op.cit.*, p.362. The uniformity of ratings in the 1540s was later departed from, until "by the 1560's there was a great variety of ratings" as the authorities sought "to take account of the problems posed by the rapid rise in general prices" (*ibid.*, pp.362, 370).
(2) *Ibid.*, p.372.
(3) Before the Industrial Revolution "the history of the country had certainly not favoured the accumulation of capital" (A.H. Dodd, "The Beginnings of Banking in North Wales", *Economica*, vol, vi (1926), p.16).
(4) For example, *L.P.H. VIII*, vol xix, pt. ii (1544), no. 340 (59).
(5) Habakkuk, *op. cit.*, p.371. The above account of the procedure in England with regard to fines is necessarily greatly abbreviated.

shire on his son, Morys, on the occasion of the latter's marriage with Elliw, daughter of Howell ap Jankyn ap Ieuan ap Rees, Elliw contributing as her marriage portion a scattered amount of land near Trawsgoed. With this as a nucleus, Moris, between 1560 and 1585, set about purchasing a considerable number of tenements in the parishes of Llanfihangel y Creuddyn, Llanafan and Llanfihangel Gelynnod, in a series of transactions. Moris's grandson, Edward Vaughan, supplemented this procedure with the tried expedient of marriage, which he contracted on two successful occasions: first with Lettis, daughter of John Stedman of Strata Florida, and secondly with Anne, daughter of Sir Thomas Jones of Abermarlais.[1] The links now forged with the important families of Jones, Stedman, Phillips and Perrot found territorial expression in the purchase, in 1630 by John, son of Edward Vaughan, of thirteen thousand acres of land extending over the granges of Hafodwen, Blaenaeron, Cwmystwyth, Morfa Mawr, Mefenydd, Penardd, Anhuniog and Doferchen, from the trustees of the Earl of Essex, for £4,300.[2] In 1637 he purchased for £755 13s. 4d. from James and Sir John Lewis of Abernantbychan in Cardiganshire nine tenements and various rights of suit of mill.[3] In 1660 John Vaughan, already a member of parliament, was deputy-lieutenant for Cardiganshire.

A better example of a family's rise on the strength of private property dealings and judicious marriages culminating in a spectacular climax, would be difficult to find. Apart from the *dénouement*, it is in principle by no means an isolated example in this region. Between 1550 and 1570 the Voyles of Haverfordwest embarked on similar lines. They were a younger branch of the family of Dafydd Foel ab Owen, ancestor of the Voyles of Philbeach.[4] They acquired some capital through operating as tradesmen locally,[5] and in 1553

(1) J. M. Howells, "The Crosswood Estate", *Ceredigion*, vol. iii, pt. i (1956), pp.71-72.
(2) N.L.W. Crosswood, I.240, 243, 246; II. 12, 13, 15, 16, 19, 20. *Vide infra*, p.45.
(3) *Ibid.*, I. 266 This purchase was preceded by a process of capital accumulation in the form of the granting of tenements by Vaughan by indenture in perpetuity for substantial consideration in cash and an annual rent (*ibid.*, II. 23, 24, 26, 31, 33, 35-45, *etc*).
(4) Dwnn, *op cit.*, vol. i, pp.71, 72, 177.
(5) Francis Jones, "Some Records of a Sixteenth-Century Pembrokeshire Estate", *B.B.C.S.*, vol. xiii, pt. ii (1949), pp.92-94. Major Jones's description of the Voyles as "merchant princes" is difficult to confirm from the Port Books. John Voyle's trading was exclusively in coasting imports, though Thomas Voyle of Philbeach handled some foreign exports (E.A. Lewis, *The Welsh Port Books, 1550-1603*, pp.49-235). *Vide infra*, pp.86-89.

John Voyle bought from Thomas ab Owen of Tenby a messuage and 140 acres of land in Crunwear parish, and another messuage and 56 acres in Amroth parish. He made a few minor additions to these small beginnings, and then purchased in 1560 several valuable "manors" and properties in the hundred of Dewsland from the Sutton family of Newgale, and ten "manors"[1] and lands in south Pembrokeshire from William Wogan of Bloxham, Oxfordshire, son and heir of the deceased Maurice Wogan. In 1566 he acquired further properties from Henry Taylor of Haverfordwest and from John Wogan of Boulston.[2] The family appears to have made hardly any further purchases of any great extent. Though they retained a place of some prominence in the ranks of the landed gentry until the late seventeenth century, they were then gradually bought out by the family of Picton Castle. Their rise seems to have been largely the result of the acumen and energy of one man: John Voyle.

After their initial large purchase, a similar policy was adopted by the Barlows and put efficiently into operation by Roger Barlow's son, John. An exchange with John Wogan of Boulston of three messuages in Boulston parish for two tenements in Herbrandston and Slebech parishes;[3] a purchase of a messuage and two acres of land in Minwear from David Mors of Lawrenny, husbandman;[4] another exchange of a messuage and three closes, six parcels of land and five gardens, for a messuage, five parcels and two pieces of land, a close, a garden, some pastures and some woods, with Margaret Phill of Slebech, widow;[5] a purchase from Owen ab Owen of Wyndshill, yeoman, of a messuage and lands in the township and fields of Slebech;[6] and, in more exalted company and on a larger scale, a purchase for £600 of seven tenements and "all the tenements in the tenure of Richard Mathewe" in Slebech parish, from John Wogan of Wiston:[7] by such calculated and considered bargainings the estate was consolidated. By the early seventeenth century the activities of the Barlows had earned them the enmity of several of their fellow landlords, and had brought Sir Richard Phillips,

---

(1) These appear to have been blocks of tenements rather than "manors" in the strict sense.
(2) Francis Jones, *loc. cit.*
(3) N.L.W. Slebech, 206 (July 1563).
(4) *Ibid.*, 235 (February 1570).
(5) *Ibid.*, 177 (May 1570).
(6) *Ibid.*, 181, 188, 198 (February 1576).
(7) *Ibid.*, 453 (September 1579).

Sir John Stepney,[1] Sir William Wogan of Wiston[2] and Sir Thomas Canon[3] into the lawcourts against them, involving them in protracted and expensive lawsuits and, almost, economic disaster.[4]

The Owens of Henllys started earlier but used similar means. Originating obscurely among the freemen of Cemais, their first representative of any significance was Philip Fychan ap Philip Richard who held lands in Bayvil in the second half of the thirteenht century. These were increased by small grants, marriages and inheritances, until by 1420 Gwilym Ddu of the family handed on to his son, Owain, the makings of a fair-sized estate. Owain increased this with commendable energy, and handed on to his son properties in Henllys Isaf, Wenallt Wood and the ploughland of Crugiau Cemais.[5] The heir had none of his father's application, but Rhys ab Owain Fychan, his son, displayed his grandfather's enterprise, and to the well-worn procedures of purchase and marriage added foreclosure on mortgages,[6] the securing of bonds from landowners who undertook not to alienate their land except in his favour, and, himself an able lawyer, the threat of litigation. His son, William Owen, another knowledgeable lawyer, thus inherited an estate of considerable dimensions. He endeavoured to cement it with the lordship of Cemais, thus incurring the hostility of the Audley family[7] and instilling in his son, George, unfortunate dreams of feudal grandeur. By 1571 nearly all the remaining independent tenants of Henllys had been bought out, and in 1583 George Owen held properties in Newport, Bury, Cemais, Newcastle, Redwalls, Cefnllynfeth, Eglwyswrw, Bayvil, Moylgrove, Pembroke, Cilymaenllwyd and Llanboidy.[8]

---

(1) *Ibid.*, 468.   (2) *Ibid.*, 4079.
(3) *Ibid.*, 3253.
(4) *Cf. infra*, p.45.
(5) B.E. Howells, "Studies in the Agrarian History of Pembrokeshire", University of Wales unpublished M.A. thesis (1956), pp.132-138.
(6) For some discussion of the nature and significance of mortgages, *vide infra*, pp. 44-48.
(7) *L.P.H.VIII*, vol. xiii, pt. ii (1538), no. 46: "I beg your help that the King may have true knowledge that the lordship of Cemais is worth, which William Owen now has for £600 , of which £50 is to pay, as appears by his obligation, and he would fain give me money to be thoroughly at a point with me. If you knew its value and the behaviour of the said William, I am sure you would have it bestowed on one that will do the King faithful service, as Owen will never do. If you will have it surveyed, the King will find that all was not true that was reported to my hindrance" (John, Lord Audley, to Cromwell, 7 August 1538).
(8) N.L.W. Bronwydd 3 (*The Vairdre Book*), f. 260.

Gradual acquisition: sometimes through the keenness of one out-standing member of a family, sometimes through what amounted to a family characteristic of business acumen, yet, on the whole, without sudden bursts of acquisitiveness or speculation born of general fluctuations in the land market. This process of the accumula-tion of land into individual hands, of which the foregoing are only a few of many possible examples, was inherently disruptive to the Welsh system of kindred rights territorially based on the *gwely* or *gafael* and, in its rigid form, essentially restrictive as regards alien-ation. But expansionist pressures from within, coupled with ex-traneous influences, had already induced adaptation and evolution in Welsh law and custom to facilitate exchange and consolidation. The outstanding feature of this development is the Welsh Mortgage. It must be emphasised that this "in its original and strict form closely resembled the *mortuum vadium* described by Glanville",[1] and is akin to the right of *ususfructus* in Roman Law by which the fruits of one man's property may be used by another as long as its substance is kept intact.[2] Since by this device the rents and profits of a mort-gaged estate were taken by the mortgagee in lieu of interest until redemption by repayment of the principal, it offered the advantage of cirumventing the illegality of usury in medieval common law through reliance upon "a doctrine derived from the canon law to the effect that a transaction was not usurious unless the creditor was certain to be owed some money in addition to the principal sum".[3] The fruits of the security in this sense represent simply the mort-gagee's compensation for having temporarily deprived himself of the use of his money. By the statute of 1545[4] the taking of interest of up to 10 *per cent per annum* was legalised and one advantage of the Welsh Mortgage thereby reduced, though the "narrow-minded successors" of medieval judges "still adhered wilfully to the letter of the ancient precedents"[5] in frowning upon "usurious bargains". The use of the Welsh Mortgage appears in general to

---

(1) *Coote's Treatise on the Law of Mortgages* (9th edn., ed. R.L. Ramsbotham), vol. i, p.35.
(2) *Cf.*, too, the doctrine of *substitutions* in early French law, prior to the *Code Napoléon* (*vide* Kenelm Digby, *An Introduction to the History of the Law of Real Property*, pp.270-271).
(3) A. B. Simpson, "The Penal Bond with Conditional Defeasance", *Law Quarterly Review*, vol. 82 (1966), pp.413-414.
(4) 37 Henry VIII, c.9.
(5) D. E. C. Yale, *Lord Nottingham's Chancery Cases*, vol. ii (Selden Society, vol. lxxix (1961)), p.12, quoting Blackstone, *Commentaries*, vol. iii, p.434.

have declined during the early part of the seventeenth century,[1] coincidentally with the evolution of the main rules of mortgages particularly as regards the establishing of redemption and foreclosure in the equitable jurisdiction.[2] In societies where money was scarce there remained obvious advantages both to the mortgagor and to the mortgagee in an arrangement less subject to the limitation of time as a bar to redemption and to the availability of cash for payment of interest. But there remains, too, the possibility that the continued use of this form of mortgage in Wales indicates the surviving influence of social disincentives against outright alienation.

Owing to these several considerations, the interpretation of the intentions of the parties to a mortgage in this period is beset with difficulties. It seems evident, however, that large-scale mortgages were, on the whole, infrequent. Three instances are outstanding. To enable him to make his purchase of 1630, John Vaughan of Trawsgoed borrowed £3,000 from the third Earl of Essex on the security of a rent-charge of £300.[3] In 1610 the nemesis of immoderate living was already hard on the heels of Sir Walter Rice of Newton, forcing him to mortgage a messuage to George Jenkins of Great Mullock, Pembrokeshire.[4] In 1612 Sir Walter settled what amounted to the bulk of his estate in Pembrokeshire on his son and heir, Henry, who undertook to settle a total of £2,410 of his father's debts, including many items to merchants of Petticoat Lane, Cheapside and Westminster, and £60 to the warden of the Fleet Prison.[5] The next six years saw further mortgages to a total of £440 by Sir Walter of various other parts of his estate.[6] By this time the emotions of his son must have been akin to those later experienced by John, son of George Barlow of Slebech. Faced with the costs of his father's long struggle at law over the lordship of Narberth and related issues, in 1635 Barlow mortgaged firstly large quantities of land in Arnoldshill, Wiston and Slebech to Sir Edward Atkins and Dame Robertah Lytton of London, in £1,000,[7] and secondly the

---

(1) R. W. Turner, *The Equity of Redemption*, p.91. Dr. Yale suggests that the Welsh Mortgage survived in use down to the nineteenth century (*op. cit.*, p.51, note 2).
(2) Yale, *op. cit.*, p.33.
(3) T. I. Davies, *op. cit.*, p.205.
(4) N.L.W. Dynevor, B/882.
(5) *Ibid.*, B/879.
(6) *Ibid.*, B/223, 880, 514, 825, 62, 746.
(7) N.L.W. Slebech, 357.

whole of the Slebech estate to Robert Parckhurst of London, in
£21,000.[1]

On a more modest scale, other mortgagors may have been motivated by the same obvious incentive of an urgent need for money.
In 1577 Henry Vaughan of Llandyfaelog, Carmarthenshire, brought
an action in Star Chamber against the Crown steward of the lordship
of Llanstephan;[2] in 1583 he mortgaged a messuage, garden, and
seven parcels of land in Llandyfaelog parish to Edward Dounlee.[3]
In 1572 and 1573 Rice ap Morgan, a Pembrokeshire gentleman,
fought Star Chamber actions arising out of alleged affrays with the
servants of Sir John Perrot;[4] in 1574 he mortgaged a tenement and
land to Owen ap Rice Philip.[5] Alban Owen's addiction to the law
in the Great Sessions,[6] and in the Council in the Marches,[7]
following hard upon like tendencies in his father,[8] may have some
bearing upon his mortgaging in £30 of a close in Nevern to George
Bowen in 1625, and a messuage and land, a close and a mill in
Moylgrove in £400 to John Lloyd of Pentre Evan in 1631.[9] But
similar explanations are less conveniently forthcoming for the
activities of such as Morys ap Richard of Llanafan, Cardiganshire,
esquire, who figures as mortgagor in 1570 of a tenement in
£13 6s. 8d. to Morrys Gwin ap Richard of Llanfihangel y Creuddyn,
gentleman, and again in 1571 of another four tenements to Ieuan ap
Griffith Gethin of Llanfihangel Gelynnod, but in 1586 as mortgagee
in a transaction with David Ieuan ap Griffith of Llanafan involving
a tenement and £20.[10]

Examination of seventeen collections of deeds and documents[11]
has revealed, for the period 1540-1639, a total of 164 mortgages,
distributed by decades as follows:

1540-9	1550-9	1560-9	1570-9	1580-9
3	3	11	12	8
1590-9	1600-10	1610-9	1620-9	1630-9
17	14	36	34	27

(1) *Ibid.*, 387.
(2) P.R.O. St. Ch. 5/V3/34.
(3) N.L.W. Muddlescombe, 818.
(4) P.R.O. St. Ch. 5/G15/25; /M60/6.
(5) N.L.W. Bronwydd, 2860.
(6) *Ibid.*, 501-502: Owen v. Thomas Lloyd, esquire.
(7) *Ibid.*, 516: Owen v. James Vaughan, gentleman.
(8) For example, P.R.O. St. Ch. 8/224/7; /226/19; /290/7; /290/8; /304/7; N.L.W.
Bronwydd, 513.
(9) N.L.W. Bronwydd, 1706, 1171.   (10) N.L.W. Crosswood, I. 60, 63, 99.
(11) N.L.W. collections (*vide* Bibliography).

The concentration in the early part of the seventeenth century deserves notice.[1] But apart from this, the variety both of the terms and of the parties involved is interesting. For relatively small sums, single messuages, tenements and parcels of lands are mortgaged, with gentlemen, yeomen and husbandmen figuring as mortgagors and mortgagees in all possible permutations. And in several instances it would seem that eventual redemption was not the intention of the mortgagor. In 1618 Morris ab Edward of Llanfihangel y Creuddyn, gentleman, mortgaged a moiety of a tenement in £40 to Edward Vaughan of Trawsgoed, redeemable at three-yearly intervals on repayment of the principal, Vaughan meanwhile to enjoy the profits of the premises, and the mortgagor covenanting to pay Vaughan's costs of levying a fine of the premises at the next Great Sessions.[2] The device of levying a fine, whereby the deforciant, or conusor, conveyed land to the complainant, or conusee, in open court, was described by Coke as "the highest and best assurance of lands",[3] invaluable in localities where, owing to the complexities of past and current practices in conveyancing, titles were readily disputed. Covenants to this effect occur frequently in mortgages of the period. They suggest the use of the mortgage as an instrument in the consolidating of estates. Again, arrangements such as that whereby in 1638 a yeoman of Llandebie in Carmarthenshire received of Henry Vaughan of Derwydd, esquire, in consideration of £40 "several closes or parcels of lands . . . to the only proper use and behalf of him the said Howell David Bedo, his heirs and assigns, forever", redeemable by Vaughan at six-yearly intervals on repayment of the principal,[4] are both distinctly reminiscent of earlier mortgage forms and suggestive of tendencies towards consolidation. Obviously by no means every mortgage was similarly intended; its flexibility either for the mortgagor as a means of raising loans, or, for the mortgagee, as an instrument for recovering rent-arrearages,[5] is apparent enough. But if, in general, "debtors were afraid of mort-

---

(1) Cf. supra, p. 45. Approximately one third of the above total mortgages were contracted before 1600 (cf. H. J. Habakkuk, "Introduction" to M.E. Finch, *The Wealth of Five Northamptonshire Families*, p.xv).

(2) N.L.W. Crosswood, I. 204.

(3) *Coke upon Littleton* (15th edn., ed. F. Hargrave and C. Butler), section 194.

(4) C.R.O. Cawdor, Box 2, no. 32. Vaughan reserved to his own use the site of a mill, some lands adjacent thereunto, and the right to work any coal on the premises.

(5) *Vide*, for example, the arrangements between Walter Vaughan of Llanelli esquire, and David and Edward Williams, gentlemen, in turn, between 1618 and 1624 (N.L.W. Derwydd, 46, 173, 216, 222).

gages and avoided them when they could" for fear of "absolute forfeiture of the estate",[1] there is reason to attribute to this form of conveyance a peculiar role in the process of gradual acquisition of land already described.

This process is further illustrated in records of litigation. When Watkin Thomas, a justice of the peace, assembled, as was alleged, a party of followers at Llwyn Iorwerth in Cardiganshire in 1594, marched them to the cottage of Edward Morris and his wife, Margaret, and removed Margaret by force, breaking her ribs and dislocating her arm, it was possession of the tenement with its dairy-house and two closes that formed the core of the dispute.[2] When Howell Thomas, gentleman, was accused in 1576 of leading a party of men and women to the house of Rees Thomas Lewis of Aber-gwili, a justice of the peace, and, upon Lewis's barricading himself indoors, pulling off the roof, breaking down the walls of the house and ejecting the justice by force, it was possession of land in Trelech parish that lay at the root of the controversy.[3] And when John Thomas of Llangadog declared in 1601 that Sir John Vaughan of Golden Grove had invited him to a feast and enticed him into exces-sive consumption of wine, he objected not in a spirit of outraged temperance but as the claimant to land in Llangadog which, in his intoxicated condition, he had been persuaded to sign away to Vaughan.[4] Whether the defendants in such highly-coloured law-suits had really been resorting to extraordinary force and subterfuge towards the satisfying of an appetite for land for which more lawful means were insufficient; or whether the plaintiffs were drawing upon fertile imaginations to buttress uncertain claims arising out of similar appetites: in the absence of more reliable testimonies than the evidence of the parties concerned, this must remain a matter of conjecture.[5] Suits in the Exchequer court, again, must be con-

---

(1) L. Stone, *The Crisis of the Aristocracy*, p.525.
(2) P.R.O. St. Ch. 5/L14/23.
(3) P.R.O. St. Ch. 5/L36/38.
(4) P.R.O. St. Ch. 5/T11/33.
(5) Owing to the loss of the Decree and Order Books of the court of Star Chamber, it is largely impossible to determine what the final decisions of the court were on suits brought there. Other sources occasionally disclose verdicts of this kind (for example, B. M. Harleian, 2143; I am indebted to Professor T. G. Barnes for referring me to this document). Exhaustive search of the Exchequer Memoranda Rolls will also indicate which party won in cases where one or other of the litigants was fined. Even in these instances, it is often difficult to conclude why the court reached a particular decision: it could have been for contempt, through a matter arising from a point of law, or through some misdemeanour not directly

sidered against a "background of imperfectly defined and badly, if not corruptly, administered areas of crown land, of tenants who held by customary tenures and payments that were unfamiliar to English farmers (and many of their lawyers) and an obstruction to the ambition of their Welsh counterparts".[1]

But the fact remains that out of 337 cases in Star Chamber between 1540 and 1625 involving men from south-west Wales, 105 were directly concerned with possession of land and the efforts of individuals, frequently involving allegations of threats, intimidation and actual force, perjury, corruption of juries, or the withholding of documentary evidence, to establish their title. A further 119 cases arising directly out of disputed title[2] were contested in the court of Exchequer between 1558 and 1625, out of a total of 261; and in the court of Chancery, in the twenty years between 1538 and 1558 alone, 75 out of 149 cases similarly. When suits brought elsewhere in common law, and before the Council in the Marches or the courts of Great Sessions, are added to these, the relative importance of this kind of plea becomes apparent. Suits are not characterised by genuine failure to reach agreement and amicable reliance upon the wisdom of the courts. There are references to the discounting of the awards of arbitrators, to refusals to accept the verdicts of minor courts and even of the central courts. Rees Philip Scarfe preferred 29 suits in various courts against Rees Prydderch of Laugharne and John Phillips of Picton over the castle and demesne of Laugharne[3] without reaching a conclusion satisfactory to himself and to the

---

connected with the plaintiff's original bill or the defendant's answer; further, bills frequently incorporated a multiplicity of charges, on any, or more than one, of which the defendant could have been fined if the charge was considered proved. In cases where no fine payable to the Exchequer was imposed it is impossible, in the absence of some chance revelation, to determine whether the bill was withdrawn, whether the defendant won, or whether some conclusion not involving a fine was eventually reached. Even so, and with full recognition of the unreliable nature of evidence drawn from *ex parte* statements, use may still be made of Star Chamber material as regards the nature of the cases involved; what was the main bone of contention, and what may be regarded as having been accepted, tacitly or otherwise, by the litigants as "common ground". "Time and again we shall have to admit that we can only conjecture the truth of the statements recorded or guess at the court's decision. This does not render the reconstruction invalid" (G. R. Elton, *Star Chamber Stories*, p.17). It is not the rights and wrongs of individual pleas but the incidental illumination which they afford that makes these records useful.

(1) T. I. J. Jones, *Exchequer Proceedings concerning Wales in tempore James I*, p.xv.
(2) This figure does not include cases relating to offices, tithes, debts, rights of court, fishing, suit of mill, *etc.*
(3) P.R.O. E112/151/55.

other parties. On the face of it, this evidence suggests competition for land in an atmosphere of hostility.[1]

4. DISPOSITION.

The formal abolition of gavelkind by the Act of Union was no guarantee of the indissolubility of these hard-won estates, once accumulated. Family commitments exercised their inevitable mor-cellating influence, in the shape of dowries and jointures. Some early seventeenth-century marriage settlements in this region reflect general contemporary concern over these consequences, which was to culminate in the evolution of the legal device of trustees to pre-serve contingent remainders.[2] Thus in 1625, in the pre-nuptial settlement of Francis, one of the sons of John Laugharne of St. Bride's, esquire, and Lettice, one of the daughters of James Vaughan of Pontfaen, gentleman, James Vaughan covenanted to convey at the next Great Sessions to trustees nominated by John Laugharne his mansion-house of Plas y Bontfaen, with messuages and land, to James Vaughan's own use for life, with remainder to the betrothed couple and thereafter to their heirs, "in default of such heirs, then to the right heirs of the said James Vaughan"; John Laugharne covenanting to convey to trustees nominated by the elder Vaughan a lordship and land to the use of Francis and his bride.[3] Inter-marryings over generations could result in interesting redistributions of capital resources. In 1601 John Stedman, esquire, of Strata Florida, covenanted to pay to Edward Vaughan of Trawsgoed £300 by instalments over two years upon Vaughan's marriage to Stedman's daughter, Lettis.[4] In 1637 John Vaughan of Trawsgoed conveyed to John Stedman of Strata Florida a number of tenements to certain agreed uses in satisfaction of a portion of £1,000 for Vaughan's sister, Jane, on her marriage to Stedman.[5]

Such eventualities notwithstanding, in Wales this period is one of transition from the concept of partible inheritance with restrictions upon alienation outside the kinship group, to the concept of the indivisibility of the inheritance as later represented in the strict settlement again restricting alienation in the interests of future

(1) But *cf. infra*, pp.78-80.
(2) H. J. Habakkuk, "Marriage Settlements in the Eighteenth Century", *T.R.H.S.* ser. 4, vol. xxxii (1950), p.17.
(3) N.L.W. Poyston, 76. Payments in goods and in cash were also involved.
(4) N.L.W. Crosswood, I.147.
(5) *Ibid.*, I. 262.

generations. Although the pattern of contemporary wills, as regards their detailed provisions, varies, there emerges in the attitudes of most testators both a desire to make adequate arrangements for surviving dependants and some ambition, expressed with differing degrees of sophistication, to preserve estates intact. Few testators were as sanguine as John Price of Gogerddan who, in 1584, left all his property in Merioneth, with one or two exceptions, to his son James, and his Cardiganshire estate to his son and heir Richard, with a bequest of £700 to his daughter Elizabeth upon her marriage.[1] In 1581 Francis Laugharne of St. Bride's devised a substantial number of tenements to be administered by six trustees until the marriages of his three daughters, to ensure their portions therefrom; his house and capital messuage to his wife, unless she should remarry; and all these thereafter to his son Rowland.[2] In his will of 1611 Alban Stepney of Prendergast abided by the dispositions made in earlier settlements in the interests of his wife and daughter-in-law, in the form of "an estate by fine unto our son, Philip Stepney", to his use after his mother's decease, with no apparent provision for reversion to the testator's heir, John.[3] But in 1625 John Stepney devised an estate of the annual value of £99 0s. 8d. to four trustees to the use of his three younger sons "for their maintenance in grammar schools until they be fit for the University" and for their specified incomes therefrom thereafter, with reversion after their decease to his eldest son and heir, Alban.[4] Walter Vaughan of Llanelli in his will of 1635 entailed his estate to his eldest son, Francis, and Francis's wife, and thereafter to their heirs according to "seniority by birth", in tail to the twentieth male or alternatively the twentieth female; reserving specified items, to the use of his widow for her lifetime, with reversion to his second son, John, who also received outright some other properties; and to the Earl of Carbery to provide maintenance for the testator's daughters.[5]

In only ten of a random sample of seventy wills from this period[6] can serious attempts at entail be found. Some include interesting provisions, such as John Vaughan of Carmarthen's insistence in 1568

---

(1) P.C.C. 41 Watson.
(2) P.C.C. 12 Butts.
(3) P.C.C. 87 Wood.
(4) P.C.C. 36 Hele; C.R.O. Cawdor, Box 10, no. 238.
(5) P.C.C. 65 Sadler; C.R.O. Museum Collection, 417.
(6) Proved in the Prerogative Court of Canterbury, and including examples of testaments by men below the rank of gentry.

that his cousin, Morris ap Rees, should administer for ten years an extensive selection of tenements to assure legacies totalling £635 15s. 10d. for the testator's ten illegitimate children, with reversion at the end of that term to his son and heir, Walter.[1] Most testators made some attempt, however ineffective it may have proved, to preserve the bulk of the main estate intact at least for their immediate heirs, provision for other children being conditional upon certain safeguards. Thus Thomas Price of Llanfihangel Genau'r-glyn, Cardiganshire, esquire, in 1623 made substantial provision in land for his second son, Edward, with reversion in default of his heirs to his brothers and their heirs in turn, and ultimately to the testator's eldest son, Thomas, and his heirs, to whom the greater part of the estate passed immediately.[2] Again, Edward Dounlee of Aberkivor, Carmarthenshire, esquire, in 1598 reserved for his son, Edward, sufficiently beloved to receive "my best armour of proof, my target of proof, my gauntlet, my dagger", in lands only those held by his father as mortgagee, the residue of the landed estate passing to the elder son, Henry.[3] Many of these testaments can only be described as naive, so dependent are they for their execution upon the goodwill of interested parties, and so vulnerable to attacks at law by dissatisfied relatives. In several, concern to provide for younger offspring must have resulted in an excessive burdening of the main estate, assuming conscientiousness on the part of trustees and executors. The concept of the sacrosanctity of an indivisible inheritance was evidently slow in achieving adequate expression in practical modern terms. In this region, an estate at this time was a unit laboriously constructed, and subject to many hazards and modifications in its transference from generation to generation.

---

(1) P.C.C. 26 Martyn. *Cf.* the Welsh practice of *cynnwys*.
(2) P.C.C. 122 Swann. Cash bequests totalling £2,000 were made to the testator's five daughters towards their marriages.
(3) P.C.C. 22 Lewyn. Edward Dounlee was a grandson of Sir Thomas Jones by his first wife, Elizabeth (*vide V. C. H. Buckinghamshire*, vol. iii, pp. 93-94).

CHAPTER TWO

Economy

1. CONTEMPORARY VIEWS AND CIRCUMSTANCES.

In Wales, as in England and in Europe at large in this period, most men depended for their livelihood directly upon the soil. This was a period generally of acute rise in agricultural prices and of significant increase in population. The immediate social and economic effects of the former of these factors depended upon the extent to which local economies were geared to the availability of money; to this, therefore, Wales was comparatively less vulnerable. As regards the latter, it has been estimated that the population of Wales rose between 1536 and 1630 from 258,000 to 375,254.[1] On the basis of Bishop Richard Davies's estimate that there were in St. David's diocese 24,161 houses, the mid-sixteenth-century population of that diocese has been calculated at 80-90,000 souls.[2] George Owen estimated from the muster books "the number of people in every hundred in Pembrokeshire" in 1588 at 6,539, and in 1599 at 7,656.[3] Mr. Leonard Owen has calculated[4] that in the middle of the sixteenth century Carmarthenshire had 34,375 inhabitants, Cardiganshire 17,320, Pembrokeshire 20,079, or a total of 71,774 out of a total for the whole of Wales of 225,826, This rose by 1670 by 11, 15 and 58 *per cent* respectively, to 88,805 out of a total of 341,674. The percentage increases for Carmarthenshire and Cardiganshire were, on this estimate, the smallest for the whole country, for which the mean increase was 52 *per cent*. Obviously, none of these conclusions pretends to be exact. But it is apparent that there was an increase in the population of this region.

Generally, such an increase, coupled with the price-rise (to which it may, indeed, have stood in causal relationship), and occurring in

---

(1) David Williams, "A Note on the Population of Wales, 1536-1801", *B.B.C.S.* vol. viii (1935-1937), p.363.
(2) Glanmor Williams, *Bywyd ac Amserau'r Esgob Richard Davies*, p.39.
(3) George Owen, *The Taylors Cussion*, pt. ii, p.83.
(4) L. Owen, "The Population of Wales in the Sixteenth and Seventeenth Centuries", *T.H.C.S.* (1959), pp. 99-113. These calculations are based on the Bishops' returns, subsidy rolls and hearth-tax returns.

predominantly agrarian economies, might be expected to have stimulated a growth in agricultural production. That this took place in the form of improved methods and increased yields has been suggested. Mr. Robert Trow-Smith has noticed a "sixteenth-century Renaissance" in English husbandry;[1] Dr. A. L. Rowse, "an undoubted improvement in the productivity of the land and in the standard of living of the bulk of the people".[2] In more specific terms, "the national average yield of corn crops was steadily rising. It had been no more than from six to twelve bushels an acre on the best farms that Walter of Henley knew. The ordinary Elizabethan farmer would have been disappointed with less than sixteen bushels in a reasonably good year."[3] But yields varied enormously from region to region as from year to year;[4] and increase, where obtained, arose less through the dissemination of new ideas than from a more intensive application of traditional methods. Little more than "the beginning of an attempt to consolidate farming practice"[5] is to be found in the writings of contemporary enthusiasts, who, far from suggesting new and revolutionary departures, advocated rather variations on long-established themes or revivals of lapsed usages. Thus Heresbach, with his indefatigable reliance upon writers of classical antiquity and the Scriptures;[6] Tusser, with his versified formulae, however neatly composed;[7] and, perhaps as significant as any, Fitzherbert, with his mourning of the marl-pits, formerly so

---

(1) R. Trow-Smith, *English Husbandry*, heading to Chapter 6.
(2) A. L. Rowse, *op. cit.*, p.94.
(3) G. E. Fussell, "Crop Nutrition in Tudor and Early Stuart England", *Agr. Hist. Rev.* (1955), p.105. *Cf.* Rowse, *op. cit.*, pp.96-97: "The improvement in stock... was notable: for 1500 an average figure for sheep has been given of 28lb., for cattle 320 lb.; for 1610, an average—true, of stock for the Prince of Wales—for sheep 46 lb., for cattle 600 lb.".
(4) Such fluctuations and their effects in this region can be traced in documents concerning government commissions and restrictions regarding the transportation of corn and other foodstuffs: *vide A.P.C.* (1550-1552), p.245; *ibid.* (1571-1575), p.116; *C.S.P.Dom.* (1547-1580), vol. ciii, no. 19; *A.P.C.* (1586-1587), pp.159, 165, 387, 110; *ibid.* (1591), p.434; *C.S.P.Dom.* (1591-1594), vol. ccxl, no. 111; *ibid.*, (1595-1597), vol. cclxii, no. 107; *ibid.*, (1619-1623), vol. cxxxix, no. 122 (ii); *A.P.C.* (1628-1629), p.319; *C.S.P.Dom.* (1629-1631), vol. clxxv, no. 66, 119 and vol. clxxxv, no. 19; *ibid.* (1631-1633), vol. clxxxviii, no. 46; N.L.W. Haverfordwest Corporation Records, 234. Sometimes these represent objections against the licensing of "strangers" to transport provisions for troops in Ireland at a time of domestic shortage.
(5) G. E. Fussell, *The Old English Farming Books*, p.20.
(6) Conrad Heresbach, *Foure Bookes of Husbandry* (1577), *passim.*
(7) T. Tusser, *Five Hundreth good Pointes of Husbandry* (1573): for example, on crop rotation in open fields ("First rye and then barley, the champion says, or wheat before barley, the champion ways", *etc.*), p.50.

much in use, which he now saw everywhere abandoned.[1] And if in the seventeenth century the possibilities of more efficient land-use attracted the attention of such sophisticated minds as Francis Bacon's, their ideas were in advance of contemporary practice. So in 1649 Walter Blith was still venting his spleen upon the open-field farmer, who met urgings of enclosure or improvement with the attitude, "No, our fathers lived well upon their land, and so will we prevent enclosure if we can; we will moil and toil rather all our days, we will keep our children at home and save charges, turn them into a field to keep sheep and kick up their heels upon a balk, look to our beasts, flit our horses and honk our oxen".[2] Advances in this sphere were never easily contrived; only under extraordinary pressures and influences could natural conservatism and circumspection be shaken.

Some such impatience was exhibited by George Owen in the course of his discourse upon agrarianship in Pembrokeshire. "This commodity of corn", he wrote, "is the chiefest that bringeth in money to the country,[3] being a country more apt for tilling than for breed, the soil being naturally dry and fit for the plough-work, but this differeth much in some part of this shire from other".[4] He classified the agricultural potential of the county's hundreds according to their suitability for arable farming, liking Castlemartin best since it "yieldeth the best and finest grain and most abundance", Rhos next, "a champion and plain country without much wood or enclosures" which "yieldeth great abundance of wheat, barley and other grain", and expressing diminishing approval of Narberth, where "by reason the country is woody[5] and enclosed the inhabitants convert more of their land to pasture", and of Dewsland, where "the negligence of husbandmen in sowing of bad and oaty feed" resulted in poor quality produce. The remainder of the county was less fruitful. Of livestock, Pembrokeshire could boast "oxen, steers, bullocks, heifers and kine of the country breed", which Owen criticised because "it

---

(1) A. Fitzherbert, *The Boke of Surveyeng* (1523), f.45b.
(2) Walter Blith, *The English Improver* (1649), p.34.
(3) *Cf.* Fitzherbert, *The Boke of Husbandry* (1548), f.26: "An husband cannot well thrive by his corn without he have other cattle, nor by his cattle without corn, for else he shall be a buyer, a borrower or a beggar".
(4) George Owen, *The Description of Penbrokshire*, vol. i, pp.55 *et seq.*
(5) Elsewhere (*op. cit.*, p. 146) Owen, somewhat inconsistently, complains of "this country's scarcity of timber and wood". Sir Francis Godolphin, writing to Burghley from the Scilly Isles in 1593, referred to "Narberth forest in Wales" as "the best place he can hear of to supply" wood for defence-works (*C.S.P.Dom.* (1591-1594), vol. ccxlv, no. 72).

procureth depopulation and maintaineth less people at work".[1]
In sheep "the country aboundeth . . . and yieldeth great profit with
little charge", for although the animals were small and their wool
coarse their flesh was sweet and wholesome. Some quantity of butter
and cheese was also produced.

These were the local resources available in what has been called
"the age of heroic achievement for Wales" in the economic sphere.[2]
Such a description seems a trifle over-enthusiastic. Though a major
obstacle to progressive farming was now statutorily removed,[3] and
land might be "brought together by purchase and exchanges",
advance was slow, particularly in the Welsh areas. There the system
of manuring was wholly inadequate, the old method of enclosing
animals by night within removable hurdles being preferred to the
carrying and spreading of dung. The sowing of the same crop of
oats over several successive years "so weakeneth the land that it
becometh very barren . . . yet cannot these doting husbands be drawn
to forego their fathers' folly". But despite these strictures, Owen was
himself sceptical of other methods, such as denshiring, on the
assumption that "this is said to be a great impairing of the
ground". The popularity of oats as a crop in the Welsh areas he
ascribed to "the use thereof in ancient time, and being brought up
therein [they] are hardly drawn to alter their custom, although it be
for the better: such force hath custom in men's nature". Against this
may be set his enthusiastic opinion of marl as a fertiliser, which "was
much used about 100 or 160 years past as appeareth by much land
marled and many ancient marl-pits yet extant, but it was wholly
neglected till about 24 years past that divers poor people began to
find commodity thereby". Sand and limestone might also be used,
though Owen's opinion was that of an old local saying, that "a man
doth sand for himself, lime for his son and marl for his grandchild".[4]

---

(1) *Cf.* his earlier remark: "I have by good account numbered three thousand young
people to be brought up continually in herding of cattle within this shire" (*op. cit.*,
p. 42). It is interesting to observe how Owen, with his legal knowledge, reflects
in his social and economic opinions something of the attitude evinced in Elizabethan legislation (for example, 39 Elizabeth, c.2: "An Act for the maintenance
of husbandry and tillage").
(2) A. L. Rowse, *The Expansion of Elizabethan England*, p.60.
(3) Gavelkind, which system of inheriting had procured the result that "in every five
or six acres you shall have ten or twelve owners".
(4) *Cf.* Barnaby Googe, *The Whole Art and Trade of Husbandry* (1614), p.20: "The
common people have a speech, that ground enriched with chalk makes a rich
father and a beggarly son". (Googe's work was an expansion of his earlier
translation of Heresbach's, *q.v.*, *supra*, p.54).

Another, probably less objective, observer noted for Wales in general that "corn, cattle and other things titheable are within these thirty years much increased in that country, and, the country being populous, the ground better tilled and the riches of men there more increased".[1] If such development did take place, there is little evidence in Owen's writings to account for it in terms of improved technical ability. In his list of the chief "wants and defects that the county of Pembroke naturally hath and of divers inconveniences in the state of the country" that "by the good industry of the people might be redressed",[2] his constructive proposals do not extend very far beyond some advocacy of enclosure. He was a careful observer and a copious chronicler, but the desire for system and for order which pervades his writings is backed by no great indication of originality in thought or in approach;[3] and the best he hoped for from the cultivation of his land was no more than his contemporaries at large felt justified in expecting, if Mr. Fussell's assessment is at all accurate.[4]

2. EXPLOITATION OF RESOURCES.

Men concerned to secure an income from land have fundamentally at their disposal two modes of procedure. They can apply themselves directly to their available resources by means of cultivation, animal husbandry, or exploitation of timber and minerals. These may be termed direct farmers, who may be content with securing sufficient from their land for their own subsistence, or may raise the level of their activity to that of an industry related to market trends, in this period inflationary. They may, on the other hand, derive a prede-

---

(1) From an anonymous tract *temp.* Elizabeth, seeking to persuade the Crown to invest in the cloth industry in Wales ("*De presenti statu totius Walliae*", *Arch. Camb.* (1915), pp.237-248).

(2) Owen, *op. cit.*, pp. 145 *et seq.*

(3) His commonplace book contains such items as "The form of an inventory for cattle to be taken in the beginning of winter", "The like to be taken in summer", "A view to be taken of the whole profits of cattle of divers dairies for the year", "A comparison of the profits of 40 kine and 400 sheep", and so on (*The Taylors Cussion*, pt. i, ff. 8, 9, 31, 34). Methodical though these are, *cf.*, in the light of Owen's declared predisposition in favour of arable, the "consistent preoccupation with the comparative profits of growing wheat and barley, and his sudden interest in new enterprises" of Robert Loder of Berkshire, " not an isolated character in his day" (G. E. Fussell (ed.), *Robert Loder's Farm Accounts, 1610-1620*, Camden Soc., vol. liii (1936), pp. xxiii, xxxi, and *passim*).

(4) *Cf. supra*, p.54. Owen's estimate of crop yield *per* acre was that a sowing of 4 bushels of wheat, 10 of barley, 18 of oats, ½ bushel of peas would yield "between the third and fourth fold increase".

termined return from the actual agrarian activity of others holding
their land from them. These are the *rentiers*, who, insofar as their
return was obtained in cash, experienced in this period a rapid
diminution in the purchasing value of what were formerly economic
rents. Obviously, these two approaches were by no means mutually
exclusive as far as their practitioners were concerned; a man might
very comfortably be a direct farmer in one portion of his estate and
a *rentier* in another. Again, landed incomes in either form might be
improved in two ways, likewise mutually compatible: by a more
intensive exploitation of available resources, or by operating more
extensively through adding to those resources. So the direct farmer
might apply new techniques, or add to his land and his stock; the
rentier might "oner" rents, shorten the terms of leases to facilitate
fresh rent-increases at each renewal, demand large fines for beneficial leases, apply more rigorously the requirements of manorial
dues and customs advantageous to himself, or simply acquire a
larger estate and thereby more tenants. All this, familiar enough in
principle, forms a convenient framework for analysis of the evidence.

To begin with *rentier* practice. From the complex assortment of
evidence relating to estate-management, some instances stand out of
private landlords increasing rents. In 1592 the lordship of Haroldston East contained seven tenants at will. One of these held a
ploughland of which half was arable and half furze. "This was but
20s. *per annum* and was raised to 50s. by Sir John Perrot at his last
repair to Ireland". The others were similarly raised, from 20s. 8d.
to 38s., 13s. 4d. to 24s., 10s. to 20s., 12s. 4d. to 24s. 8d., and so on, or
approximately doubled.[1] In 1624 William Powell, a "poor man",
petitioned the Bishop of Lincoln, saying that he and his ancestors had
long held in the hamlet of Newton two houses with their appurt-
tenant land, one at an annual rent of eleven shillings, the other at
fifteen shillings. George Barlow had dispossessed the petitioner of the
former and had raised the rent of the latter to fifty shillings. The
petitioner had paid this rent for some years, but "since Mr. Barlow
returned to Pembrokeshire he threateneth to put your poor petitioner
out of this tenement also unless your petitioner will give him £5
per annum for the same, being more than the same is worth; and yet
refuseth to make unto your petitioner any lease or copy thereof, but
will have him hold it as tenant at will."[2] At the beginning of the

(1) P.R.O. L.R. 2/260/102b-103.
(2) N.L.W. Slebech, 3245.

seventeenth century Thomas ap Jevan, who held a messuage, tenement and land in the Crown grange of Ystlwyf in Carmarthenshire,
accused John Morgan Wolfe of levying rents far in excess of the
£3 6s. to which he was accustomed and, on his refusal to pay, ex-
pelling the tenant from his holding.[1]

But instances such as these are not necessarily typical. Moreover,
the foregoing appear to have arisen as a result of exceptional circumstances. The raising of rents on the Perrot estate, if proved, coincided
with his departure for Ireland to take up the expensive post of Lord
Deputy there. The allegation against Barlow constituted only one
feature of his main struggle with his tenants over his manorial rights
in Canaston, Robeston, Wilfrey and Newton, rack-renting being
perhaps an item dragged in to discredit the landlord.[2] The action
against Wolfe, himself a quite frequent litigant,[3] was a rare instance
of a lawsuit apparently arising directly from the alleged imposing of
extortionate rents. Certainly as numerous and possibly more significant are examples of rents not keeping pace with the estimated
improved value of land. A survey in 1618 of the manors of Bier and
Penally, conducted by Sir John Stepney and Thomas Canon, showed
the total free rents paid there to be 16s. 3d., the total husbandryhold
rents £59 0s. 3d., and the total censoryhold rents £32 4s. 9d.,
whereas the land held by husbandryhold was valued at £196 13s. 6d.,
and the censoryhold land at £84 9s.[4] In Llwynyrebol and Blaen-
gwythno in 1609 the total leasehold rents came to £11 10s. 5d. for
land valued at £76 5s. 10d.[5] Perrot's former manor of Eglwys
Gymyn in Carmarthenshire yielded in 1609 a total rent of
£26 1s. 8½d., whereas the property was valued at £94 10s. 10d.[6]
£10 1s. 11d. was paid by the tenants of Cwrtmaenorforion,

(1) P.R.O. E112/146/59.
(2) N.L.W. Slebech, 3082. In this petition to the Crown by Thomas David Morris
    on behalf of himself and "3 or 4,000 other" tenants of Narberth lordship, the
    main accusations were Barlow's imposing of unaccustomed dues and services
    upon his tenants, multiplicity of lawsuits and encroachments upon commons.
    Rack-renting should in this context be considered in company with a charge
    that Barlow had refused to contribute to a benevolence to the Crown, into which
    refusal the tenants read treasonable tendencies. *Vide infra*, p. 69.
(3) Mostly in the court of Exchequer, where in Elizabeth's reign Wolfe was involved,
    from 1580 onwards, in ten actions: as plaintiff, P.R.O. E112/59/34, 38, 46, 54(i),
    E112/61/22; as defendant, E112/59/9A, 23, 40, 42, E112/17/108. Of these, some
    represent more than one suit arising out of a single dispute: for instance, the
    affair of Lamentation Chapman, *q.v., infra*, p. 205.
(4) P.R.O. L.R. 2/206/75-117. They valued both arable and pasture at 2s. 6d. an
    acre, meadow at 5s., heath at 1s.
(5) *Ibid.*, /216-225.
(6) P.R.O. L.R. 2/258/3-18.

formerly the Earl of Essex's, valued altogether at £68 2s. 8d.[1]
Between 1583 and 1594 George Owen's income from rents paid by
customary tenants in Bayvil actually fell from £5 1s. to
£3 13s, 8d.[2] In the eight manors and six granges surveyed by
Gilbert Thacker in 1607 in Carmarthenshire and Pembrokeshire, the
total value of leasehold land was £867 10s. 10½d., but the corresponding rents paid amounted to no more than £176 10s. 9½d.[3]

These examples raise further problems. First, they illustrate the
difficulty of improving rents on manors or lordships containing
numbers of freehold tenants[4] and tenants holding for long terms.
Eglwys Gymyn, for instance, contained seven freehold tenements
yielding a total of 14s. 4½d. a year, and a dozen tenants holding
leases for 99 years, many dating from the days of Henry VIII.
Secondly, instances taken from surveys of Crown land—by far the
most extensive evidence available—may not be representative of the
activities of private landlords on the spot, who would have been
more aware of the anomalies which existed and, it might be assumed,
more likely, where impelled by a desire for economic rents, to
resolve them. On Crown properties, indeed, despite greater diligence
in surveying in later years, rents still lagged far behind estimated
values, and adjustment often proved difficult. In a survey of 1570[5]
one Richard Gibbon was described as holding a messuage and one
and a half carucates of land in Leweston: "upon the measuring
hereof fifteen acres of this content were found wanting, but yet I
found good to enter it thus by reason of the common reputation of it,
and have allotted to this tenement by view of the jury six acres one
rood found to be encroached by Matthew Morse among his freehold, and this by the privity and consent of both parties". A sad
comment, perhaps, on both the difficulties and the efficiency of
earlier administration; but another entry in the same survey carries
another implication. Roger Marcroft held a messuage and two carucates of land in Haverfordwest. The premises "hath been rented as
in the record at 100s., which was belike when the country was in
such great disorder as the tenant found special defence by the aid of
the castle (near which it lieth) for himself and his goods; and I find
that the forty shillings continued in arrears and could never be gotten.

(1) P.R.O. L.R. 2/205/200-206.
(2) N.L.W. Bronwydd, 3 (*The Vairdre Book*), ff. 210, 216. *Vide infra*, p. 81.
(3) B.M. Lansdowne, 169, f.116.
(4) Freehold tenure tended to predominate, of course, in Welshry areas.
(5) P.R.O. L.R. 2/238/20-37.

Wherefore, being brought to £4, *it will be higher rented than any land in all these parts*".[1]

It is just conceivable that the surveyor's meaning in this phrase was "any Crown land", but since the whole object of this survey would appear to have been the standardising of rent levels on Crown land "in all these parts" in accordance with a desirable scale, this seems unlikely. The more reasonable interpretation is that an economic rent as conceived of by a Crown steward or surveyor would be higher than that required by any local rentor.[2] This differs strikingly from the disparity found by Dr. Kerridge between rent increases on certain Crown manors and those on the Herbert and Seymour estates, where the reverse is convincingly demonstrated.[3] Perhaps our surveyor was not an honest man; one grows weary of suspecting behind every official pen a lying hand, but is bound to admit the possibility. For south-west Wales the absence of detailed rentals prohibits the forming of firm opinions; but the foregoing juxtaposing of instances from Crown land and from private estates suggests, at least, that the degree of rent increase found necessary and viable on certain estates in certain parts of England may not have been parallelled here.

Another aspect of the question of rents tends to develop this impression. It has been argued that the process of commuting rents into cash payments had begun in parts of Wales before the fall of Llywelyn the last.[4] Yet the seventeenth century saw widespread continuation in this region of the paying in kind of customary dues and services.[5] The inhabitants of the granges of Llanycrwys, Traethmelgan, Cefngwlith, Gwyddgrug and Casta were in the

---

(1) *Ibid.*, /23.

(2) Some landlords averred greater sympathy with their poorer neighbours than with the Crown's, or any other magnate's, desire for augmented revenue (*vide infra*, p.68).

(3) Eric Kerridge, "The Movement of Rent, 1540-1640". *Econ. H.R.*, ser. 2, vol. vi (1953), pp.16 *et seq.*

(4) T. Jones Pierce, "The Growth of Commutation in Gwynedd during the Thirteenth Century", *B.B.C.S.*, vol. x, pt. iv (1941), pp.309-332. In the Welsh areas, "it is evident that before the final Conquest the process of commutation had been carried much further in South Wales than in large parts of North Wales many years later"; and in the Manor, or Englishry, "even by the end of the thirteenth century commutation had already made considerable advance, and it would seem that in Wales the movement was at least not behind that in contemporary England, and in some respects it was in advance" (William Rees, *South Wales and the March*, pp.223, 177).

(5) For cash-payments in Iscennen, Carnwyllion, Kidwelly and Llandovery of rents termed *cyfed, cyd, comorth, gwestfa*, etc., *vide* P.R.O. D.L. 42/120/4-6; S.C. 12/30/8.

reign of Elizabeth still alleged to be obliged to pay annually 260 days' work to Sir Henry Jones.[1] In 1624 Henry Rice of Newton, Carmarthenshire, esquire, leased to Rees ap John David Gwilym of Llandebie two tenements at an annual rent of £5 *plus* two days' reaping at every harvest, carriage of four horse-loads of coal from the coal-pit to the mansion-house at Newton, two capons yearly upon demand, one bushel of pure winnowed oats by the hoop or pack of the market measure of Llandeilo Fawr, to be delivered between 1 November and 1 January yearly, the grinding of all corn at Rice's new mill, and a heriot of the tenant's best beast.[2] The tenants of the manor and grange of Morfa Mawr in Cardiganshire in 1605 were expected by their landlord, Anthony Stanley, to supply labour for three days a year on the demesne of harvest-time, work for two days with horses and three harrows at sowing or harrowing time, work for one day with oxen to carry stones and for one day with a team of oxen to carry wood and other fuel.[3] Alban Stepney was alleged to have tried to recover from the clients of three water corn mills farmed by him in Haverfordwest the payment of their tithes in kind in excess of the old cash payment of 26s. 8d., the suggestion being that such a payment would be more advantageous to the landlord than the former cash payment.[4] In 1614 William Barlow of Cresswell in Pembrokeshire found difficulty in collecting from Thomas Phillips of Cilsant and Thomas Bowen of Robeston the sixty bushels of barley, sixty bushels of oats and twenty bushels of wheat they owed him by way of tithe.[5] The tenants of the grange of Ystlwyf owed in 1600 thirty stones of cheese, 22 rams, 22 lambs and 22 bushels of oats annually.[6]

In some places a definite scale for commutation appears to have been reached. Tenants in the grange of Anhuniog in Cardiganshire paid yearly rents of four teals of meal (20s.) and 3s. 4d. a year for

---

(1) P.R.O. E113/67/1511. In this and other instances taken from documents relating to lawsuits, the quantity of dues payable may have been in dispute but the concept of payments in kind is clearly operative.
(2) N.L.W. Dynevor, A/24.
(3) P.R.O. E112/145/36. The court found for the tenants (P.R.O. E124/1/399), though the plaintiff was not satisfied and brought a fresh suit.
(4) P.R.O. E112/151/26. Stepney was also alleged to have sought to attract custom to his mills by carrying the grain of clients at his own expense, changing the courses of streams, and so on. The leader of the opposition to him was William Warren, who prosecuted the matter over several lawsuits in Exchequer, Stepney countering with actions in King's Bench and winning at least three of the Exchequer suits (P.R.O. E124/1/72b, 131, 173, 223b; E123/29/96, 156).
(5) P.R.O. E112/151/45.
(6) P.R.O. E112/59/9A; /59/42: dispute over title.

commortha, four pounds of wool (2s.), three and a half teals of oats (21d.), twelve capons (4s.), half a sheep (12d.), one day's work (6d.), ten teals of wheat (66s. 8d.), one porker (2s. 4d.), one hundred eggs (12d.).[1] So explicit a scale was sometimes acceptable to neither party. In 1608 the stewards of the Earl of Essex in the grange of Mefenydd attempted to recover from the tenants two shillings a truck on the ancient rent of seven trucks of oats each containing one bushel of Winchester measure, and 26s. 8d. on each of three teals of oaten meal each containing four bushels. The tenants protested that they had been accustomed to smaller cash equivalents. The stewards tried not so much to compel payment at the new rate as to obtain payment in kind, but with this the tenants persistently refused to comply.[2] Several of the foregoing examples are drawn from formerly monastic property, by this time in private landlords' hands; some refer to tithes. But the same feature as regards payments in kind is clearly evident in the leases of the period which are not affected by these factors.[3]

The survival of payments in kind, in Tawney's view, can indicate two things.[4] First, "where money was scarce, tenants were sometimes allowed to pay in kind as a concession to their interests". That money was scarce in south-west Wales seems very probable. Secondly, the survival of non-cash payments supplies "a link between the vanishing subsistence cultivation and the growing commercial economy". This would suggest that the greater the growth of a commercial economy, the greater the demand for payments in cash. The converse seems equally valid.

The protection afforded by custom to tenants against arbitrary increases in their rents or fines is well-known. Crown surveyors in Cardiganshire and in Pembrokeshire recorded the predictable affirmation by freeholders that their fines on alienation, exchange or admittance, were fixed and certain. The sums involved varied, from commote to commote, from manor to manor; occasionally it is apparent that opportunities for free exchange by deed and release had resulted in a lapsing of customary procedures. But it seems clear that loaded inquiries were met with declarations unfavourable to the *rentier* landlord. In the commotes of Perfedd, Cyfoeth y Brenin and

---

(1) P.R.O. E112/145/51. The definition of dues in money terms does not exclude the possibility that actual payments were made in kind.
(2) P.R.O. E112/145/50.
(3) *Vide infra*, p.65.
(4) R. H. Tawney, *The Agrarian Problem in the Sixteenth Century*, p.211.

Llanilar in Cardiganshire, on the death of every freeholder his heir
paid a heriot or relief of ten shillings (Cyfoeth y Brenin) or 7s. 6d.
(Perfedd and Llanilar) on entering into his inheritance.[1] In the
manors of Bier and Penally there was no entry-fine, the land being
taken by the Rod with a payment of a penny each to the steward,
clerk and bailiff.[2] In St. Florence[3] the entry-fine was twopence
an acre, as was the alienation-fine at Reynalton[4]. In Narberth two
payments on decease or alienation obtained: 7s. 6d. in the Welsh
tenure, a shilling in the English.[5] In Templeton "upon the death
of every freeholder the lord ought to have twelvepence for relief",
and upon alienation, which was conducted "by deed and release, and
such other assurance and conveyance as is used by course of the
common law, and yet by the custom the same alienation ought to
be presented by homage in the lord's court; and upon that present-
ment the vendor shall pay fourpence to the steward for striking out
his name, and the vendee shall pay twelvepence".[6] In Ysgeifiog the
freehold tenants knew that they should pay a lump sum of five
shillings "upon every alienation or alteration of possession of any
part of their lands, be it more or less that is so alienated", and five
shillings relief.[7] In the Carmarthenshire lordship of Clinton the
alienation fine was five shillings; yet in St. Clears, within the same
lordship, the fine was "twelvepence due to the three portreeves there
for the same alienation or exchange, that is to say, fourpence to the
portreeve of Train Clinton, fourpence to the portreeve of Train
March and fourpence to the portreeve of Train Morgan".[8]

Tenants holding by base tenure were, of course, less immune.
The vulnerability of copyholders varied with local custom: they
might possess estates of inheritance; they might hold for life or lives;
their fines, in either instance, might be fixed or arbitrable. The benefits or otherwise to landlord or tenant of conversion of copyhold into
leasehold varied likewise in accordance with the nature of the copyhold. The conversion of copyhold for life or lives at arbitrable fines
into leasehold for an equivalent term need represent, in practical
terms, no immediate economic gain to either side other than the

(1) P.R.O. E134/3 Cas. I/E24.
(2) P.R.O. L.R. 2/206/88.
(3) P.R.O. L.R. 2/206/230.
(4) P.R.O. L.R. 2/260/20.
(5) P.R.O. L.R. 2/206/160b.
(6) P.R.O. L.R. 2/260/45b-46.
(7) P.R.O. L.R. 2/260/91.
(8) P.R.O. L.R. 2/260/182-185.

formalising of the landlord-tenant relationship. Further, the legal position of the sixteenth-century lessee for years was notably superior to that of his earlier counterpart.[1] The position of such a tenant became immediately disadvantageous only when landlords set out deliberately to demand high fines for beneficial leases or high rents for short terms

The available evidence relating to leasing policy on south-west Wales estates is, it must be said, extremely scattered and unsatisfactory. Out of thirteen collections of documents examined, yielding a total of approximately 240 leases,[2] only in one instance does there survive a sequence sufficient to indicate landlord policy on a single estate. The absence of contemporary estate surveys prevents any estimate of the relationship of fines to the values of properties leased,[3] or of the effect upon rents and fines of improvements made upon leased property, of the presence thereupon of buildings, or of the inclusion in leases of conditional clauses and reservations. Apparent leases which are in effect conveyances or mortgages further diminish the available evidence: witness John Vaughan of Trawsgoed's activities prior to his purchase from the Lewises of Abernantbychan in 1637,[4] or the device of lease and release evolved to defeat the Statutes of Uses and Enrolments, of which these collections contain several examples. The variety of the properties involved further obscures general attitudes: leases of mills or the profits of fairs are hardly comparable with leases of land. Payments in kind or services supplementing cash rents render it impossible to estimate the total amounts of rents demanded. The vast majority of these leases involve such payments, which sometimes constitute the entire rent, sometimes an appreciable proportion of it, sometimes are commutable into cash payments at either the lessor's or the lessee's choice, and sometimes are incidental: their occurrence is nonetheless highly significant.

Conclusions based on such evidence can only be very tentative. But it does not emerge that these landlords were over-inclined to

---

(1) Kenelm Digby, *op. cit.*, pp.241-245.
(2) N.L.W. Bronwydd, Derwydd, Dynevor, Eaton Evans and Williams, Haverfordwest Corporation, Crosswood, Llwyngwair, Maesgwynne, Maesnewydd, Muddlescombe, Poyston, Probyn, Slebech.
(3) For a discussion of this relationship in general, with the more sophisticated approaches developed in the early seventeenth century and the gradual realisation of aristocratic landlords that high rents and short terms yielded better returns than high fines and long terms, *vide* L. Stone, *op. cit.*, pp.318-322.
(4) *Vide supra*, p.41, note 3.

exploit their leasehold tenants. In Muddlescombe, within the Englishry of Kidwelly, between 1611 and 1639, Francis and Walter Mansell issued an extant total of 84 leases to their tenants. In these leases the average annual rent is £2 17s. 2½d.[1] Where cash fines are stated to have been exacted, the average rent is £2 5s. 7d. These fines varied enormously, from a maximum of £40 to a minimum of £2. In many instances, though the amount of the fine is not explicitly stated such a fine may perhaps be assumed from the phrase "valuable consideration", taken to imply a financial transaction as opposed to a lessor's non-fiscal motive expressed in such phrases as "good causes and reasonable considerations".[2] In these instances the average annual rent is £2 13s. 5d. But the average rent where there is neither cash fine recorded nor "valuable consideration" noted is £4 6s. 10d. There appears, therefore, to be some reason to assume that the exaction of a cash fine had an effect upon the rent beneficial to the tenant. But the outstanding feature of these leases is that terms remain constant throughout the period, with a few exceptions, at 21 years or three lives. The exceptions relate not to the exaction or non-exaction of cash fines, but rather to the nature of the premises: there are, for example, three leases of mills[3] for, respectively, one life, eleven years and fourteen years, each at a rent well above the average.

The predominance of 21 years or three lives as the standard term of a lease remains true for each of these collections, limited in usefulness as they are. In the Bronwydd papers, 12 out of 25 leases were for this term; the highest recorded fine (£33) was for a lease of 13 years, the rent in this instance being stated entirely in kind.[4] In the Dynevor collection, in 1607 an extraordinarily high fine (£70) was paid to Sir Walter Rice of Newton by John ab Ievan ap Rees of Llanegwad, gentleman, for a seven-year lease on several tenements in Llanarthney at a rent of £1 per annum; ten years earlier the same lessor had leased a messuage and land in Llanedi for two lives to a

---

(1) Making no allowance for rents in kind.
(2) But even this latter phrase does not necessarily exclude fines in cash: for example, N.L.W. Bronwydd, 934, where the phrase "for divers considerations him moving" introduces a lease for which a fine of £40 was paid.
(3) N.L.W. Muddlescombe, 1620: four mills with land to a widow at a rent of £5 6s. 8d. per annum, "for divers good and valuable considerations" (dated 1620); 1357: two mills to two yeomen at £17 per annum, "for good causes and considerations" (dated 1633); 1348: one mill to a gentleman for £10 per annum, "for good and valuable considerations" (dated 1636).
(4) N.L.W. Bronwydd, 2330: Philip Bryne of Llangynllo, gentleman, leasing a tenement and land to Ievan ap Lewis, yeoman, in 1589.

yeoman at a rent of two shillings *per annum* and apparently no fine
at all.[1] Such scattered instances prove very little. The only other
sequence that is at all meaningful in this assortment is one of sixteen
leases by the mayor and corporation of Haverfordwest, where terms
of 99 years remain constant throughout the sixteenth century, falling,
in five seventeenth-century leases, to 21 years and three lives, and
three of 7, 7, and 11 years respectively, two of which are on the
profits of a fair and of a shambles, and none containing any specific
mention of a cash fine. Elsewhere, George Owen tabulated his
leasehold tenants. Of 44 in 1583, five were for term of life, 33 for 21
years, one for twenty years, one for fourteen, two for ten, one for
eight and one for three. In 1594 he listed 25 leases, of which three
were for life, one for eight years and the rest for 21 years. This list
was added to until 1607, during which time nine more leases were
added: one for 99 years, two for life, three for 21 years, one for
twelve years, one for seven and one for six.[2] If some inclination
towards shortening terms may here be detected, the balance of the
evidence is in general against such a conclusion.

On occasion, fines alleged to have been arbitrarily increased in defiance of customary rights were contested in the lawcourts. Thomas
Bowen in Manorbier demanded from some of his tenants there fines
increasing over a succession of three tenants from £9 to £12, from
ten shillings to £4, and from £1 to £6, granting leases to those who
offered the highest fines; so, at least, his tenants asserted, regarding
this as an unprecedented and indefensible innovation, and endeavouring, in a lengthy lawsuit, to show that their fines were fixed by
custom.[3] In 1625 Sir John and Alban Phillips were alleged to have
raised Rice Lougher's fine on a tenement in the manor of Walwynscastle with the specific intent of securing his eviction.[4] Here is
conduct in the character of grasping landlordism, such as drew from
George Owen a lamentatious plaint for the poor tenant who "two
or three years ere his lease end . . . must bow to his lord for a new

---

(1) N.L.W. Dynevor B/90, B/777. *Cf. supra*, p.45.
(2) N.L.W. Bronwydd, 3 (*The Vairdre Book*), ff. 261, 207-208.
(3) P.R.O. E134/8 Jac. I/H7. The weakness in the tenants' case lay in the readiness
    of a few of their number not only to pay the sums asked by Bowen but also to
    try to outbid their neighbours. Also, *cf. infra*, p.74, note 4.
(4) P.R.O. E112/151/69. The defendants attempted to sidetrack this Exchequer
    suit with a counter-action in the Pembrokeshire Great Sessions, where their
    influence might have been expected to earn them some credit. Lougher secured
    an injunction against this, but owing to his failure properly to examine witnesses
    he lost face and, possibly, the action (P.R.O. E124/35/220; E124/36/67.)

lease and must pinch it out many years before to heap money together".[1] But that the landlord Owen should have condemned this
practice is as significant as the content of his remark.[2] It is an
attitude matched by that of George Devereux, who, writing to
Salisbury in 1611, declared, "I am to entreat your honourable favour
to my poor neighbours who are likely to be oppressed by a mighty
man, whom they are not able to encounter withal . . . He will undo
them all, which were great pity, for they and their ancestors have
always, time out of mind, lived honestly upon that which he will
impose such fines upon them . . . that they are not able to pay without
their utter undoing".[3] In fact, instances of protests against increased
fines are not numerous: certainly not when compared with the
appeal to custom from another quarter and from another motive.

   Custom, as Tawney suggested, has two faces:[4] that which pro-
tects the tenant, and that which rewards the lord. There is considerable evidence of the anxiety of landlords to wring the maximum
benefit from rights which they in their turn might claim to be long-
established. Whilst the agents of the Earl of Essex fought protracted
actions at law with tenants in several Cardiganshire granges over
rents and services in general, including such dues as *cylch march*,[5]
local gentry were usually more explicit. It was the refusal of tenants
to grind corn at the mills farmed by him that troubled Lewis Powell
of Greenhill, Pembrokeshire, the defendants answering that they had
always been used to grind their corn wherever they chose, and
pointing out that Powell's mills were both too small and too
dependent upon the ebb and flow of the tide to function efficiently.[6]
Edward Vaughan of Trawsgoed appeared similarly concerned to
wrest as much as he could out of his two mills in the grange of
Cwmystwyth, the tenants retorting with the neat point that they

---

(1) Owen, *The Description of Penbrokshire*, vol. i, p.190.
(2) *Cf.* W. Harrison, *Description of England* (1577): "Forget not also such landlords
     as use to value their leases at a secret estimation given of the wealth and credit
     of the taker, whereby they seem (as it were) to eat them up, and deal with bond-
     men; so that if the lessee be thought to be worth £100, he shall pay no less for
     his term, or else another to enter with hard and doubtful covenants. I am sorry
     to report it, much more grieved to understand of the practice" (quoted in L.
     Stone, *Social Change and Revolution in England*, p.124). Professor Stone
     considers that the country parson Harrison's analysis "of the evils of the day is
     perhaps more a product of conservative prejudice than of accurate observation"
     (*op. cit.*, p. 121).
(3) P.R.O. S.P. 14/66/45.
(4) R. H. Tawney, *op. cit.*, p. 128.
(5) P.R.O. E112/145/51, 52, 53, 55; E112/146/109.
(6) P.R.O. E112/151/58.

were obliged to grind at the grange mills only the corn actually
grown by them on grange land, and other corn, whether purchased
or otherwise acquired, they might grind where they pleased.[1] Sir
Richard Price of Gogerddan met similar objections.[2] In Carmarthenshire David Hopkin, a gentleman of Llanwrda, endeavoured to
recover his rights to the ancient payment of *amobr*, a sum of ten
shillings payable upon the marriages of the daughters of tenants in
Caeo, Manordeilo and Cethiniog: a claim which stamped him in
his tenants' eyes as "a young man of a very greedy and covetous
disposition".[3]

In several cases, monastic leasing policy prior to the Dissolution[4]
may have effectively frustrated alternative methods of improving
rentier incomes. But apart from this, prominent landlords placed great
emphasis upon their customary rights. Having clashed with the
Prince of Wales over his title to the alleged manors of Canaston,
Newton and Newhouse, Wilfrey and Robeston, and Taff Wood,
George Barlow spent a great deal of money in proving his claim,[5]
only to find the tenants refusing to recognise his title and yield him
dues and services, in particular as relating to manorial courts other
than those of the lordship of Narberth.[6] Driven to recklessness he
purchased that lordship too from the Prince,[7] but still met great
opposition to his demand for payment of dues in return for such
privileges as common of pasture and estovers[8] within the premises,

(1) P.R.O. E112/145/41.
(2) P.R.O. E112/145/32.
(3) P.R.O. E112/59/15.
(4) *Vide supra*, p. 33.
(5) Having initially striven to show from ancient deeds and records that Wilfrey was
a manor distinct and independent from the lordship of Narberth (N.L.W.
Slebech, 3185), and then offered to abandon his claim to Wilfrey if he might
retain the other manors (*ibid.*, 3044), he eventually succeeded in proving that he
had purchased all five manors from the Crown in 1602 (*ibid.*, 3087, 3116, 3094-6,
3098) and obtained a decree in Chancery confirming his title to them (*ibid.*, 4303)
(6) Barlow was ready to concede that the tenants of Wilfrey were "customary
tenants of inheritance, in nature freeholders, having a fee simple and perpetuity
to them and their heirs forever", and acknowledged the right of these fee-simple
tenants to convey their lands as they wished, as long as this were not prejudicial
to the lord's inheritance, if they would do suit and service at the leet court of
Slebech (*ibid.*, 3066).
(7) His son claimed that there had been paid "£2,000 and £56 rent *per annum*, which
is £23 *per annum* more than he doth or shall receive for the same for many years
to come. And he paid 50 years' purchase and almost if not fully a treble rent for
all the demisable lands, most whereof is estated for a life or two now in being
and 40 years in reversion. Which considered, the rate of his purchase was so
great as no subject usually giveth more, if so much" (*ibid.*, 3078). The tenants
themselves had offered a price for the lordship (*ibid.*, 3265).
(8) *I.e.*, their right to a reasonable amount of wood for fuel or repairs.

both parties fighting to the last ditch to maintain what they evidently
believed to be their just demands.[1] Sir Thomas Canon's attempt
to secure payment in return for common of pasture in the manor and
forest of Coetrath, and to ensure suit and service at his manorial
court there, prompted the tenants to appeal to the King, and
threatened their landlord's career of local service to the Crown.[2]
And George Owen's efforts in the cause of more than archival
accuracy to prove Cemais a feudal barony show an urge to exercise
feudal rights such as wardship therein to his own profit.[3]

   This persistence with ancient rights is suggestive rather of a retro-
spective than of a "progressive" attitude on the part of landlords. In
localities where freehold tenure predominated, *rentier* opportunity
was necessarily limited; but elsewhere the evidence does not suggest
the exploitation of their tenants by commercially-minded landlords.
Nor in the sphere of direct farming is the rapid development of a
commercial economy apparent. Reliance upon mixed farming is to
be found at all social levels and in most districts. In 1605 John Gibbon
of St. Florence, who farmed about 52 acres, had twenty of these
under crops, and owned in addition livestock to the total value of
£26.[4] In 1629 James Bowen of Llwyngwair had thirty head of
cattle, valued at £13 17s. 6d., 141 sheep, valued at £14 2s., four
hogs and one sow, worth 6s., four geese and two ganders, valued at
2s., and corn totalling £15 in value.[5] In 1575 Lewis ab Owen ap
John of Llangadog in Carmarthenshire left to his daughter Margaret
two oxen, eight kine, three heifers, two yearling heifers, one bullock,
45 sheep, five mares, two horses and a colt, together with all his
corn.[6] In 1584 John Price of Gogerddan left his wheat to be divided
equally between his sons Richard and James, and kine and sheep to

(1) For the consequences upon Barlow of this struggle, *vide supra*, p.45. The tenants
    complained that they were so impoverished by maintaining lawsuits that they
    could not continue the fight in the courts, and so they fell back upon petitions
    to the Prince's Council (*ibid.*, 3240). There was great bitterness on both sides,
    Barlow being accused of recusancy and potential treason, and he, for his part,
    announcing to the tenants that he would "crush and crack them like fleas"
    (*ibid.*, 3248).
(2) *Ibid.*, 3194, 3253.
(3) P.R.O. St. Ch. 5/05/2. Also, *vide* F. Jones, "The Roll of Wards of the Lords
    Marcher of Kemes", *B.B.C.S.*, vol. x, pt. i (1939), p.83.
(4) N.L.W. Probate Records: Diocese of St. David's (Archdeaconry of St. David's)
    1605.
(5) E. D. Jones, "An Inventory of a Pembrokeshire squire's chattels", *N.L.W.
    Journal*, vol. viii (1954), pp.222 *et seq.*.
(6) P.C.C. 19 Pyckering.

his mother.[1] Thomas Canon's certificate of William Scourfield's estate in 1622 included "in oxen, kine, horses, *etc.*, £200 3s. 6d.; in sheep and lambs, £118 6s.; in corn in the barns and in the earth, £67 5s."[2] George Owen's "survey of a farm"[3] ascribes, out of a total acreage of 375½, 103 to arable, 30 to meadow and 199 to pasture, valuing the arable at £8 13s. 4d. and the pasture at £8 19s. 8d.

But there is also considerable evidence, not confined to upland regions, of emphasis upon pastoral farming, with sheep predominating over cattle. The stock ascribed to Robert, Earl of Essex, in Carmarthenshire at the time of his attainder, totalled 1,973 sheep, 128 kine, 467 wethers, with another 32 kine, a bull and 360 sheep rented to his tenants, the whole valued at £870.[4] On the demesne of the castle of Laugharne Rees Phillips was said to keep two thousand English sheep, a hundred young cattle, 166 milch kine, twenty stud mares and colts, and a stallion.[5] On Sir John Perrot's demesne at Robeston there were three hundred sheep valued at 3s. 4d. each (£50), thirty kine in calf at 22s. a head (£33) and eight oxen at 33s. 4d. each (£13 6s. 8d.).[6] John Scurlocke's two hundred sheep and hundred lambs at Herbrandston were worth considerably more than his fourteen kine.[7] But the chief recommendation of these animals lay in their tolerance of hard living rather than in the excellence of their quality. The coarse wool of local sheep earned Welsh woollens a bad name.[8] Sir Thomas Perrot, attempting to persuade Burghley to procure a royal pardon for his father, emphasised the meagre material profit that the Crown stood to gain by his execution, saying that Sir John's stock of cattle and sheep was of no great value, "being mostly of the Welsh breed".[9] Moreover, the pastoral character of the medieval Welsh economy is familiar

---

(1) P.C.C. 41 Watson.
(2) P.R.O. Wards 5/51.
(3) Owen, *The Taylors Cussion*, pt. i, f. 25; though Owen's mysterious references in this survey to "the county of B" and the market towns of "A", "B" and "D", prompt some doubt as to how far the survey is representative of local conditions, or how far it may be hypothetical or transcribed from elsewhere.
(4) P.R.O. E178/3327.
(5) P.R.O. E112/151/36.
(6) P.R.O. L.R. 2/260/71b.
(7) N.L.W. Probate Records: Diocese of St. David's (Archdeaconry of St. David's), 1618.
(8) "The final verdict on the quality and worth of Welsh cloth shows that it was at once coarse, poorly made, and expensive" (T. C. Mendenhall, *The Shrewsbury Drapers and the Welsh Wool Trade in the XVI and XVII Centuries*, p. 21).
(9) *C.S.P.Dom.* (1591-1594), vol ccxlii, no. 28.

enough; "sheep-farming, dairy-keeping and cloth-weaving[1] were
the staple branches of industry in medieval Wales".[2] The population of north Carmarthenshire, north Pembrokeshire and the whole
of Cardiganshire has been described as being almost wholly occupied
in the fifteenth century in the rearing of sheep and cattle.[3] To
identify in this period some blurring of the economic distinction
between upland and lowland is not to recognise an economic
revolution.

In this connection, one symptom of change in the rural economy
may be the development of enclosure. The nature and degree of
change implicit in that term is susceptible to exaggeration; for the
term "enclosure" is capable of many meanings. Four interpretations
of it have been put forward by Dr. Slicher van Bath,[4] who
suggests that each "involved the partial or complete disintegration of
the open fields" and tended to the advantage of the large landowner.
Since a considerable proportion of the available evidence for this
region consists in lawsuit records, it is important to remember that
in law this same term does not necessarily imply erection of physical
demarcations in the shape of hedges, fences or ditches:[5] "for every
man's land is in the eye of the law enclosed and set apart from his
neighbour's, and that either by a visible and material fence as one
field is divided from another by a hedge, or by an ideal, invisible
boundary, existing only in the contemplation of the law, as when one
man's land adjoins to another's in the same field".[6] Viewed in this
light, there is a peculiar significance in the form of writs of trespass
issued out of the courts of Great Sessions. The writ *transgressus vi et
armis, transgressus clausum fregit*, or *transgressus vi et armis clausum fregit*

---

(1) For the decline of the cloth industry in this region, *vide infra*, p.85.
(2) E. A. Lewis, "The Development of Industry and Commerce in Wales during
   the Middle Ages", *T.R.H.S.*, new ser., vol. xvii (1903), p.139.
(3) T. I. J. Jones, "The Enclosure Movement in South Wales", University of Wales
   unpublished M.A. thesis (1936), p.52.
(4) "(1) Combining plots, scattered about the open fields, into united areas of far m
   land, surrounded by hedges; (2) reversion of ploughland to pasture; (3) enlarging of the big landowner's property by combining several plots into one, and
   destroying the dwellings on them; (4) seizure of the common waste by the large
   landowners, with a simultaneous decrease or even complete abolition of the
   rights of the commoners, or, in other words, the remaining farmers" (B. H.
   Slicher van Bath, *The Agrarian History of Western Europe, A.D. 500-1850*,
   p.164).
(5) Hereinafter termed "physical enclosure".
(6) Earl Jowitt, *The Dictionary of English Law*, vol. i, p. 395: quoting Blackstone
   Commentaries, iii, 290. A "boundary" is defined as "the imaginary line which
   divides two pieces of land from one another" (Jowitt, *op. cit.*, p.270).

apparently indicates the breaking of an enclosure by use of force. In fact, the *close* involved is simply a man's rights over his own property; and the accompanying force may be exercised by sheep, cattle, pigs or any other animals simply by straying upon the same.

Suits of this type occur with undiminishing regularity throughout this period, and suggest a marked absence of physical enclosure. In 1619 Henry Griffith of Pembrokeshire claimed that his neighbour, the yeoman Thomas James, had allowed his animals to cause damage in this way to the value of one hundred shillings to Griffith's crops of wheat and rye as well as to grass and hay,[1] there being apparently nothing to prevent their access to these. In 1551 William Owen of Cemais charged the husbandman, James Turner of Gwern y Gwythill, with a similar offence.[2] In 1621 Sir Robert Mansell prosecuted John Palmer of Laugharne similarly, the damage in this case being estimated at £60.[3] In Pembrokeshire in 1563 it was the yeoman Henry Jones's turn to prosecute William Jenkins of Cilgerran, esquire, the damage being estimated at £20.[4] Even so scientifically-minded a man as Robert Record had apparently no defence against the blind intrusion of the animals of a weaver and a tanner upon his property at Tenby.[5] In 1635 Stephen David, a gentleman of St. Dogmael's, was still exposed to the intrusion of the animals of his gentle neighbour, William Sandhowe, upon his premises,[6] just as Hugh Gwynne, gentleman, of Llannerchaeron in Cardiganshire, had been from another quarter forty years earlier.[7]

In explanation of the decline of "Rudwall custom, which was that no action of trespass lay for pasture in open fields out of enclosures", George Owen indicated not the growth of physical enclosure but the consolidating of strips into individual holdings.[8] It is this, together with the process of encroaching upon the waste, that represents the most common form of "enclosure" at this time, in which both large and small proprietors participated. John Prydderch's allegation against Thomas John Thomas in the court of Exchequer was that he "hath enclosed and united to his own lands about four acres of woodland": terms repeated by the defendant in

---

(1) N.L.W. Wales 25/111/10.
(2) N.L.W. Wales 25/8/13.
(3) N.L.W. Wales 19/70/13.
(4) N.L.W. Wales 25/24/1.
(5) N.L.W. Wales 25/80/3.
(6) N.L.W. Wales 25/143/9.
(7) N.L.W. Wales 18/51/3b.
(8) Owen, *The Description of Penbrokshire*, vol. i, p.193.

his answer.[1] It was for the "defacing of boundaries" in his efforts
to gain possession of land in the parish of Llannerchaeron that Thomas
Price, esquire, indicted his fellow justice of the peace, David Lloyd
of Abermâd, in 1600;[2] for "moving" the boundaries of several
messuages and tenements in Carew that Sir John Carew sued Edward
Webb and John Phillips of Picton in 1614;[3] and for "ploughing
up" boundaries that Charles Bowen and three others were prosecuted in 1620 by John Gwyther.[4]

Objections to these activities, though sometimes insinuating as a
defendant's motive such regrettable aims as "bringing and reducing
the inhabitants to stand in awe and dread of his great weight and
power",[5] frequently affirmed the need to retain ancient "meres
and bounds". [6] Alban Stepney of Prendergast, claiming on behalf
of the tenants of Rosemarket in 1586 that Morris Walter had encroached upon common land "and the arable hath converted into
pasture contrary to the laws and statutes", emphasised that the
defendant had "utterly taken away and caused to be taken away divers
hedges which were the known meres and ancient boundaries".[7]
In a survey of 1623 of Crown manors in Pembrokeshire[8] reference
was made to a comment by surveyor Robert Davy in 1578 to the
effect that enclosures in the freeholds adjoining the manor of
Staynton threatened encroachment upon Crown property there.[9]
Nearly fifty years later the surveyors reported of this same locality:
"Whereas the lands of these tenements do lie divided among the
tenants in small parcels lying intermixedly, whereby the tenants

---

(1) P.R.O. E112/146/68. Thomas was described in the bill as "a covetous and ill-
    disposed person".
(2) P.R.O. E112/59/24(A).
(3) P.R.O. E112/151/50.
(4) P.R.O. E112/151/60. The main dispute was over whether Gwyther's fine was
    fixed or arbitrable, a charge of converting arable into pasture being incidentally
    introduced. Gwyther brought actions in Chancery, Exchequer and Hereford
    Great Sessions, and appears to have lost them all (P.R.O. E124/29/67-68b).
(5) P.R.O. St. Ch. 8/290/7.
(6) Cf. "the value attached in the [Welsh] laws to the meer crosses of stone or wood,
    which, according to Giraldus, medieval Welshmen frequently moved to their
    own advantage" (William Rees, op. cit., pp.15-16).
(7) P.R.O. E112/62/2. A special commission jury later held that although Walter
    had "enclosed with hedges and ditches" pieces of Crown land which he claimed
    to hold by lease, he had left intact "the meres, bounds and landskares" (P.R.O.
    E178/3485/36 Elizabeth).
(8) P.R.O. L.R 2/206/38-39.
(9) "Forasmuch as the above-mentioned freehold adjoineth and lieth with the said
    ... lands ... it was not fit to let ... for fear of encroachment. But the said free-
    holders have since raised enclosures which now they make the bounds between
    their freeholds and the said lands" (ibid., loc. cit.).

cannot make full profit of their tenements, and thereby they are the less valuable in the letting, it were convenient in our opinion for his Highness's profit and for the benefit of the tenants, that by view of a jury in every manor or by some other direction from your Lordships the land were viewed and by exchange made entire, as near as may be, or sorted in such parts as the tenants may enclose and thereby make their best profit. . . . Notwithstanding" this proposal, the survey ends, "the ancient landskares and meres betwixt the pieces [should] be preserved".

This concern for ancient landmarks is a salutary reminder of the composition of landed property at that time. In 1631 Sir Walter Mansell of Muddlescombe leased to a mason and his two sons several "parcels of lands", some bearing such names as "*y llain*[1] *a'i phen i'r ffordd fawr*", "all which parcels of lands are situate, lying, being within the several fields of Mores and Siagog within the said lordship of Penbre".[2] In 1609, in Gerrard Bromley's survey of the lordship of Kidwelly, the jury for the commote of Kidwelly "say that they cannot make any perfect boundary of the said foreignry in respect that divers lands of the Welshry are intermingled among the lands of the foreignry".[3] In general, the variations in the form, development and distribution of open-field and strip-plot systems[4] are as well-known as is the post-Restoration persistence of traditional communal husbandry, presenting in "large areas especially of midland England . . . practical barriers to alternate husbandry".[5] But preoccupation with the development of "enclosure", and attempts to estimate its growth on the basis of ambiguous indications in contemporary documents, can obscure the extent to which individual holdings at all levels of society in this period were still made up of scattered parcels of "lands". Despite some modern controversy over the interpretation in detail of "lands" and their attributes,[6] the prevalence of this term in contemporary documents[7] should

---

(1) Defn., piece, narrow strip.
(2) N.L.W. Muddlescombe, 1594.
(3) P.R.O. D.L. 42/120/52b.
(4) For some discussion of open-field agrarian structure in Wales, *vide* P. Flatrès, *Géographie rurale de quatre contrées Celtiques*, pp.412-433.
(5) C. Wilson, *England's Apprenticeship, 1603-1763*, p.145.
(6) *Vide, inter alia*, M. W. Beresford, "Ridge and Furrow in the Open Fields", *Econ. H.R.*, ser. 2, vol. i (1948), pp.34-45; Eric Kerridge, "A Re-consideration of some former Husbandry Practices", *Agr. Hist. Rev.*, vol. iii (1955), pp.26-40; H. A. Beecham, "A Review of Balks as Strip-Boundaries in the Open Fields", *ibid.*, vol. iv (1956), pp. 22-44.
(7) Examples of this and of scattered holdings are to be found in P.R.O. D.L. 42/120; L.R. 2/206, 238, 258, 260.

present a counterbalance to over-ready recognition of "enclosure" in any of its more portentous senses.

For "enclosure" may mean[1] the development of large single units, as at Somerton in 1593 in the shape of "one entire tenement . . . of 100 acres, whereof 30 acres are arable ground, 4 acres are meadow, and the residue, being 66 acres, consisteth of moor, heath and furze, being pasture ground; it lieth all together and is enclosed".[2] It may also disguise the continued existence of "nine pieces in George Owen's close called George Owen's great close or park";[3] or "7 acres lying in a close containing 11 acres".[4] Its possible indication of reversion of ploughland to pasture is qualified by such instances as John Phillips of Picton, esquire's, holding in Robeston in 1623 of "arable in a close called Woodwaye, arable in a close called the Hill Park, arable and meadow called Hookes Meadow".[5] If "enclosure", in the form of the enlarging of their property by big landowners through amalgamating farms and destroying the dwellings thereon, is exemplified in Thomas Lloyd of Cilciffeth's activities in buying the lands of freeholders and turning them into sheep-walks and dairies to the "utter decay" of the said freeholders and depopulation of the lands so annexed:[6] so may the same broad descriptive term apply to the activities of such husbandmen as "one Rees Thomas Howell [who] hath not only erected one cottage in and upon some part of the said mountain, but also hath enclosed some part of the said mountain containing by estimation two English acres".[7] And if seizure of the common waste was perpetrated by Edward Dounlee, esquire, and Harry Vaughan, gentleman, who "enclosed . . seven acres or thereabouts . . . and converted the same to their own use" upon "a mountain called Althkanatha [sic] . . . wherein the freeholders of the said foreignry have time out of mind been accustomed to have free and common of pasture for all manner of cattle";[8] so was a like appetite indulged by David Thomas Llewelyn ap Howell of Conwilgaeo, yeoman, who "enclosed with

(1) To consider the alternatives suggested by Dr. Slicher van Bath (*supra*, p.72).
(2) P.R.O. L.R.2/260/223b.
(3) N.L.W. Bronwydd, 1264.
(4) P.R.O. L.R. 2/260/32b.
(5) P.R.O. L.R. 2/206/141.
(6) N.L.W. Bronwydd, 7149. This allegation was one of a series of imputations against Lloyd arising out of his alleged abuse of his authority as a justice of the peace.
(7) P.R.O. D.L. 42/120/159b-160.
(8) *Ibid.*, f.51b.

hedges and ditches" a common of 41 acres of mountain land and 21 acres of pasture, valued at best at a penny a year.[1]

"Enclosure", in any of its several meanings, was therefore engaged in during this period by men from all levels of society and with an indistinguishable variety of purposes and effects.[2] As long as "closes" may mean anything from physical barriers incorporating "gates . . . [which] are so narrow and straitened . . . that neither cart nor horse laden with hay and great loads can pass that way";[3] to "one close joining to the great orchard wall, having the wall on the north side and Milton leys on the west side";[4] to "closes" whose holders "had some [persons] to keep the cattle from coming into them",[5] or "one other close . . . which lay open to the mountain":[6] it is dangerous, in the absence of additional evidence, to attribute to such units, when baldly referred to, a precise and recognisable role in the improvement of actual agrarian practice. Where supplementary descriptions are lacking, "enclosers" cannot be credited with motives beyond those of acquisition and consolidation, such as prompted Edward Hugh, gentleman, in 1609 to lease from a neighbour yeoman several parcels of lands, "the biggest of the said four parcels . . . being environed with the lands of the said Edward on the east and west parts, and adjoineth on the north to the highway . . . The second parcel is separated from the first by the lands of the said Edward . . . The third parcel, being about half an acre, . . . goeth directly between the lands of the said Edward to the said highway; and the fourth, being about half an English acre, . . . adjoineth to the lands of the said Edward . . . and is on all other parts compassed about with the lands of the said Edward".[7] Consolidation may be an advisable preliminary to effective technical improvement; in itself it does not necessarily imply that such improvement simultaneously went forward. Without corroborative proof of technical advance, it is difficult to regard "enclosure" as representing other than a part of a process of more extensive farming.

(1) P.R.O. E178/3350.
(2) E. C. K. Gonner argued that enclosure was not necessarily "subversive of the open field system, but in some cases, it was essential to its practical and effective working" (*Common Land and Inclosure*, pp.108-109).
(3) N.L.W. Wales 28/163/1.
(4) P.R.O. L.R. 2/260/32.
(5) P.R.O. D.L. 42/120/108b. *Cf. supra*, p.56, note 1.
(6) *Ibid.*, f. 101.
(7) N.L.W. Muddlescombe, 2008.

That this period witnessed gradual accumulation of land into individual hands—a process already long in operation—has already been shown.[1] Whether the litigation of the time in this connection arose more out of unadulterated acquisitiveness than out of genuine uncertainty as to title, is often obscure. George Owen, with his accustomed regard for Tudor legislation, made the point that formerly in "the counties of Carmarthen and Cardigan... all lands and tenements passed by surrender in the lord's court according to the laws of Howell Dda, so that in these countries you shall find no deeds, releases, fines nor recoveries of any lands before 27 Henry VIII except in certain boroughs", whereas Pembrokeshire people, with some exceptions, "used here to pass all their lands according to the ceremonies of the laws of England".[2] The preamble to that statute,[3] itself less effective than the authorities had hoped, amply illustrates the confusion then existing in England concerning the transference of land. Furthermore, contemporary documents are illustrative for this region of the indecisiveness of customary practices in this connection. In 1631 Nicholas ap Rees, a gentleman of Cenarth, describing the procedure whereby "the freehold owners of lands within the lordship or manor of Emlyn were accustomed to hold their lands within the said lordship or commote by the rod or virge, ... deposeth that he saw the virge or rod used in form above mainfested at such time as one Harry ap John of Cryngae, deceased, was steward under Sir Henry Jones, knight ... being above three-score years now last past; ... and he knoweth of no other estate but by the virge or rod passed all that time". To this interesting deposition Thomas ap Rees David ap David, a gentleman of Cilrhedyn, added "that he had no other estate, deed or writing upon the said premises and for the possessing and holding thereof but by the said rod or virge".[4] In 1632 Lord Carbery complained that his

---

(1) *Vide supra*, pp.40-50.
(2) Owen, *op. cit.* , vol. i, pp.169-170.
(3) 27 Henry VIII, c. 10 (The Statute of Uses): "Divers and sundry imaginations, subtle inventions and practices have been used, whereby the hereditaments of this realm have been conveyed from one to another by fraudulent feoffments, fines, recoveries, and other assurances craftily made to secret uses, intents and trusts", *etc.* Whilst no such preamble amounts to an objective statement of historical reality, the statute, with the supplementary Statute of Enrolments (27 Henry VIII, c.16), clearly aimed, *inter alia*, at the necessary "restoration of the publicity of conveyance"; but, owing to the abandoning of the original draft proposals for the latter statute, "the ingenious conveyancer had not much difficulty in evading the obligation to enrol imposed by this makeshift piece of legislation" (W. S. Holdsworth, *A History of English Law*, vol, iv, pp. 460, 467).
(4) P.R.O. E134/6 Cas. I/M1.

tenants in Emlyn had been transferring their lands independently of this procedure.[1] None of the defendants nor deponents denied this, but many pleaded ignorance as to the proper custom.

Uncertainty of this sort pervaded the whole province of land tenure at this time, from essential details of manorial custom to the definition of the boundaries of estates and parishes. In 1609 in the course of a dispute over whether a certain parcel of land was a part of the manor of Eglwys Gymyn, Rees John Davy, an eighty-years-old yeoman, deposed that he knew it was because "about sixty years now last past he (among others) went in procession with a number of the parishioners of the said parish round about the same parish to tread the bounds and limits thereof; and coming to the said parcel, called *y maen dalfa*, alias maynstone, the eldest sort of the company, some of them being about eighty years of age, did then shew and declare to this deponent and the rest that the said parcel was part of the said parish . . . and did lie within the same".[2] The custom of beating the bounds is familiar enough; its implications are obvious. In 1631 Edward Vaughan of Trawsgoed's claim to mine for lead on his own freehold gave rise to disagreement over how far the parish of Llanfihangel y Creuddyn was separate and distinct from that of Llanafan, the opinions of those who had "walked the bounds", and the degree to which a particular brook constituted a meaningful boundary, being variously appealed to by the parties.[3] Further, in the fundamental sphere of land-measurement there was significant inconsistency. George Owen observed in 1593 that in Cemais and Castlebigh 12 feet equalled 1 pole, 2 poles in length and breadth formed a yardland, 40 yardlands a stang, 4 stangs an acre, 10 acres an oxland, 12 oxlands a ploughland and 10 ploughlands a knightfee; whereas in Woodstock, Ambleston and Reynalton 11 feet made a pole, 2 poles a yardland, 40 yardlands a stang, 4 stangs an acre, 8 acres an oxland and 8 oxlands a ploughland, with "no certainty of any knightfee".[4] And so it is not surprising to find one

(1) P.R.O. E134/6 & 7 Cas. I/H3.
(2) P.R.O. E134/6 Jac. I/H12.
(3) P.R.O. E134/5 & 6 Cas. I/H11.
(4) P.R.O. L.R. 2/260/21. Elsewhere Owen noted that "in Pembrokeshire the pole differeth almost in every hundred of the shire from other, for in some place the pole is but ix foot, and in some place xii foot, and so differing between both". Attempting to reduce "the same briefly into a table", he admitted that this might "seem to miss in some particular hamlet or townred which perchance of late have altered". As to weights and measures, "they use difference as well from the unual measure of the realm as in divers parts among themselves within the shire" (*op. cit.*, vol. i, pp.133, 135, 137).

man estimate a piece of land in Milton in Pembrokeshire at 24 acres worth 5s. 6d. an acre, and another the same piece at 20 acres worth 6s. 8d. apiece.[1]

Again, it would be foolish to ignore the possible contribution to this uncertainty, in the shape both of misunderstandings and of opportunities for abuse and exploitation, of the legacy of Welsh law, with its attemps from the early thirteenth century to reconcile individual accumulation of land with the "complex of customs, including the prohibition of alienation", which had "severely restricted . . . freedom to dispose of land at pleasure".[2] What Professor Jones Pierce has elsewhere termed "the adjustment of Welsh medieval arrangements to the manorial framework of English property law in the sixteenth century"[3] should not be allowed to obscure, simply through contemporary adjustments in legal terminology, the surviving influence of former practices. Another historian, commenting on the Exchequer Decrees, has held these to be "of vital importance inasmuch as they detail the attempts of the Crown lawyers of Queen Elizabeth to solve the intricate problems which were the legacy of the tribal system in the Principality".[4] It seems, in short, that either of two constructions may be placed upon lawsuits arising out of disputes over title: that each party genuinely believed himself to have a rightful claim to the property in question, neither being able to produce incontrovertible proof of this; or that the opportunity to take advantage of an indeterminate situation was being grasped. Whereas it is now, in many instances, impossible to arrive at a just view of each matter, these considerations must qualify opinion as to the degree of acquisitiveness exhibited at that time.

Even so, the evidence as a whole suggests that landowners seeking to increase their landed incomes tended rather towards more extensive farming than towards any other of the alternatives here under consideration. Over and above the numerous indications of accumulation and consolidation apparent at all levels, there is positive evidence of the activity of leading gentry in this direction. Between 1583 and 1594 George Owen's income from land increased from

(1) P.R.O. E134/20 Jac. I/T8.
(2) T. Jones Pierce, "Social and Economic Aspects of the Welsh Laws", *Welsh Hist. Rev.* (Special No. 1963), p.42.
(3) *Id.*, "Medieval Cardiganshire—a Study in Social Origins", *Ceredigion*, vol. iii, pt. iv (1959), p.283.
(4) E. G. Jones, *Exchequer Proceedings (Equity) concerning Wales*, p.vii.

£160 18s. 2d. to £251 4s. 1d.[1] The greatest single contribution to this increase was the growth in income from the demesne land[2] at Bayvil, coupled with the addition of that of Eglwyswrw, from £13 to £60. Newshipping, which "in times past . . . consisted only of a messuage and thirty acres of arable and ten acres of furze and pasture", was increased in size by Sir John Perrot to well over a hundred acres, partly by purchase and partly by the addition of "parcels of ground taken from tenements in Newton", and "used by him as his demesne and . . . for maintenance of his house".[3] To the demesne at Carew Perrot added 118 acres purchased from Lady Jones, together with some other purchases. Newshipping was described as a "dairy", suggesting some measure of specialisation in husbandry,[4] though the survey of that property notes several parcels of arable and distinguishes between items which "lie together in one piece" and others lying "amongst other grounds". Evidence of more intensive farming practice is sparse or ambiguous; there remain clear indications of landowners extending their activities in the sphere of direct farming.

Finally, the mineral deposits of this region were sufficiently inviting to attract the attention of influential outsiders, such as Sir John Poyntz of Acton, Gloucestershire,[5] Sir Richard Lewkenor, Chief Justice of Chester[6] and Sir Hugh Myddelton of Denbigh and

---

(1) N.L.W. Bronwydd, 3 (*The Vairdre Book*), ff. 209-210, 259-261.
(2) This conclusion depends upon the meaning of Owen's phrase "*scitus manerii*" in this connection. Meaning, strictly, "site of the manor", it may also denote "site of the manor-house" or "site of the demesne lands of the manor"; this last, in the context, is the only reasonable interpretation. (I am grateful to Mr. Reginald Lennard and to Mr. F. W. Brooks for their views on this point).
(3) P.R.O. L.R. 2/260/33b-34, 216-221. The degree to which customary tenants suffered through annexation of parts of their holdings by Perrot is difficult to estimate in the absence of indications as to what proportion of their tenements was appropriated. Items as large as "fifteen acres in a croft . . . sometime belonging to the tenement wherein Thomas Gibbon dwelleth" seem exceptional, most items of this sort amounting to one or two acres.
(4) "Dairy", a term occurring elsewhere in George Owen's writings (for example, *The Taylors Cussion*, pt. i, ff. 31-34) and in surveys, denotes some emphasis upon pastoral farming; *cf.* Daniel Defoe, writing in 1727 of southern England: "All the lower part of this country is full of large feeding-farms, which we call dairies" (*Tour of Great Britain*, vol. ii, p.41). But *cf.*, too, Owen's "order to lay down the whole profit and commodity of a farm or dairy stocked by the owner thereof as well of the corn as of all other profits thereof arising", in which corn amounted to £80 out of a total gross profit of £192 (*op. cit.*, ff. 33-33b).
(5) P.R.O. E112/146/81: coal, lead and iron mines in Kidwelly. Poyntz was Chamberlain in the Exchequer (*C.S.P. Dom.* (1623-1625), p.670).
(6) P.R.O. E112/145/77: lead mines in the parish of Llanfihangel y Creuddyn.

London.[1] Insofar as industrial development depended on the availability of coal (if only to a limited degree in this period) and of means of transport, these conveniences were here present; insofar as it depended upon the availability of capital for investment, the resources of local men were herein deficient. As regards coal, Walter Vaughan of Golden Grove worked mines in Llangennech, Llwynhendy and Kidwelly.[2] In 1609 "one Thomas Lloyd of Llangennech, gentleman, hath and doth work coal-works at a place called Allt Llangennech", and "one David Vaughan, gentleman, hath wrought coals at or near a place called Llwynhendy".[3] In Pembrokeshire "small pits were to be found in a broad belt from Coetrath to St. Bride's Bay".[4] How far these represent commercial undertakings is doubtful. The jury of 1609 affirmed "that there are coals found, wrought and digged in the said common called Mynydd Mawr the use whereof the said tenants . . . had for all the time whereof the memory of man is not to the contrary for necessary fires and burning of lime as part of their freehold";[5] of Lloyd's and David Vaughan's activities, "what the quantity and yearly value thereof is they know not". There were coal-mines at Nolton in 1593, but the profits were "nil, for that it is casual".[6] Despite some increase in activity, immediate domestic needs, such as prompted Owen Nash to dig up stone coals in 1551,[7] continued to outweigh commercial incentives. "The country people," wrote George Owen, "dislike with the selling of [sea-coal] . . . lest in time it grow so scarce that the country shall want it".[8] An anonymous author of a memorandum "against the transportation of sea-coals" agreed that "the veins of Wales are no more than needful for that country".[9]

Landowners' rights to extract metallic mineral ores on their estates were complicated by the principle of Crown ownership over all mines of precious metals, interpreted in 1568 as including "all

---

(1) *C.S.P. Dom.* (1623-1625), vol. clxxxiv, no. 15. In 1625 the projector William Gomeldon estimated that these Cardiganshire silver and lead mines might be made to yield £10,000 yearly, adding that they had been worked in ancient and modern times (*ibid*, no. 14).
(2) F. Jones, "The Vaughans of Golden Grove", *loc. cit.*, p. 104.
(3) P.R.O. D.L. 42/120/160b-161.
(4) B. E. Howells, "The Elizabethan Squirearchy of Pembrokeshire", *The Pembrokeshire Historian*, vol. i (1959), p. 26.
(5) P.R.O. D.L. 42/120/188.
(6) P.R.O. L.R. 2/260/66b.
(7) N.L.W. Wales 25/8/14b.
(8) Owen, *op. cit.*, vol. i, p.57.
(9) H.M.C. *Cal. Salis. MSS.*, vol. xiv, p.330.

ores that contained the slightest trace of gold or silver".[1] Royal licencees occasionally encountered unwarranted competition from local men. In 1618 Edward Vaughan of Trawsgoed, Sir Richard Price of Gogerddan and Thomas Jones were alleged to have stopped the working of lead mines at Cwmystwyth in an endeavour to deprive Sir Anthony Ashley of the premises in the interests of William Wingfield and Matthew de Questor.[2] Philip Vaughan, with four accomplices, and Morgan Thomas Herbert, a gentleman of Cwmystwyth, with two others, were alleged to have stolen ore from the mines of Poyntz and Lewkenor respectively.[3] This may indicate some jealous aspiration on the part of local landowners, themselves as a rule poorly placed to secure patents and concessions, to tap these deposits on their own account.[4] John Canon, enjoying the position of feodary, was authorised in 1623 to "undertake the working" of lead mines upon his Pembrokeshire estate, "which yield 60 lbs. of lead and 8 ozs. of silver per cwt. of ore", the sheriff of Somerset being ordered "to send him ten or twelve of the most skilful workmen from the Mendip mines to assist him".[5] In Cardiganshire Edward Vaughan entertained similar notions;[6] but although "the owners of lands containing mines royal" were afforded some measure of "preference over others in obtaining leases of them", those of Cardiganshire were reserved for Myddelton "in recompense for his industry in bringing a new river into London".[7] In 1636 the person authorised by "the Governors, Assistants and Society of the City of London of and for the Mines Royal . . . to search, dig and mine for ores and metals" in Carmarthenshire was no local gentleman but one Henry Murrey.[8] Moreoever, estimates by contemporary projectors of the output likely to be derived from their proposed undertakings were notoriously optimistic. If the records of maritime commercial activity through the ports of south-west Wales provide any indication of the quantity of minerals mined in that locality, output there was not impressive.

---

(1) L. Stone, *Crisis of the Aristocracy*, p.339.
(2) P.R.O. E134/15 Jac. I/H18.
(3) P.R.O. E112/146/81;/145/77. Myddelton's mines also suffered (*vide C.S.P.Dom.* (1623-1625), vol. clii, no. 22).
(4) *Cf.* the advantage of technical expertise in the appointment of Robert Record to supervise the royal mines and the royal mint in Ireland (*C.P.R.* (Edward VI), vol. iv (1550-1553), p. 144).
(5) *C.S.P.Dom.* (1623-1625), vol. clii, no. 9.
(6) *Vide supra*, p. 79.
(7) *C.S.P.Dom.* (1623-1625), vol. clvi, no. 6; vol. clxxxiv, no. 15.
(8) *Ibid.* (1635-1636), vol. cccxxvi, no. 68.

3. MARITIME COMMERCE.

Although companies, notably of weavers and tuckers, existed at
Carmarthen[1] and at Haverfordwest,[2] gild life had never been
strong in Wales,[3] and individual traders were comparatively un-
hampered by restrictive regulations. In consequence, there was in
this regard some opportunity for spontaneous expansion of commercial activity and for the participation of country gentlemen
therein. Moreover, there was some tradition, however modest, of
maritime commercial enterprise. Ships having some association with
Tenby and Milford traded to Bristol in the fifteenth century.[4]
From the fourteenth to the mid-sixteenth centuries butter, cheese,
wool, skins, hides and cloth constituted "the staple and surplus
produce of the country" in the form of exports.[5] The availability
of excellent harbours,[6] and the need of Elizabethan armies in Ireland
for supplies, furnished additional conveniences and incentives.

But for the Elizabethan period it has been observed that "none of
this [foreign] trade of the South Wales ports was on a large scale",
and that apart "from cloth and coal and a little grain, butter and
cheese, South Wales had not much to offer to the outside world".[7]
Despite its basic truth, this statement is in many particulars mis-

---

(1) The Carmarthen weavers received their charter in 1574 and the tuckers in the
    same year (C. A. J. Skeel, "The Welsh Woollen Industry in the Sixteenth and
    Seventeenth Centuries", *Arch. Camb.* (1922), p.236). At about this time there
    were also formed companies of tanners, cordwainers, hammermen, tailors,
    saddlers and glovers (Glyn Roberts, in *A History of Carmarthenshire* (ed. J. E.
    Lloyd), vol. ii, p. 18).
(2) D. J. Davies, *The Economic History of South Wales prior to 1800*, p.55.
(3) David Williams, *A History of Modern Wales*, p.90.
(4) E. M. Carus-Wilson, *The Overseas Trade of Bristol in the later Middle Ages*,
    Bristol Record Society Publications, vol. vii (1937), pp. 218-289. Without
    additional corroboration too much reliance should not be placed on simple
    statements in port records concerning these vessels' ports of origin. *Cf.* M. I. J.
    Brugmans, "Les Sources de l'Evolution Quantitative du Trafic Maritime des
    Pays-Bas (XIIe- XVIIIe siècles)", in M. Mollat (ed.), *Les Sources de l'Histoire
    Maritime en Europe*, p.421: "Le lieu d'origine et le lieu de destination ne sont
    pas toujours indiqués d'une manière uniforme".
(5) E. A. Lewis, "A Contribution to the Commercial History of Medieval Wales",
    Y Cymmrodor, vol. xxiv (1913), p.95. The evidence there presented of "the
    import (excepting wine) and export customs of Wales from Michaelmas 1301 to
    Michaelmas 1547" (*ibid.*, pp. 124-133) shows no very great quantity even of these.
(6) Carmarthen had a "fair haven", Milford "one of the fairest and capablest
    harbours of this realm" (H.M.C. *Cal. Salis. MSS.*, vol. ix, p.292).
(7) T. S. Willan, *Studies in Elizabethan Foreign Trade*, pp.86-87. As regards the
    coasting trade, Mr. Willan concludes that "in the first half of the seventeenth
    century Milford shipped coastwise mainly agricultural produce" (*The English
    Coasting Trade, 1600-1750*, pp. 178-179).

leading. Firstly, "in the early sixteenth century cloth manufacture migrated from Pembroke, Carmarthen and Monmouth to the centre and north";[1] and in consequence it was the raw material rather than the manufactured commodity that was available from the south-west in this period. "The lower part of the shire", wrote George Owen, "vent and sell their wool to Bristol men, Barnstaple and Somersetshire, which come twice every year to the country to buy the wool. The upper parts, as Cemais and Cilgerran, sell their wool weekly at the market of Cardigan which is bought by North Wales men and wrought by them to white cloths which they sell to Shrewsbury men".[2] Confirmation of this comes from the clothiers of Bristol themselves, who "have most of their wool out of Pembrokeshire, being 100 miles distant, which ever heretofore hath been transported by sea from Milford Haven unto the port of Bristol by port cockett",[3] the necessary transport being apparently furnished by the clothiers rather than by local merchants.[4] When in 1622 the Privy Council sent letters to "the most discreet and sufficient clothiers of every shire of this kingdom where any kind of woollen cloths, kerseys, cottons or dozens be made", the 25 shires so addressed included Denbigh, Merioneth and Montgomery, but neither Cardigan, Pembroke nor Carmarthen.[5] Secondly, the commodities passing through the local ports were of a much greater variety than this comment suggests. The foreign and coasting import and export trade of the port of Milford and its members between 1550 and 1603, as represented in the extant port books, involved 102 different kinds of commodity, ranging from almonds to wire, from livestock to millstones.[6]

Simple quantitative comparisons between different ports on the evidence of subsidy and custom duties paid, especially between London and the ports of remoter regions, are obviously unreliable as an index of actual trading activity, if only because of the problems

(1) T. C. Mendenhall, *op.cit.*, p.3.
(2) Owen, *op. cit.*, vol. i, p. 57.
(3) P. McGrath, *Merchants and Merchandise in Seventeenth-Century Bristol, Bristol Record Society Publications*, vol. xix, pp. 142-143. This, a petition against government restrictions upon the free shipping of wool, may to some extent exaggerate the importance of this source of supply.
(4) "The said Bristol clothiers have ever heretofore transported the said country wools to Bristol" (*ibid., loc.cit.*).
(5) *A.P.C.* (1621-1623), pp.190-191.
(6) This total, compiled from E. A. Lewis, *The Welsh Port Books, 1550-1603*, pp. 49-235, takes no account of different types of corn, wool, coal, *etc.*

of administration.[1] Three points emerge, however, from an analysis of the Welsh port books.[2] A relatively large number of merchants used the ports of south-west Wales, but of these a high proportion made very few voyages each, involving, for example, only a few frises or a few tons of culm. Exceptional as was Sir Francis Godolphin's shipment of 100 packs of charcoal and thirty small oaks to St. Ives in 1593,[3] it highlights the manner in which individual merchants engaged in occasional transactions for specific purposes *via* these ports. Secondly, of those who did engage in regular trading ventures there was a great prominence of men, like Jethro Biggs of Carmarthen, who made no claims to gentry status. Thirdly, the names of leading gentlemen make rare appearances in the port books.

Between 1550 and 1603 sixty-five of the local merchants trading through the ports of south-west Wales would have claimed to be gentry.[4] Closer examination of this apparently impressive number shows that the amount of trade handled by them was small. The coasting export of wool totalled 24,324 stones, together with 360

(1) For example, for what it is worth, P.R.O. S.P. 12/281/107 provides an account of customs received on all kinds of cloth from 37-43 Elizabeth. The ports entered are London, Sandwich, Chichester, Ipswich, Southampton, Yarmouth, Newcastle, Hull, Poole, Exeter, Dartmouth, Bristol, Boston, Lyme, Plymouth, Fowey, Cardiff, and always last, nearly always least, and sometimes omitted altogether, Milford. By far the greatest part of the total was invariably derived from London: a fact to which the inefficiency of provincial customs officials was no doubt contributory. In any event, Milford's contribution is notably modest:

Year	TOTAL: (All ports in England and Wales, except Berwick)	MILFORD
37 Eliz.	£5,027 16s. 0d.	22s. 10d.
38 Eliz.	£3,958 15s. 4d.	—
39 Eliz.	£3,893 4s. 4d.	7s. 4d.
40 Eliz.	£4,883 16s. 0d.	6s. 4d.
41 Eliz.	£4,763 19s. 3d.	—
42 Eliz.	£4,974 8s. 1d.	9s. 2d.
43 Eliz.	£6,718 1s. 10d.	3s. 4d.

(2) The following discussion is based upon a statistical analysis of the port books as published by E. A. Lewis. Totals have been compiled for the import and export, foreign and coasting, of each separate commodity, with the activities of gentry tabulated apart. For full tabulated details, *vide* my "Gentry of South-West Wales, 1540-1640", University of Oxford D.Phil. thesis (1964), pp.368-409.
(3) Lewis, *op. cit.*, p. 159. Godolphin "devoted all his ability to his mining affairs and public business within the county" (A. L. Rowse, *Tudor Cornwall*, p.54); though *cf. supra*, p. 55, note 5.
(4) This figure has been arrived at by checking the names of merchants in the *Port Books* against Lewis Dwnn's *Heraldic Visitations*.

tods, 2 fardels, 20 sacks, 24 bags; the gentry contribution amounted to 10 sacks. Similarly, 40 measures, 1,630 quarters and 1 sack of rye were exported, the gentry contributing 80 quarters; of wheat, 128 measures, 1,000 bushels, 350 quarters, 2 sacks and 200 barrels, gentry merchants further contributing 100 quarters and 240 barrels. The employing of factors by gentry may conceal their actual trading operations. In 1571 Alban Stepney complained to the Privy Council that Sir John Perrot, when in Ireland, took from Stepney's factor £100-worth of the wheat he had transported there for the victualling of the army, "and neither showeth any cause why he hath taken it from him, nor yet appointed any order to pay for it".[1] Merchants and shipmasters were separately entered in the port books; there are instances where the former in fact signify factors, acting for the royal purveyor of Munster,[2] or for busy merchants who were simultaneously occupied on their own account.[3] A factor might be either a shipmaster or travelling salesman to whom the merchant, himself remaining at home, entrusted his wares, and who sold these and brought back others; or a permanent resident abroad, who sold his employer's cargo when it arrived and arranged for return cargoes;[4] or, conceivably, a representative in the home ports, with full responsibility over his employer's maritime commercial affairs. In general, the coasting trade was lacking in formal organisation, so that merchant seamen might "at one point . . . be masters and merchants, at another they might be masters carrying goods for a merchant, at yet another they might be shipping goods in a boat of which they were not master".[5] But however far arrangements might vary for individual shipments, it is unlikely, if the leading gentry regularly relied upon factors to conduct their seagoing trade on their behalf, that their own names would figure as merchants at all in the port books. Yet the names of Perrot,[6] Edward Dounlee,[7] Hugh Owen of Orielton,[8] John Scourfield of New Moat,[9] Sir

(1) *A.P.C.* (1571-1575), pp.51-52, 190.
(2) Lewis, *op. cit.*, p.200; Richard Wogan, factor for Captain John Woods.
(3) *Ibid.*, p.203; Richard Perrot, factor for William Gibbon in a cargo of wheat and malt for Waterford; Gibbon himself entered as merchant in a similar cargo for Dublin.
(4) T. S. Willan, *Studies in Elizabethan Foreign Trade*, p.3.
(5) *Id., The English Coasting Trade, 1600-1750*, pp.52-53.
(6) Foreign import: "newlonde" fish, 19,000; salt (bay and French), 26 tuns.
(7) Foreign export: coal, 10 weys.
(8) Coasting export: corn: barley, 60 bushels; pilcorn, 26 bushels; wheat, 40 bushels.
(9) Coasting export: corn: pilcorn, 40 qrs.; rye, 80 qrs.; wheat, 100 qrs.; barley-malt, 20 qrs.

John Vaughan,[1] to name only a few prominent gentlemen, do so
occur—sometimes concerned only in single shipments, on occasion,
perhaps, of special importance, but sufficient to cast doubt on their
consistent reliance upon factors. The occasional appearance of these
names can only suggest that their owners' participation in sea-going
trade was itself only occasional.

Apart from these somewhat more complex aspects of trading
organisation, there are some instances of the formation of simple
trading partnerships. Of men claiming gentry status, Thomas Bowen
of Kidwelly conducted all his sea-going trade in partnership with
Henry Vaughan of the same town and Thomas Floyd of Glyn. All of
Morgan Powell's foreign trade, both import and export, was conducted in partnership with his half-brother, Thomas Powell of
Haverfordwest; his coasting trade, far greater in variety if not in
quantity, he conducted alone. Humphrey Toy took into partnership
for his foreign import of skins and sugar Jenkin Ievan Philip of
Carmarthen, a man apparently his inferior in social rank. It may be
suspected that partnerships were negotiated chiefly for purposes of
foreign trade, when the added cost of launching, and risk attendant
upon, the venture could be better sustained if shared.[2] Out of 23
commodities traded in partnership, seventeen were foreign and only
six coasting enterprises. Yet when John Howell in 1565 was partnered
by Roger Collin in shipping cloth from Carmarthen to Bristol, and
in 1587 was exporting cloth and importing salt to and from France
on his own,[3] there is reflected some increased capacity on the part
of the trader. Even so, it seems incredible that men could rise to the
social prominence of the Toys in Carmarthen[4] or the Powells in
Pembroke on the profits of the amount of trading atttributable to
them from the port books. John Palmer of Laugharne figures as a
bigger, certainly more frequent, trader than his namesake of Tenby,
yet the latter called himself a "gentleman", a status to which the
latter made no apparent claim. Thomas Powell, who appears to have

---

(1) Foreign import: English horses, 3.
(2) Even trade in home waters was not lacking in hazard. In 1588 Thomas Perrot
    wrote to Dr. Julius Caesar on behalf of Hugh Bowen, who "being a younger
    brother and desirous to get his living by honest trade of merchandise beyond the
    seas, about two years past had certain goods in a Scottish ship freighted by men
    of Dublin in Ireland, who were met and taken on the seas by certain men-of-war
    of Plymouth" (B.M. Add. MSS., 12507, f.188).
(3) Lewis, *op. cit.*, pp.76, 141.
(4) Humphrey Toy, at his death, owned, in addition to property in town and county
    including a shop and stalls in the market-place, a tannery containing a stock of
    hides to the value of at least £100 (P.C.C. 22 Pyckering).

concentrated on his own account upon foreign ventures, particularly exports, with very few coasting cargoes, never reached in Haverfordwest the position won by his half-brother, a much more cautious merchant relying largely on the coasting trade, in Pembroke.[1] Again, John Voyle can scarcely have founded the fortunes of his family on the profits of the coasting import trade credited to him in these records.[2]

The unwisdom of estimating the quantity and nature of maritime commerce in this locality on the evidence of the extant port books alone, is obvious. Much trade must have gone unrecorded, for customs officials, when diligent, cannot have had an easy task. Thomas Powell and Martyn Beynon refused to pay a total of £132 due on 92 tuns of wine brought by them into Milford in 1615-1616.[3] Thomas Vaughan, John King and George Williams appeared equally obdurate in Tenby and Carmarthen.[4] If the smuggling activities of Lewis Davy of Tenby[5] were detected, not all local men would have been as conscious of their public duty as John Elyot of Erwer was anxious to appear to be.[6] If people like Erasmus Saunders, mayor of Tenby, and Griffith Dwnn chose to convey "forbidden and unaccustomed wares" to Portugal, beyond appealing afterwards to the Privy Council there was little that John Kiste, searcher of Milford, felt he could do to prevent it, especially if violence was

---

(1) Morgan Powell, like his father, Lewis, was mayor of Pembroke. He was the only son of Lewis's first marriage to the illegitimate Mary Lloyd, the second marriage, to Katherine Huwl of Trewent, producing two sons and three daughters (Dwnn, *op. cit.*, vol. i, p.126).

(2) Which totalled: brass, 8 cwt.; grocery wares, 12 coffers; iron, 15 tuns; oil, 6 tuns; pewter, 10 cwt.; wool, 12 packs. *Cf. supra*, pp.41-42.

(3) P.R.O. E112/146/98. Beynon admitted the fact, but claimed immunity and freedom from paying the dues required of him, on the grounds that as a burgess of Carmarthen he enjoyed the liberties of the town under a charter of 38 Henry VIII. Although the court ruled that he must surrender his wines or the value thereof, this was because the liberties granted under the said charter were not sufficiently clearly defined to allow for exemption in this instance, the suggestion being that there might well be other occasions when such immunity would apply (P.R.O. E124/25/49b.).

(4) P.R.O. E112/146/66.

(5) P.R.O. E159/330/12 (5 Edward VI). He was arrested for smuggling fifteen pieces of wool, three measures of woollen cloth and ten measures of white woollen cloth, with other goods, into Tenby.

(6) P.R.O. E159/331/10 (6 Edward VI). Elyot's servant, George Wethers, stated that his master confiscated at Llanstephan forty frises which were being smuggled out of the country, and that he was impeded in this by the mayor of Tenby and others, who took the said goods out of his hands after he had seized them to the King's use. On another occasion Elyot detained the ship of "one Ivan", a Breton, thereby incurring the indignation of the French ambassador and the displeasure of the Council, who instructed him to make amends (*A.P.C.* (1552-1554), p.6).

offered him when he strove to prevent them.[1] Customs officials were themselves prone to error and corruption, as sheriff Hugh Gwynne of Pennarth claimed to have discovered on rescuing the cargo of a ship wrecked at Dinas Dinlle that included malt, rye, cheese, wheat and butter, in quantities not consistent with the entry at the customs house at Pembroke.[2] Where bribery and intimidation failed, there was always evasion; and people who employed "sinster practices" in the wool trade, for instance, by conveying the wool to "secret and obscure places" where it was sold to "foreigners" to take out of the country, conspired against not only the profits of customs but also the prosperity of the locality itself.[3]

But whilst the weaknesses of the major single surviving source of evidence must accordingly be recognised, alternative indications of maritime commercial enterprise by the men of this region are no less sparse and ambiguous. The port books disclose occasional ventures on their part to Spain.[4] In January 1571 Richard Holland, Richard Nash and several other Carmarthen merchants complained to the Privy Council that "divers goods and merchandise of theirs have been stayed in Portugal by commandment of the King there".[5] In 1583 four Pembrokeshire merchants were fined sums ranging from ten shillings to £2 by the Bristol Company of Merchants trading to Spain and Portugal; and in the same year a Carmarthen merchant and another from Haverfordwest were in debt to the Company to the tune of £5 and £1 respectively.[6] Why

(1) *A.P.C.* (1577-1578), p.196. But Kiste himself was not unimpeachable. On another occasion he allegedly contrived the sequestration of George Clerk from executing his duties as searcher of Milford. A commission of investigation cleared Clerk, but Kiste managed to cast doubt upon its findings and secure the setting up of another commission. Under cover of all this he was himself, supposedly, trafficking with pirates from France (P.R.O. E112/59/2(i)). In 1578 Clerk was in trouble, in company with John Vaughan, the then customer, and their assistant William Blackhurst, before the Great Sessions, for various misdemeanours, including the concealing of goods (N.L.W. Wales 7/9).
(2) P.R.O. St. Ch. 5/H69/23.
(3) Despite efforts in 1607 to confine all wool transactions to the towns of Haverfordwest, Pembroke and Tenby (N.L.W. Poyston, 58), by 1631 the decline of the Pembrokeshire wool trade was still far from being arrested (*C.S.P.Dom.* (1631-1633), vol. cxcii, no. 70).
(4) For example, a shipment, by Mylo Wilson of Pembroke and John Laugharne of St. Bride's, of 10 tuns of coal, 4 cwt. white leather, 10 qrs. rye, 3 qrs. barley, in April 1567 (Lewis, *op. cit.*, p.89).
(5) *A.P.C.* (1571-1575), p.6. Attempts to recover these goods proved vain; in April 1578 compensation was paid (*C.S.P. Dom.* (1566-1579: *Addenda*), vol. xxv, no. 92).
(6) P. McGrath, *Records Relating to the Society of Merchant Venturers of the City of Bristol in the Seventeenth Century*, Bristol Record Society Publications, vol. xiii, pp.83-84.

the Company, membership of which required an entrance fee of £5,[1] imposed these penalties is not specified, but since it was empowered to discipline traders who trespassed upon its privileges, it seems likely that these men were interlopers.[2] If this was so, it confirms one's impression, from the available evidence, of the casual nature of the sea-going trade of south-west Wales. It is an impression reinforced by contemporary statements as to the quantity of local shipping suited to trading ventures. Apart from one fifty-tonner trading to France and Bristol, the seven vessels of Carmarthen, Laugharne, Gwendraeth, Burry and Marros in 1566 were wholly engaged in the coasting trade.[3] In 1611 this representation of available shipping resources was largely confirmed in the deposition of Walter Philpin, a merchant of Tenby, in an action against Richard Barret of Haverfordwest and others for evasion of butlerage and prisage.[4] Asked how many merchants and ships there were in south Wales, Philpin said that he could not say with certainty, but that in Carmarthen there was one ship or flyboat of about 40 tons, in Tenby one small ship of about 30 tons, and in Milford two small ships of 40 and 26 tons respectively. The people of Carmarthenshire and Pembrokeshire, he believed, bought most of their wines from Bristol; "and his reason therein is for that there is very small quantities of wine brought into south Wales".[5] However suspect in its details this deposition may be, its implications are consistent with available evidence. The maritime trade of the region languished in this period.

Dr. Mendenhall has noted a failure on the part of the Welsh gentry "to take advantage of their prestige and location to manage the Welsh cloth industry", to handle which "no capitalist group" emerged. That "scattered, vaguely-organised industry" remained inefficient in itself; control over the marketing of its produce passed outside Wales "to more capitalistic, more strategically-located

(1) C. T. Carr (ed.), *Select Charters of Trading Companies, 1530-1707* (Selden Society, vol. xxviii), p.xxiii.
(2) The list of the Company's members in 1577, as partially published, includes no names from this region (V. M. Shillington and A. B. W. Chapman, *The Commercial Relations of England and Portugal*, pp.313-326).
(3) P.R.O. S.P. 12/39/27; printed in Lewis, *op. cit.*, pp.315-318.
(4) P.R.O. E134/8 Jac. I/E3. This deposition was largely, and of course predictably, supported by those of Bateman, Rice Prickarde, Jenkin Davids and others.
(5) "The country of Wales has long since been troubled with unwholesome malt, so that great quantities of wine were then brought by Frenchmen into this country and discharged without paying of impost", to which Welshmen were in any case not liable owing to their being required to pay upon the death of every Prince "a great sum of money called mises" (*ibid., loc. cit.; cf. infra*, p.105).

middlemen".[1] A corresponding failure on the part of the local gentry is apparent in the general economic condition of this region. The gentry's attitude and example had an important influence upon the economic development of their community as a whole. The importance of their political example was no less.

(1) T. C. Mendenhall, *op. cit.*, pp.212-214.

CHAPTER THREE
Politics

1. PARLIAMENT.

In the course of the Reformation Parliament, to which the first Act of Union was presented in its last session,[1] the institution of Parliament emerged as "a true legislative assembly".[2] In the subsequent period, when "the Reformation forced people to think critically on issues of transcendent importance to their consciences", the House of Commons was transformed "into an assembly mainly of gentlemen, most of whom were there because they ardently desired to be: men of character, education and wealth, who, given the occasion, were likely to display independence of mind":[3] culminating, in Professor Notestein's phrase, in "the winning of the initiative by the House of Commons", until "by 1629 it had become exceeding powerful".[4]. It was in this situation that Welshmen, newly emancipated by the Act, obtained their first real parliamentary opportunity.[5] It is according to its standards that their contribution must be judged.[6] If the period was one of "apprenticeship" for Welshmen in Parliament,[7] it was no less so for Parliament itself with its emerging responsibilities, and for the gentlemen in general

---

(1) W. Rees, "The Union of England and Wales", *T.H.C.S.* (1937), p.28.

(2) G. R. Elton, *The Tudor Constitution*, p.229: "A marked change came over the nature of Parliament as a consequence of the long and vital sessions of the Reformation Parliament".

(3) J. E. Neale, *Elizabeth I and her Parliaments*, vol. i, p.21.

(4) W. M. Mitchell, *The Rise of the Revolutionary Party in the English House of Commons, 1603-1629*, p.xi.

(5) For the attendance of Welshmen in Parliament in the fourteenth century, *vide* T. F. Tout, *op. cit.*, vol. ii, p. 15.

(6) Owing to the incompleteness of the sources now extant, it must be recognised that many of the activities of individual members may be impossible to trace. In 1614, for instance, Robert Wolverston, member for Cardigan, secured after the dissolution the support of the King in delaying a lawsuit before Chancery "because he had in the Parliament house showed himself forward in our service" (J. P. Collier (ed), *The Egerton Papers*, Camden Soc. (1840, p.464)—though there is no record of his having therein showed himself at all (*vide* T. L. Moir, *The Addled Parliament of 1614*, pp.148-149). Wolverston was a "stranger" member, and so this instance does not directly affect a view of the local gentry; what his "service" might have been can be the subject only of unprofitable conjecture. Despite this qualification, one can do no more than interpret the evidence that is available.

(7) A. H. Dodd, "Wales's Parliamentary Apprenticeship, 1536-1625", *T.H.C.S.* (1942), pp.8-72. *Cf.* Neale, *loc. cit.*: "Mary Tudor's reign marks a stage in this apprenticeship to future greatness" of the House of Commons.

who increasingly constituted its membership.

Between 1540 and 1640 about ninety men represented the seven south-west Wales constituencies.[1] They included Englishmen, such as Sir Conyers Clifford, and Welshmen from other shires, such as William Awbrey of Brecknock.[2] However, representatives of forty-eight local families found their way to Westminster, some more frequently than others. The Jones family of Abermarlais could boast a member on thirteen separate occasions to 1563, but after that date their influence waned in Carmarthenshire before that of the Vaughans of Golden Grove, who might have made a similar boast seventeen times to 1640. For Pembrokeshire and Haverfordwest Sir John, Sir James and Sir Thomas Perrot sat on a total of nine occasions; for Cardiganshire the Prices of Gogerddan sat similarly thirteen times between 1553 and 1621. The Wogans sat, when at all, exclusively for the county seat of Pembrokeshire, whereas the Stepneys of Prendergast represented four separate constituencies.[3] But for a merchant gentleman like Griffith Higgon of Carmarthen, election to parliament was in 1553 a solitary peak in a long record of public service by his family.[4] If there was some tendency towards the predominance of a few families, this could certainly be broken, as when Sir James Perrot failed to find a seat for this region in 1625. The long holding of a seat or seats by one family may as well be accounted for by lack of competition as by overwhelming political influence.

The baldness of the records of parliamentary proceedings for the beginning of this period may or may not conceal some activity by the early members.[5] The first mention of one of them by name occurs in the record for Friday, 29 January 1563, when Giles Clinket, servant to Sir John Perrot, arrested in London on a plea of debt, had the privilege of the House granted:[6] his master presumably pleading

---

(1) Cardigan county and borough, Carmarthen county and borough, Pembroke county and borough, and Haverfordwest. This survey is largely based on W. R. Williams, *Parliamentary History of Wales;* Browne Willis, *Notitia Parliamentaria;* M. F. Keeler, *The Long Parliament;* M. E. Jones, "The Parliamentary Representation of Pembrokeshire", University of Wales unpublished M.A. thesis (1958).
(2) Members respectively for Pembroke (1593) and Carmarthen (1554).
(3) Pembroke county, Pembroke, Haverfordwest and Cardigan.
(4) His family had supplied several mayors and bailiffs of Carmarthen; he himself was high sheriff of the county and mayor in 1551 (Williams, *op. cit.*, p.51).
(5) The Parliament of 1559 dealt with a bill concerning Great Sessions in Pembroke and another concerning frises in south-west Wales (D'Ewes, pp.48, 54; *C.J.*, pp.55, 59). Up to 1553 several members remain unidentified.
(6) D'Ewes, p.83; *C.J.*, p.64.

the favourable precedent of Ferrers's case twenty years earlier. The member for Carmarthenshire had evidently noted this, for a week later he sought similar immunity for six of his servants, arrested on three actions of trespass for causing a riot in London. But this request caused long argument; the matter was committed for further examination to Mr. Sackville, Mr. Sidney, Mr. Mason and others, who found that the affray, which had resulted in damage to the value of three thousand marks, seemed to have been begun by Sir Henry Jones's servants. They were consequently delivered to the custody of the serjeant-at-arms, and released only after their master had bailed them in £500:[1] an incident that may thereafter have disillusioned him with Parliament and killed his interest in it.[2]

Indeed, apart from Sir John Perrot's service on the committee of seventy-five members to confer with the Lords on the twin matters of the Queen's marriage and the declaration of a successor[3] that were to cause Peter Wentworth such perturbation, the activities of the members for south-west Wales proved rather more of a nuisance than an advantage to the House during the first thirty years of their regular appearance in the Commons chamber. This situation was highlighted in 1571 with Haverfordwest's error in returning an alleged excommunicate as member, in the person of John Garnons, a Herefordshire gentleman, who had previously represented the borough of Pembroke in 1554.[4] The member for Carmarthen county in the brief session of 1571, John Vaughan of Golden Grove, proved rather more useful, as became one who had been a gentleman-usher at Court. He served on the committee on a bill for "certain offences to be made treasons" in April,[5] and in May took part in deliberations with the Lords upon two occasions, firstly over the bill "for increase of tillage and maintenance of the navy", and secondly "upon matters concerning the Queen of Scots".[6] Vaughan

---

(1) D'Ewes, p.84; *C.J.*, pp.64-65.
(2) According to Professor Dodd (*op. cit.*, p.12) he probably sat again for Carmarthenshire in 1571 and was nominated to a committee; other sources give John Vaughan as the Carmarthenshire member in that year.
(3) D'Ewes, p.126.
(4) D'Ewes, p.156; *C.J.*, p.83. Also, *cf. infra*, p.132. Garnons's religious lapse can at worst have been no more than temporary. He was appointed, in company with one William Rudhale, in 1586 to investigate recusancy in the county of Hereford (Williams, *op. cit.*, p.160).
(5) Somewhat ironically, in view of William Vaughan of Penbre's alleged remark to Vaughan's servant at Llanegwad ten years previously: "Thou knave, I will send thee to the traitor John Vaughan, thy master, to the Council" (N.L.W. Wales 19/21/12).
(6) D'Ewes, pp.165, 187, 206; *C.J.*, pp.91, 95.

dying in 1574, the county elected his son, Walter,[1] to follow him—
an election that occasioned the House further embarrassment, for
Vaughan was discovered to be outlawed for debt and therefore ineligible for election. The matter was investigated by the Speaker,
Mr. Knollys and Mr. Townshend,[2] who found that the debts "weie
all grown by reason of suretyship for other persons, and not for his
own debt or causes, and withal, that yet nevertheless he had, to his
own great charge and hindrance, very honestly compounded and
taken order for all or the most part of them already".[3] This mis-
judged paragon of virtue was therefore not only allowed to "stand
and continue as in his former estate of the good opinion of this whole
House, sufficiently purged and discharged of the said suspicion", but
was also soon placed on an appropriate committee, for the bill
"against the excessive multitude of attorneys in the court of Common Pleas".[4] But this early prominence was not sustained; this
was Vaughan's final appearance by name in the records, though he
sat again for Carmarthenshire in 1593 and 1597.

John Price of Gogerddan, member for the county of Cardigan,
having remained hitherto in obscurity, now made two committee
appearances, to consider "the reformation of errors in fines and
common recoveries in the county palatine of Chester and in Wales",
and the proposal that a "convenient sum of money be out of hand
prepared" for the maintenance of the armed forces,[5] this being the
whole of his active service in parliament. Even so, Price's record,
however modest, was more impressive than that of Alban Stepney
of Prendergast, burgess for Haverfordwest. This worthy's prolonged
unobtrusiveness in the House[6] was relieved in February 1585 when
Anthony Kirle of the Middle Temple served him with a subpoena
out of the court of Star Chamber and followed this up with a writ
of attachment: which documentary persecution sent Stepney hotfoot
to the House, claiming privilege. Kirle's excuse was simply that he
did not know the object of his attentions to be a member of parliament: a state of ignorance shared, perhaps, by many of those present.

---

(1) Professor Dodd (*op. cit.*, p.15) says "brother", but Williams (*op. cit.*, p.43),
    Dwnn (*op. cit.*, vol. i, p.214) and Major Francis Jones (*op. cit.*, p.103) indicate son.
(2) I have in these instances described such members by titles as noted in contem-
    porary parliamentary records.
(3) D'Ewes, p.294; *C.J.*, pp. 122-124.
(4) D'Ewes, p.298; *C.J.*, p.127.
(5) D'Ewes, pp. 253, 288.
(6) He was member for Haverfordwest (1572, 1584-1585 and 1586-1587), for
    Cardigan (1588-1589) and for Pembroke county (1604-1611).

But the House was sensitive on matters of privilege. Kirle was committed to the custody of the serjeant-at-arms and ordered to reimburse Stepney for all his expenses in this affair. Five days later authority relented and Kirle was released, having begged pardon on his knees, taken the oath of supremacy and paid Stepney £3 6s. 8d.[1] In short, apart from Gelly Meyrick's appearance on a couple of committees,[2] and those occasions when the Welsh members served likewise as a body,[3] only two local residents sitting for south-west Wales constituencies played, according to the records, any significant part in the parliaments of the sixteenth century. One of these, who figured upon a single occasion, was Edward Dounlee, member for Carmarthen. He presented John Penry's *Supplication in behalf of Wales* to the parliament of 1586-1587, and spoke "of the great idolatry begun again in Wales to an idol; of the number of people that resort to it; of the solitary character and closeness of the place . . . and what ignorance they live in". For this service he appears to have lost his place on the commission of the peace, and did not again secure membership of the House.[4] The other was Sir John Perrot.

Having represented Carmarthenshire in 1548[5] and Pembrokeshire in 1563,[6] Perrot displaced Stepney at Haverfordwest in 1588-

<hr>

(1) D'Ewes, pp.347-350. The case was cited as a precedent in 1589 (*ibid.*, p.431); *cf. infra*, p.101.
(2) Williams (*op. cit.*, p.52), Willis (*op. cit.*, vol. iii, p.126) and Glyn Roberts (*History of Carmarthenshire* (ed. Sir J. E. Lloyd), vol. ii, p.464) agree that Meyrick sat for Carmarthen borough in 1588. In 1597 he sat for Radnor and was a member of two committees, one dealing with vagrants and the other with the relief of mariners and soldiers (D'Ewes, pp.575, 588).
(3) The knights sat collectively on the committees for the subsidy in 1585 and 1593; on monopolies and the abuse of patents of privilege in 1597; on the bill concerning beggars and the relief of vagabondage in the same session; again, this time with all the Welsh burgesses, on the bill for repairing the bridges of Caerleon and Newport; and in 1601 on the bill for the abbreviating of Michaelmas term (D'Ewes, pp.356, 474, 555, 561, 565, 634). The members for Carmarthen, Cardigan and Pembroke boroughs also served in 1593 on the committee considering "the statutes already in force for the relief of the poor and the punishment of rogues", but none of them was native of south-west Wales. They were Sir Thomas Baskerville, Sir Ferdinando Gorges and Sir Conyers Clifford, of whom only the first could claim particular local connections: a Baskerville was sometime mayor of Pembroke and husband of Lord Ferrers's daughter (*L.P.H. VIII*, vol. xiii, pt.i (1538), no. 320).
(4) J. E. Neale, *Elizabeth I and her Parliaments*, vol. ii, pp.153, 194; but *cf. infra*, p.186.
(5) Succeeding as member Richard Devereux, deceased.
(6) Perrot was associated in London in 1555 with a group of "young bloods" who "intended to resist such matters as should be spoken of in the Parliament other than liked, and that they did very sore mislike such Catholic proceedings as they perceived the Queen and all Catholic men went about, as indeed they did everywhere declare themselves to be right Protestants" (Testimony of John Daniell, quoted in Conyers Read, *Mr. Secretary Cecil and Queen Elizabeth*, p.108).

1589[1] and was promptly placed on the committee for the bill on informers and informations upon penal statutes, acting as its spokesman in the House. He accompanied to the Lords the bills on purveyors and proclamations in fines; served on the committees for the bills on mortmain and the pier of Hartlepools, the importing of salted fish and salted herrings[2] and the relief of the city of Lincoln; was one of a deputation of ten to the Queen in March; and took charge, in the absence of the Vice-Chamberlain, of the committee for the bill on hue and cry, and reported its deliberations to the House. On 26 March he introduced his own bill on the embezzling of Crown armour and armaments, saying that the Queen had intimated to him her view that such pilfering offended the welfare both of herself and of her subjects; and on the same day he notified the House of the royal concern at "the small number of the members of this House presently attending the service of the same, the one half at the least supposed to be absent". Having on 28 March conveyed the bill "against forestalling, regrating and ingrossing" to the Lords, he addressed the Commons on the following day on the question of "the great practices and treasons heretofore intended against her Majesty's person, state and kingdom", being himself one of those who felt that the repeated plots and conspiracies against the Queen that were contrived by Spain warranted a declaration of open war against that country:[3] a speech savouring somewhat of irony in view of the ultimate fate of its deliverer. In a session lasting less than two months Perrot had displayed an energy and a variety of application and interest in sharp contrast to the habitual supineness of his south-west Wales colleagues. But by 1593 and the next parliament he was dead, convicted of the activity which his final parliamentary oration had denounced.

Only three very different circumstances brought this region into prominence in the last three parliaments of Elizabeth's reign. The first was the bill for the restitution in blood of Sir Thomas Perrot, son of Sir John, which was speedily passed.[4] The second was an

---

(1) Stepney had to resort instead to the Cardigan boroughs, thereby interrupting a striking sequence of "stranger" representatives of that constituency, running from 1584 to 1628. *Vide* J. E. Neale, "More Elizabethan Elections", *E.H.R.*, vol.lxi (1946), pp.20 *et seq.*
(2) An industry of which he might have claimed to speak from first-hand knowledge (*vide supra*, p.87).
(3) D'Ewes, pp.436-437, 443, 445, 448, 453-454.
(4) *Ibid.*, pp.510-511. Sir Thomas had been elected member for Pembroke county in 1593, and was through this bill enabled to take his seat.

attempt by John Phillips, member for Pembroke county, to push
through a bill proving the lordship of Llanddowror[1] to be in Carmarthenshire rather than in Pembrokeshire. Heywood Townshend
took a less charitable view of Phillips than he had of Vaughan.[2]
Advised by a young lawyer of Lincoln's Inn, he understood that the
lordship had been acquired from Morgan Phillips of Picton by
George Owen, who had married Elizabeth, daughter of William
Phillips, the original farmer of it; and that Morgan's son, John, was,
through this bill, attempting "to strengthen his estate and to overthrow
the right, title and interest of the said George". Townshend con-
vinced the House that Llanddowror was in Pembrokeshire, "which,
being shewed to the House and put to the question, the greater voice
was No, No, No, and so the bill was rejected".[3] If Townshend's
report of the affair is accurate, Phillips seems to have been unfairly
treated. By his will, dated 27 February 1573, William Phillips had
left all his lands in Iscennen, Carmarthenshire, and Walwynscastle,
Pembrokeshire, to his daughter, Mary, who married Alban
Stepney.[4] All the residue of his estate, including the manor of
Llanddowror, went to his brother, Morgan Phillips, who in his
will[5] divided his lands into three parts: one to the Queen in
assurance of ward and relief during the minority of the testator's
heirs, and the profits of the other two parts to be collected towards
the marriages of his three daughters, with the whole, including the
lordship of Llanddowror, to be inherited by Morgan's son, John,
when he came of age. John therefore had every legal right to that
particular lordship, for George Owen's marriage to William
Phillips's daughter gave him no title to it. Townshend, however
excellent his intentions to defend the integrity of Parliament, appears
to have been completely misinformed on all counts. Nevertheless,
it seems evident that Phillips was attempting to use his public office
to further a private claim.

Thirdly, there was a disputed election. In Cardiganshire the
borough member had apparently always been returned by the
borough of Cardigan; but in the 1601 election "the sheriff of the

(1) Not Llandovery, as indicated by Professor Dodd (*op. cit.*, p.13), from whose
interpretation of this affair my own differs in detail. The lordship of Llanddowror
had been ascribed, together with those of Laugharne and Llanstephan, to Pembrokeshire in 1536 and to Carmarthenshire in 1543.
(2) *Cf. supra*, p.96. The present parliament was that of 1597-1598.
(3) H. Townshend, *Historical Collections*, p.267.
(4) P.C.C. 10 Peter.
(5) P.R.O. C142/208/193; P.C.C. 38 Brudenell.

shire,[1] after he received the writ, sent his warrant to the bailiffs of
Aberystwyth to choose a burgess". They did so, "*viz.* Dr. Awbrey,
and returned him burgess for Cardigan and Aberystwyth, and
shewed in the indenture the election to be made by both towns". The
burgesses of Cardigan meanwhile elected William Delabere[2] on
their own account without a writ from the sheriff, and notified
Delabere by letter of his election; whereupon he, having failed to
contact the sheriff, delivered his letters of election to the Clerk of the
Crown, paid his fees and was admitted. Then Awbrey arrived, and,
not unnaturally, objected. Several points arose. As the county court
was held alternately at Aberystwyth and at Cardigan, each might
claim parity with the other. The House was undecided as to whether
it had the power to fine the sheriff, and if so whether he had in fact
acted incorrectly and deserved punishment. The matter was accordingly referred to the committee for privileges and elections: at which
Sir Edward Hoby commented that "Awbrey and Delabere, the one a
civil, the other a common lawyer, he might say to them as the Duke
of Milan said of the thief, it is no matter whether goes first the
hangman or the thief".[3]

Parliament was dissolved before the matter was satisfactorily
decided. This was unfortunate, for in James I's first parliament it
happened again. This time the offending sheriff was Sir Richard
Price of Gogerddan, whose conduct was even more ambiguous.
Having instructed the mayor of Cardigan to proceed to the election
of a burgess for that town, he, "minding to make choice of a friend
of his . . . proceeds to the election of another in Aberystwyth", in the
person of Delabere once more; and, on receiving the indenture of
the mayor of Cardigan to the effect that that borough had elected
William Bradshaw,[4] he returned both indentures to Westminster.
The House, understandably annoyed, ratified Bradshaw's election
and instructed the serjeant-at-arms to arrest the irresponsible
sheriff.[5] Price may well have misunderstood the function of contributory boroughs, which, after these upheavals, later refused to

---

(1) Even he, Sir Thomas Jones, was not a Cardiganshire man.
(2) Williams (*op. cit.*, p.37) gives Delabere's first name as Richard. He hailed from
    Gloucestershire, Awbrey being a member of a prominent family of county
    Brecknock.
(3) D'Ewes, p.628.
(4) At that time an alderman of Cardigan, he was the eldest son of John Bradshaw
    of Presteigne, county Radnor (*cf. supra*, p.31).
(5) *C.J.*, p.170.

contribute to Bradshaw's salary of £25 as he claimed.[1]

Most prominent by far of the south-west Wales members in this parliament was Sir Robert Mansell, sitting for Carmarthen county, but again he was not a native of that region.[2] John Lewis, member for Cardigan county, and Alban Stepney, now sitting for Pembroke-shire, were named to "the committee . . . for conference touching the union";[3] and Stepney was soon after claiming privilege again from a suit brought against him by William Warren, who was committed to the serjeant-at-arms for his boldness.[4] Stepney was amongst those who considered the restitution in blood of Sir Gelly Meyrick's children, Roland and Margaret; and he rounded off his personal parliamentary record with a report that one Parker, a member of Convocation whose reliability was doubtful, had played cards throughout one Saturday night, "and one asking how he could preach the next day, take no care of that for he was prepared":[5] a statement damaging to its subject and suspiciously vindictive on the part of its utterer. With Captain Richard Cuny, the member for Pembroke borough, given leave to depart on 5 March, and Walter Rice, sitting for Carmarthen borough, distinguishing himself by being fined double the usual amount for non-attendance,[6] Sir James Perrot was otherwise left to represent south-west Wales with little support from his colleagues.

With the exception of his father's one active session, Perrot

---

(1) P.R.O. E112/151/29(i). The defaulting boroughs included both Cardigan and Aberystwyth, with Tregaron, Talsarn, Lampeter and Trerhedyn. Bradshaw's bill was dismissed in the Exchequer court, the defendants successfully demurring that as the plea " is grounded on a penal law" it could not be heard there (P.R.O. E124/5/44b).

(2) Though he held some land there (cf.supra, p.73). Mansell, Treasurer of the Navy, was a scion of the house of Margam. He served on over forty committees and made at least three speeches.

(3) C.J., pp.179-180. For this conference with James "to hear him explain his own meaning in the matter of the Union . . any member of the House, being no committee, hath liberty to accompany them to the King".

(4) Warren, on grounds reminiscent of those of the earlier offender Anthony Kirle (cf. supra, p.97), explained "that he indeed did know Mr. Skepweth (sic) to be a member of this House at such time as he served the said subpoena on him, but for his excuse protested that he then thought Mr. Skepweth would not have attended this session which he partly believed by reason he had so heard and partly because the last session Mr. Skepweth, being high sheriff, made that an occasion to stay in the country". The House imposed upon him the comparatively light penalty of an admonition and three days in the custody of the serjeant-at-arms (D. H. Willson (ed.), The Parliamentary Diary of Robert Bowyer, 1606-1607, pp.45-46. Also, C.J., p.269).

(5) C.J., pp.291, 313. He also served on a committee for explaining a statute on Welsh cottons (ibid., p.281).

(6) Ibid., p.451.

emerges as the only one of these members who may be spoken of as having enjoyed anything approaching a parliamentary career. Having sat inconspicuously for Haverfordwest in 1597, he soon became prominent in the 1604 parliament, beginning with membership of the deputation of a hundred commoners and forty peers who met with the King to discuss "the blessed and happy Union of these two kingdoms" of England and Scotland,[1] and continuing over about forty more committees. His main interests, foreshadowed by his writing of anti-papist tracts during Elizabeth's reign, were matters of religion and morality. As early as 5 May 1604 he was delivering "a long and learned discourse touching matters of religion, and concludeth with a motion to send to the Lords for further conference"; and his opinion was thought desirable on such matters as "the bill for a public thanksgiving to be given to almighty God every year on the fifth day of November", on ecclesiastical grievances, "to direct some proceedings in courts and causes ecclesiastical", and recusants. But his efforts covered a great variety of subjects. In March 1606 he backed the royal request for money by referring to Queen Elizabeth's debt of £400,000 (which was exceeded by the Crown's present embarrassment) and suggesting that relief of the royal wants should be reciprocated by redress of the subjects' grievances, proposing a committee to consider both. He served on several committees for the maintenance of husbandry and tillage, and for the reformation of unlawful fishing; on a committee for free trade; another for safeguarding the poor from drinking beer brewed from malt of inferior quality; and yet another on alehouse keepers.[2] His views upon matters of law were evidently respected,[3] for he was amongst those who considered the "reformation of the abuses in the court of Marshalsea", the question of naturalising certain individuals, the reform of "abuses of wide and wasteful writing of English copies in courts of record", and the "reformation of one branch of a statute . . . for restoring to the Crown the ancient jurisdiction over the state spiritual and ecclesiastical". He was placed in June 1607 on the committee for privileges; and the House's confidence in him was neatly demonstrated when, in the case of certain

(1) *Ibid.*, p.172.
(2) This last was a matter of sufficient significance to constitute the immediate cause of a clash between Lords and Commons in 1621.
(3) He was admitted to the Middle Temple on 9 January 1591 (*Register of Admissions to the Honourable Society of the Middle Temple*, vol. i, p.61)—though this in itself represents no guarantee of legal learning (*cf. infra*, p.195).

peers' pages who had tricked other pages into pawning their masters' cloaks in order to pay wine reckonings, it was Perrot's assurance that was taken for the appearance of the offenders before the Commons on the following day.[1]

It was a commendable record but, as far as the representation of south-west Wales is concerned, a lonely one. In the brief parliament of 1614 the sheriff of Carmarthenshire, Rhys Williams of Edwinsford, took upon himself the function of sustaining that electoral confusion which seemed to be the locality's only other route to renown, by refusing to ratify the election of one Mr. Thomas, Recorder of Carmarthen, for that borough, on the remarkable grounds that no borough in the shire was eligible to return a member as there was no recognised shire-town. The member for Cardiff[2] explained with ponderous simplicity that "the shire-town [was] not a name of a town but the denotation of it, as the principal town of the shire", and that if Williams's objection were accepted the House would have to "turn out all the burgesses for Wales".[3] The committee to which the matter was referred had yet to report when parliament was dissolved; by which time only Perrot, again, had made a positive contribution. He had passed the period since the previous dissolution in pursuit of recusants,[4] and now proposed that every member of the House should receive communion by a certain date, in order that papists might be excluded. He followed this up by urging for a committee to consider the proposals of the Bills of Grace, declaring that delay therein might harm the interests of the Crown. He joined the committee to protest against the undertakers,[5] contrived both to defend Thomas Wentworth and to recommend fair treatment for Bishop Neile,[6] and drew attention

(1) *C.J.*, pp.199, 258, 282, 287, 292, 296, 308, 310, 326, 329, 342, 347, 351, 374, 384, 387, 404, 417, 426.
(2) Matthew Davies, a Middle Temple lawyer, and a very active member.
(3) *C.J.*, p.461.
(4) On 13 March 1612 he wrote to Salisbury from Beaupre in Glamorgan to the effect that "Christopher Hawkes, sent by his lordship, had not sincerity nor skill enough to apprehend a Jesuit as he promised. Certain Jesuits and priests keep up intelligence among the recusants resident in Worcestershire, Monmouthshire, Herefordshire and South Wales. If some trusty professed romanist would come amongst them he might discover and reveal much of their haunts and practices" *C.S.P.Dom.* (1611-1618), vol. lxviii, no. 75).
(5) *I.e.*, courtiers who meddled in elections to secure the return of members favouring the Crown.
(6) Neile, in commenting in the House of Lords upon the violence of Wentworth's language in attacking impositions, was considered to have impugned the loyalty of the entire House of Commons.

to those members who, owing to the distance of their seats from the Speaker's Chair, were rarely placed on committees[1]—a point of procedure which may provide some excuse for the backwardness of so many of Perrot's neighbours. Vociferousness on some of these issues was indiscreet. Upon the dissolution of parliament Perrot, amongst others, was commanded by the Privy Council "not to depart the town without leave first had from his Majesty".[2]

In the 1621 parliament, despite the failure of Privy Councillors and Crown dependants to re-assert control over committee nominations, the representatives of south-west Wales did not greatly attract attention. Harry Vaughan of Carmarthen served on one committee,[3] and his county colleague and kinsman troubled the House only to the extent of requiring a ruling on whether his elevation to an Irish peerage disqualified him from sitting. Lewis Powell, for Pembroke borough, did not even bother to attend and may eventually have been unseated when John Wogan, sitting for the county, made his only form of recorded intervention during an extended period in parliament before 1640,[4] when he informed a committee[5] that the contributory boroughs had not been admitted to the poll.[6] Sir Richard Price, the wayward sheriff of the 1604 Cardigan election and now member for the county, declined to draw further notice to himself. Apart from occasional instances, such as the bill for the free trading of Welsh cottons and frises throughout England,[7] when the Welsh members served collectively on committees, Perrot was left to set a solitary shoulder to the Commons wheel.

He did not long leave the House in doubt as to his intentions. It was he who proposed, almost immediately, that all members should take communion as "a touchstone to try our faith . . . a blessing by it on all other consultations". On the same day, 5 February, he joined in a discussion begun by Sir Edward Gyles on freedom of speech and expanded to include such matters as recusancy, supply and the royal assent and prerogative. Perrot's speech amounted almost to a statement of policy. Beginning with a plea, "if we differ with our equals

---

(1) *C.J.*, pp.461, 464, 469, 496, 501.
(2) *A.P.C.* (1613-1614), p.460.
(3) *C.J.*, p.614.
(4) Wogan sat for Pembrokeshire in 1614, 1621, 1625, 1626, 1628 and 1640.
(5) Presumably the committee for returns, elections and privileges, on which Perrot served (*C.J.*, p.507).
(6) M. E. Jones, *op. cit.*, pp.74-75.
(7) *C.J.*, p.534. The proposal for a committee came, in fact, from Perrot.

to have it done in love, if with our superiors to have it done with respect", he went on to affirm that questions of supply and the Commons' grievances should be treated "as twins", with no consideration of the one without the other. He objected to the guidance in the King's speech that "matters of state" were not to be treated of in the Commons chamber, on the grounds that this restricted ability to receive petitions against the Church, and moved that the King be petitioned to define the phrase, which might well be extended in meaning to include recusancy, monopolies and foreign policy. He opposed a conference with the Lords, on the grounds that their treatment of the Commons in the last parliament had been uncooperative. In short, he emerged as a leading voice of opposition in matters of fundamental difference with the Crown. Ten days later he took advantage of a debate on supply to make a veiled reference to the laxness of the Crown's policy on religion, saying "that his Majesty may have his due out of the recusants' estates. The Queen had £18,000 *per annum* when not a fourth part of the recusants as now, yet now the King [has] but £6,000 *per annum*". Religious matters were increasingly dominating his mind; in March he launched an attack on Sir Henry Spiller for having monopolised the office of investigating recusants' lands, saying that Spiller "taketh upon him to make out writs and to do divers other things not belonging to him". This earned him a rebuke from the Chancellor of the Exchequer, who considered that Perrot "has exceeded his authority", and, rather apprehensively, "that searching of records is dangerous". The House meanwhile had been considering a proposal that Wales should be exempt from contributing to the new subsidy "until they have paid their mises".[1] Perrot supported the exemption, and momentarily carried the House with him; but five days later a message from the King declared that "no prince was ever so well-used by any House of Parliament as he from this" and "giveth thanks both to the whole committee and to those of Wales in particular for their readiness to yield him the subsidy", promising to be "more ready to help all just grievances than they to desire it". Perrot displayed further antagonism towards the Lords by greeting a request from them that certain gentlemen be asked to give evidence on oath on a matter concerning inns and hostelries with the opinion that there was no precedent for this, and that it was "a disreputation

(1) *Cf. supra*, p.91, note 5.

to the gentlemen to be drawn upon oath, as not trusted". But however sensitive he was to the rights of the Commons in general, and upon so delicate a matter in particular, he remained for the moment sufficiently open-minded to greet the royal expressions of regret at the accusations against the Lord Chancellor with the words, "This message [is] most cordial to us", and proposed that the King be thanked "by some near the Chair" for his "gracious message".[1]

This was only a momentary pause in his spate of criticism. In April he revealed that although in accordance with the King's request a contribution had been levied to relieve the wants of the Palatinate,[2] much of the money collected remained in the hands of private persons, a leading offender being the sheriff of Pembrokeshire.[3] In June the House supported, with "general acclamation and waving of hats", his call for a declaration that "we will (if the King shall require it) adventure ourselves and all our estates in defence of religion", hoping thereby to encourage the King to a more positive Protestantism in his negotiations with foreign states. Disappointed in this, he attempted to lash the Commons into a warlike mood with a violent speech after the summer recess. Beginning by quoting Aristotle on liberality, he exhorted the House to remember its responsibility towards religion in general and the Palatinate in particular, and the diligence of former monarchs in opposing Turks, French, Spaniards and Irish alike, and in upholding the just cause in the Low Countries. England was poorer, but money was still to be had: with a magnificent air of modern parsimoniousness he called attention to the £200,000 spent annually on tobacco which would maintain an army of 15,000, the lavishness of noble and gentle spending in London, the £1,500,000 East India Company, the great quantity of plate. He called for an immediate vote on supply, which should be expended on the armed forces, pointing out that the whole of Wales contained only one barrel of gunpowder; and promised for his part to pay his share of the subsidy to the full, towards the "assurance of our religion at home, and the Jesuits, the Pope's Janissaries, banished". This was followed the next day with an equally enthusiastic speech, which Perrot concluded, a

---

(1) *Ibid.*, pp.509, 525, 537, 544, 549, 550, 557, 563.
(2) On 1 April 1621 the delegates of the Protestant Union in the Empire had signed the Mainz Accord, committing themselves to neutrality, and the belated English assistance sent to the Elector Frederick of the Palatinate, to futility.
(3) *Ibid.*, p.594. The sheriff in question was Alban Phillips of Great Nash.

little warily, with the hope "that if his Majesty hath conceived any displeasure against any member of this House for free speaking here, he would be pleased to remit it". He ended this session with a glowing review of its achievements, protesting that there had been no conscious attempt to stir up trouble, and whilst detecting royal displeasure at the violence of the complaints against popery and at the belligerent attitude, nevertheless proposing a petition to the King "specially to send home the papists according to the laws", and the setting up of a "committee for our liberties".[1]

With so articulate and lively a member from their ranks,[2] the quiescence of the others from south-west Wales is almost distressing. Two explanations may be offered. Perrot himself was an exceptional man, in political maturity far in advance not only of his Welsh colleagues but of most of the other members too. Whatever the merits of modern analyses of the social and economic preconditions of revolution, it remains a key to understanding of the Civil War that the reigns of the first two Stuart kings coincided with the emergence of some remarkable individuals in whom ripeness of intellect and power of leadership fused to an outstanding degree. After the Pyms, Hampdens and Cromwells, Perrot deserves to be counted at least in the second rank; and far behind such as these trailed the main body of gentlemen, whose comprehension of the nature of affairs was but dim, and whose participation in parliamentary proceedings rarely went further than their physical presence, pricked possibly into spasmodic animation by some immediate issue. Secondly, Perrot's opinions, definite as they were and fiercely expressed, were never those of the locality which in name he represented. Few aspiring political leaders would be loth to gather a body of supporters around them; but Perrot seems to have been quite out of sympathy with his neighbours. There was little puritanism and less anti-popery in south-west Wales.[3] Its most outspoken member might as well have sat for Berwick-on-Tweed for any indication he gives of the temper of his constituency.

But the peak of his career was now past. There was some dispute, for all his prominence, over the propriety of his election for Pembrokeshire in 1624, though the committee for privileges held that

(1) *Ibid.*, pp.639, 645, 648, 664.
(2) Perrot's activities were, of course, not limited to those above outlined. He made in this parliament about seventy speeches and sat on more than twenty committees, ranging from electoral reform to the problem of drunkenness.
(3) *Vide infra*, pp.185-194.

"the election and return of Sir James Perrot is due and good", on
the grounds that complaint had not been received within six weeks
of the beginning of the session.[1] He again proposed at the outset
that all members take communion. He was still active on many
committees, including those for the presenting of recusants, for sea
coals, for the apothecaries' bill, and for privileges. He once more
exhibited a grasp of legal technicalities in his contribution to the discussion of the case of one Mrs. Thomas, whose estate had been
sequestered for debt, in breach of an earlier settlement. Vociferous
as ever against recusants, Perrot in April, when each member reported on the recusant situation in his own constituency, named his
own wife.[2] He was loud in his condemnation of the Lord
Keeper;[3] by now his distrust of the Lords and of the Crown had
hardened, for he cautioned the House when feeling ran high
against Spain that what was said should be reported to them by word
of mouth only and not in writing, and met the King's request for
six subsidies and twelve fifteenths with criticisms of the amount demanded and requests for royal assurances as to the uses to which
the money would be put.[4] In fact, Perrot's increasing tendency
towards indiscriminate opposition may well have led his fellow
members to regard him as a man sincere but excessively rebellious.
There was some indication of this in May when Sir James, sent for
to go to a committee of the Lords, declared that he would "not do
it without leave of the House": which, a little tiredly, "left to him
to do as he will in it".[5] At all events, he made in this parliament far
fewer speeches than in the last; and the authority of his utterances

(1) C.J., p.798. The unfortunate Lewis Powell's election for Haverfordwest was also
disputed, by Sir Thomas Canon.
(2) Ibid., pp.692, 694, 704, 713, 776. In consequence of this last it was later resolved
(ibid., p.788) that they should not be presented to the Lords or to the King whose
children, though recusants, were of mature age, and who were known to be
Protestants, these being seven in number, including Perrot, who had already suggested such a practice. The members for Cardigan and Carmarthen reported
that their counties were free of recusants, although Sir William Awbrey, formerly
the member for Cardiganshire, was presented by the member for Brecknock. It is,
perhaps, significant that the the clerk did not know the name of the Carmarthen
member, who should join those for the counties of Caernarvon, Flint and
Merioneth, noted by Professor Dodd (op. cit., p.63) as being in like obscure case.
(3) On the Lord Keeper's having presented one Dr. Grant to a living in place of the
rightful presentor's nominees, Perrot spoke twice (C.J.., pp.700, 785), declaring
that the fault was great; that ignorance of law was inexcusable in a judge; and
that other alleged offences of a similar nature confirmed doubts regarding the
Lord Keeper's integrity.
(4) Ibid., pp.728, 741.
(5) Ibid., p.793.

was in part diminished and in part superseded by those of more re-
strained members such as Mansell.

Even so, Perrot far outshone all the other members for south-
west Wales. Sir Walter Devereux, sitting for the Pembroke boroughs, served on a few committees mainly concerned with circumstances at law affecting certain individuals;[1] as did Richard
Vaughan of Carmarthenshire on one or two more, such as that
"to enable . . . Prince Charles to make leases of land, parcel of his
Highness's Duchy of Cornwall". The "Mr. Lewis" who considered
"the naturalising of Sir Robert Anstruther, Sir George Abercromby
and John Cragge" may have been the member for Cardiganshire,
as the "Mr. Vaughan" who looked into "the inning and gaining of
the Erith and Plumstead marshes" may have been the member for
Carmarthen.[2] On such matters as the sale of butter and cheese, the
burning of moors and "the prostrating of weirs upon the river Wye",
all the Welsh members continued to sit collectively.[3] But it is
noteworthy that when a committee of twenty-four was set up to
consider a bill for the repeal of a branch of a statute that was causing
some confusion in Wales, the only member from the south-west
nominated to it was Sir James Perrot.[4]

The first parliament of Charles I saw the failure of Perrot to find
a seat,[5] and the subsequent complete silence in the Chamber of
the representatives of south-west Wales. At the next, with parliament
meeting in the aftermath of the government's hapless foreign policy,
Perrot was anxious to win Haverfordwest for himself once more,
but Canon held the seat, and not until the last two months of the
session did Perrot find his way back to the House.[6] In consequence

---

(1) For example, "on Mr. Egerton"; and "for the sale of lands of Thomas Cope"
(ibid., pp.687, 691, 737).

(2) Ibid., pp.731, 753, 761, 762.

(3) Ibid., pp.753, 764.

(4) Ibid., p.730. The bill was concerned with the position of the four English border
shires consequent upon the Act of Union. Cf. infra, p.169.

(5) John Wogan of Wiston won the Pembrokeshire seat, from which, in the previous
election, Perrot had ousted him. Haverfordwest was won by Sir Thomas Canon.
Perrot, whose petition, with Sir John Savile's, was given precedence by the committee for privileges, complained of electoral misdemeanours by Wogan, and
argued further that the sheriff had been incapacitated by the death of the late
King, but the committee's ultimate decision is not recorded (C.J., p.806; S. R.
Gardiner (ed.), Debates in the House of Commons in 1625, Camden Soc., new
ser., vol. vi (1873), pp.6, 53-54).

(6) Perrot complained against electoral misdemeanours by Canon, the matter being
referred to the committee for privileges; its report, if any, is not recorded. That
he won some by-election must be assumed from his later presence in the House.

he served on only about a dozen committees, including one for drawing up a petition to the King "wherein the desire of the House may be intimated to his Majesty for the rectifying and augmenting of his revenue", and another for "the preservation of the ecclesiastical jurisdiction".[1] His interests had not changed, but no speech of note came from him now. And he had no disciples from his own country. On 5 April Sir Richard Vaughan was licensed to return home to Carmarthenshire on account of his father's illness.[2] John Wogan gave voice only to secure his own privileged immunity from two lawsuits, and Canon earned like privilege with service on two committees: a contribution half-matched by James Lewis of Cardiganshire.[3]

Between the dissolution of this parliament and the summoning of the next, events moved rapidly. The government's foreign policy evoked fears of an alliance between France, Spain and the Papacy. Money, men and ships were demanded for abortive European expeditions, strongly disapproved of by many thinking men, and provided with much reluctance.[4] Yet the elections of 1628 saw the return of no protesting members for south-west Wales; indeed, those who were sent to speak from here in Parliament on behalf of oppressed constituencies were much the same as those who had failed to speak at all in previous sessions. Perrot, gradually assuming the mantle of a patriarch, found the hot opinions of more youthful days somewhat muffled by its folds. He still served on committees dealing with recusancy and the abuse of the sabbath,[5] but increasingly he was becoming preoccupied with matters of procedure, privilege and law.[6] These interests he seems to have shared with Sir Thomas Canon, now sitting for Haslemere,[7] who had joined him on the committee for privileges, and was also associated with him on the committee that weighed a bill "against the procuring of judicial places for money or other reward, and against giving and taking of bribes"; and with Henry Vaughan, in considering the matter of "the contempt of Langford and another". Vaughan was

---

(1) *C.J.*, pp.852, 855.
(2) Vaughan had evidently been present earlier, for he, with 83 others, held conference with the Lords on 7 March (*ibid.*, p.832). The roll-call of the House at this time was exceptionally lacking in Welsh absentees (*ibid.*, p.844).
(3) *Ibid.*, pp.840, 865.
(4) *Vide infra*, pp.121-123.
(5) *C.J.*, pp.877, 888, 904, 930.
(6) *Ibid.*, pp.899, 908, 911, 913, 929.
(7) *The Order and Manner of the Sitting of the Lords and Commons*, p.12.

also active, amongst one or two other matters, in censuring the
King's printer;[1] and Sir Walter Devereux, now holding a seat
distant from south-west Wales, was briefly active in framing a bill
"to avoid suspicion of injustice in any member of the Commons
House of Parliament".[2] But Sir Richard Vaughan again spent
much of the session in the country;[3] John Wogan, Hugh Owen
and James Lewis might just as well have done the same; and the great
days of John Vaughan of Trawsgoed lay in the future. Perrot
roused himself on one occasion to declare, in a discussion on two
allegedly Arminian bishops, that "it is said that these two bishops
were before the Council on their knees and with tears did disclaim
the opinions, but we see their facts. Dr. Laud, Bishop of London,
entertained for his household chaplain one that did dispute the
Arminian points, who said, 'What the Arminians hold and write he
would maintain and believe'". He offered to support this testimony
upon oath,[4] but his invitation was not taken up by the House. In
short, in a session in which routine legislation was supplanted by
controversy of great implication and lasting significance, the members from south-west Wales remained as subdued as ever.

In the light of all this, Professor Dodd's view of a growth in the
"political consciousness" of the Welsh members, who were "neither
puppets nor mouthpieces, but genuine representatives of Wales at
Westminster",[5] must, for this region, be qualified. There are
grounds for suggesting that patronage and activity in the House went
hand in hand. The interest of the Earl of Pembroke may have had
some effect in the constituencies of Montgomeryshire, Monmouthshire, Cardiff and Glamorgan; and Beaumaris was a pocket borough
of the Bulkeleys of Baron Hill. For this last Charles Jones was a
member from 1624; and the others had amongst their representatives the recurring names of Mansell, Stradling and Herbert itself.
Indeed, apart from Radnor, for which Charles Price sat from 1624
onwards, and the Denbighshire constituencies which sent Sir Thomas

(1) C.J., pp.919, 921, 922, 923. The printer was accused of having, by selective
publishing of the Petition of Right and the King's answers, misrepresented both.
Professor J. Gwynn Williams considers the Vaughan herein concerned to have
been John of Trawsgoed and not Henry ("Sir John Vaughan of Trawscoed,
1603-1674", N.L.W.Journal, vol. viii, pt. i (1953), p.45, note 26).
(2) C.J., p.874. Devereux sat for Tamworth in 1626 and 1628.
(3) He was licensed to depart on 27 May (ibid., p.905).
(4) Cobbett's Parliamentary History of England, vol. ii (1625-1642), p.458. Cf. supra,
p.106.
(5) Dodd, op. cit., pp.67-72.

Myddelton and Sir Eubule Thelwall to the House, no other Welsh constituencies could claim for their representatives the prominence and distinction that was won by those who sat in seats of "influence". If, apart from one important phase, the constituencies of south-west Wales elected their members without very great interference, for the most part, from outside political potentates, only one of these, and he not untouched by the finger of patronage,[1] escaped the slough of mediocrity. Secondly, there is reason to doubt the view that "on broader issues . . . her [i.e., Wales's] members often spoke with divided voices; but at least they spoke, or at any rate voted. It is nonsense to represent Stuart Wales as politically ignorant or indifferent".[2] It is no less nonsense to attribute the virtues of individuals to the groups into which they may conveniently be categorised. In south-west Wales political awareness was a rare quality. Professor Hexter, protesting that he "takes faith and freedom rather seriously himself", is "inclined to think that a good many men in the mid-seventeenth century took them seriously too".[3] This persuasion may sound ingenuous. If it holds any truth for Britain generally, then south-west Wales was a backwater.[4]

2. THE REALM

If the men elected to participate in central politics failed to reveal much capacity or interest therein, it would be unreasonable to expect more from those who stayed at home. Yet however far south-west Wales might lie from the whirlpool of affairs, some ripples were bound to disturb its accustomed stagnation. When the royal favourite Robert, Earl of Essex, resolved to act upon the overthrow of his love of the Queen by his love of himself, the interest of his supposedly adoring Welsh tenants might be expected to have quickened.

The Devereux, having profited materially at the time of the

---

(1) Perrot himself was something of a *protégé* of Pembroke's. *Vide*, for example, the dedication to his *Chronicle of Ireland* (ed. H. Wood, p.2): "Your lordship's (much more than can ever by me be merited) favours and furtherances extended towards my unworthy self are chains strong enough to fasten on me duty, faith and service as far as I am able . . . to perform any oblation worth the offering unto such a personage".
(2) A. H. Dodd, "Wales under the Early Stuarts", *Wales through the Ages* (ed. A. J. Roderick), vol. ii, p.60.
(3) J. H. Hexter, *op. cit.*, p.149.
(4) Mr. E. G. Jones ("The Caernarvonshire Squires, 1558-1625", University of Wales unpublished M.A. thesis (1936), pp.123-124) inclines to a similar view of that shire's representatives' activities in Parliament.

Dissolution by consolidating and extending their monastic holdings, and politically through the decline of the house of Dynevor following the fall of Rhys ap Griffith, had by the middle of the sixteenth century emerged as the leading family of this region. Their early opposition to the reforming zeal of Bishop Barlow had yielded before the opportunity of acquiring the manor of Lamphey.[1] In common with so many contemporary Welsh families, and with as much conviction as most, they claimed descent from the ancient princes of Wales; they had held the Chief Justiceship of South Wales; they were elected to Parliament, in particular representing Carmarthenshire,[2] and held the mayoralties of several boroughs. From these authoritative heights of blood, office and possessions, they assumed naturally a position of leadership; and although this may not have secured for them freedom of action in all spheres,[3] there is some justification for Laws's opinion that if anyone might have considered himself prince in Pembrokeshire, the second Earl was he.[4] From his birth in 1567 until 1584 he had spent a good deal of his time in that shire,[5] and had recruited into his household local men, among them Gelly Meyrick,[6] son of the former

---

(1) Glanmor Williams, "The Protestant Experiment in the Diocese of St. David's", pt. i, *B.B.C.S.*, vol. xv (1953), p.222. *Vide infra*, p.175.

(2) The first Earl of Essex was referred to as "Gwallter o'r Devrasiaid, Iarll Caerfyrddin" (David Mathew, *The Celtic Peoples and Renaissance Europe*, p.339).

(3) For instance, P.R.O. St. Ch. 2/17/271. According to the mayor and corporation of Carmarthen, Richard Devereux, after engrossing corn in defiance of their admonishings, had, through his servants led by one Thomas Awbrey, attempted to impose his will by force, procuring assaults upon the mayor and affrays in the town. Legal action was taken against him.

(4) Laws, however (*The History of Little England beyond Wales*, p.314), tends towards hyperbole. He attributes to Essex plans for securing home rule for Wales, and particularly for Pembrokeshire. He considers, further, that "the inhabitants of South Pembroke had followed the fortunes of the house of Devereux with a devotion resembling that of a Scottish clan to their chief" (*A Short Account of the Great Civil War as it affected Tenby*, p.7).

(5) G. B. Harrison, *Robert Devereux, Earl of Essex*, p.7.

(6) Meyrick is a classic example of a minor gentleman who rose to a position of authority and prosperity primarily through service in a noble household. Entering Essex's service in 1579 when the Earl was at Cambridge (H. E. Malden (ed.) "Richard Broughton's Devereux Papers", *Camden Miscellany*, vol xiii (1924), p.21), he rose to be steward of his household, was knighted by him at Cadiz, and like him was executed after the revolt. The rhyme composed in satirical celebration of Essex's liberal distribution of honours after Cadiz probably refers directly to Meyrick: "A gentleman of Wales/with knight of Cales / and a Lord of the north countrie; / a yeoman of Kent / upon a rack't rent / will buy them out, all three" (W. B. Devereux, *Lives of the Devereux Earls of Essex*, vol. i, p.370). In this connection, *cf.* Essex's like activity in Ireland (1599), when he "made sixteen new knights, probably in reward of future service" (John Chamberlain to Dudley Carleton, *C.S.P.Dom.* (1598-1601), vol. cclxxii, no. 1.).

chancellor of St. David's who later became Bishop of Bangor and
who had been allied with Barlows and Devereux against Bishop
Ferrar.[1] His contact with the region was further reinforced by the
romantic marriage of his sister;[2] and to this his own career added
an emotional lustre enhanced by his personality.[3] He of all men
might have hoped to draw from the local gentry support for a cause
which, though essentially his own, could be and was coloured with
political and religious implications sufficiently imprecise to afford
general appeal.

His lieutenant, Meyrick, certainly thought so. From about 1595
he set about the positive task of recruiting Welsh support for Essex.
His activities centred upon two regions: the March, old home of
unrest, where his personal interest largely lay;[4] and the south-west.
His efforts were not untrammelled by opposition, from both high
and low. Pembroke, President of the Council in the Marches, rejected his nomination for the post of deputy-lieutenant of Radnorshire in terms which hinted that he at least scented danger: "I know
that Sir Gelly Meyrick is a knight; I hear that he is rich. I mislike
not his credit and envy not his wealth. But I also know that he is
the Earl of Essex's household servant, not residing in Radnorshire,
and born and bred elsewhere, nor of kin to any there, only brought
thither by marriage to his wife . . . Why the Earl of Essex's service—
which should rather disable him—should cause this last to be preferred, I cannot conceive. If his lordship cannot endure that I should
recommend any but them who are only devoted to him, I will

(1) For the indictment against Ferrar, and Meyrick's prominence in this, *vide* John
Foxe, *Acts and Monuments*, vol. vii, p.17.
(2) Lady Dorothy Devereux married Sir Thomas Perrot in 1583 at Broxbourne in
Hertfordshire, in circumstances of great secrecy and not a little disorder, thus
uniting the two families of greatest influence in south-west Wales (B.M.
Lansdowne, 72, ff.10 *et seq.*). Essex espoused Sir John Perrot's cause at the time
of the latter's attainder, pledging himself to "employ what poor strength he has
to the uttermost", and supplicating Burghley on his behalf (*C.S.P.Dom.* (1591-
1594), vol. ccxlii, no. 4).
(3) On the occasion of his Irish expedition of 1599 the bard Evan Lloyd Jenkin
composed a lengthy poem in Essex's honour, reminiscent of the vaticinatory
verses addressed to Henry Tudor: "With the Earl of Essex, the famous reined
deer, / many went in anger against the enemy— / lords, knights, captains, fine men:
/ may we send our prayers after them . . . May the children in their cradles, the
women a-sitting, / the old man who guards the home, / the parson from the
pulpit, and all the world, pray / God to grant strength to the deer" (E.D. Jones,
"The Brogyntyn Welsh MSS.", *N.L.W.Journal*, vol. vi (1949-1950), p.154.)
(4) He had married Margaret Lewis, daughter of a high sheriff of Radnorshire and
a member of parliament, and had gained thereby the estate of Gladestry
(Jonathan Williams, *History of Radnorshire*, p.82).

recommend none at all".[1] Susan Morgan of Whitland, a lady with a strong antipathy to powerful men,[2] wrote to Essex in 1598, "Most of them that wears your honour's cloth in this country is to have your honour's countenance, and to be made sheriffs, lieutenants, stewards, subsidy-men, searchers, sergeants on the sea, mustermen—everything is fish that comes to their net. When the last sheriffs were made your lordship should have come to your chamber and said, 'Lord Meryke [sic] I have made all the sheriffs thou would'st have me make in Wales save one'. So with their offices and brags they oppress all her Highness's poor subjects".[3] To this were added allegations that Meyrick was accustomed to connive in murders and to conceal felons.[4]

But whatever the truth of these remarks, Meyrick's methods were unlikely to alienate more support than his favours won; for Essex was a diligent patron. As early as 1585 he had written to the Justice of Assize, Serjeant Puckering, "I am desirous to countenance my friends and servants in their country as far forth as I am able".[5] His intention upon that occasion had been to place Alban Stepney and David Lloyd Griffith in the commission of the peace for Carmarthenshire, and David Lloyd ap Hugh and David Lloyd ab Evan for Cardiganshire. Not all his efforts were successful. Walter Vaughan of Golden Grove, called to account for having, when high sheriff, released a prisoner for no apparent reason, grew to rue the day of Essex's intervention on his behalf, and eventually wrote directly to Puckering, "Whereas you supposed that I wrote a great complaint to the Earl of Essex to procure his last letter unto you, upon my credit, and as tract of time shall surely try, my letter purported no other meaning but only my heavy fine and the heinous machination in the Star Chamber".[6] The tone of the Earl's own letters to Puckering became less peremptory. Putting forward the names of Rees Thomas Lewis and David George Powell for the commission of the peace in Carmarthenshire, he wrote in 1587, "I will commend none unto you but those that I am persuaded are very fit ... Except there be some cause to the contrary I would be willing to give them some credit in the country, therefore herein I commend them both

(1) H.M.C. Cal. Salis. MSS., vol. viii, p.233.
(2) She greeted the attainder of Sir John Perrot with joyful exclaimings, on the grounds that "no justice can be had as long as the great devil lives. God bless her Majesty, who doth help us all" (B.M. Lansdowne, 72, f.67).
(3) H.M.C. Cal. Salis. MSS., vol. viii, p.423.   (4) Ibid., vol. xi, pp.125-127.
(5) B.M. Harleian, 6993, f.116.   (6) Ibid., 7002, f.6. Cf. infra, p.146.

to your good favour".[1] Yet even at this early date at least ten of the justices of the peace of south-west Wales could be described as "certain serving-men in livery . . . belonging to the Earl of Essex".[2] The representation of south-west Wales constituencies in the parliament of 1593 was virtually monopolised by the Essex connection, with four of the seven members being, moreover, "stranger" knights. It was this situation, coupled with the rivalry of Court factions, that inclined the authorities concerned to interpret allegiance to the Earl as a disqualification for local government appointments: a development that drew strong protests from Essex,[3] and that indicates how menacingly powerful his position had become.[4]

So when, about Michaelmas 1600, Sir Gelly and his brother, Francis, "travelled much the most part of Carmarthen and Pembroke shires, . . . making great cheer and feasting with their friends";[5] and when Sir George Devereux, "uncle of the Earl of Essex, being in the commission of the peace in counties Pembroke and Cardigan, . . . came down upon the sudden with one man only attending him at Christmas last, and did ever since (as yet he doth) sojourn at the house of John Barlow in Slebech";[6] when Carmarthenshire's leading gentleman was Meyrick's son-in-law, with others, such as David and William Gwyn of Kidwelly, closely related to him: rumour might well murmur meaningfully of the Earl, "I can tell the man hath many friends in many places of England, and espcially in the Welsh shires of Carmarthen, Pembroke and others adjoining, as far as the sea-coast".[7] Coercion, blandishments, ties of blood and tradition—all these were Essex's to exploit.

Yet when the die was cast in London in February 1601 the men of

(1) *Ibid.*, 6994, f.74. Essex was in fact simply following his father's example. For instance (*C.S.P.Dom.* (1547-1580), vol. xc, no. 8), Walter Devereux's letter on one occasion to Burghley condemned Sir Henry Jones and David Phillips as sheriffs for Carmarthenshire, and recommended Rhydderch Gwyn and Thomas Williams in their stead.
(2) In Cardiganshire, John Stedman, James Lewis, John Lloyd, Maurice ap Richard, Walter Vaughan; in Carmarthenshire, Philip Williams, David ap John ap Gwillim, Morgan John Harry, Owen Dwnn; in Pembrokeshire, George Wyrriott (B.M. Lansdowne, 53, f.182).
(3) B.M. Harleian, 6997, f.74. Philip Williams in particular was mentioned by Essex as having been removed from the commission of the peace for "retaining unto me".
(4) In Radnorshire, for instance, the continued freedom of one Harry Prosser of Walterston, an alleged double-murderer, was attributed to Meyrick's continued support and protection of him (H.M.C. *Cal. Salis. MSS.*, vol. xi, pp.125-127).
(5) *Ibid.*, p.135.
(6) *Ibid.*, pp.92-93.
(7) *Ibid.*, p.134.

south-west Wales were conspicuously absent. Of them, only Philip Williams[1] and John Vaughan joined Meyrick amongst eighty-five conspirators imprisoned.[2] Williams was discharged without bonds, indictment or fine; Vaughan was discharged upon bond; and only Meyrick remained steadfast to the noose's end. A few from the south riding to London in the company of Price, Meyrick's servant, heard half-way that the revolt was miserably over, and hastily "returned posting back again".[3] John Birt, the litigious public notary[4] in whom public duty and private vindictiveness should after the revolt have found an ideal opportunity for mutual expression, could do no more than trot out the time-worn imputations of recusancy against the Barlows and hint that the inconveniently-named sheriff, Devereux Barret, was a "known professed follower" of Essex, in support of his thesis that Pembrokeshire was full of hotheads and rebels of threatening disposition.[5] John Vaughan, in whom Sir Gelly had reposed sufficient confidence to convey "the greatest part of the goods and plate"[6] he possessed "to the number of twenty or a dozen trunks" from his own home to Golden Grove for greater safety before the revolt, now hastily transferred his allegiance, protested that the suspicions against him arose from his zeal in seeking out recusants and were fomented by such, denounced the "untrue and slanderous articles preferred by his enemies against him", and, in several letters, begged Cecil's favour.[7]

---

(1) Possibly former secretary to Sir John Perrot (*C.S.P.Dom.* (1581-1590), vol. ccxxxiv, no. 67), who had given evidence against him at his trial (*State Trials*, vol. ii, f.190).
(2) *A.P.C.* (1600-1601), pp. 483-487 (this list is not exhaustive). Spurrell (*op. cit.*, p.114) mentions David William Parry, the Carmarthenshire sheriff of 1568, as well, but his authority for this is not apparent.
(3) H.M.C. *Cal. Salis. MSS.*, vol. xi, p.43.
(4) He was accused by John Lewis of Llangrannog of making corrupt gain out of the office of sheriff (*vide infra*, p.155). Later charges suggested that he took physical vengeance upon Lewis and upon his servant, Owen ap Howell, in particular dragging the latter from his sick-bed, binding him with ropes and haling him before a justice of the peace on a charge of treason. Following the revolt, it was further alleged, he clapped both Lewis and his servant in Cardigan gaol on unsubstantiated charges (P.R.O. St. Ch. 5/L47/6 (f.18), /P44/15, /P52/21, /H47/38). His son was no more popular, being slanderously called a horse-thief (N.L.W. Wales 19/70/3).
(5) H.M.C. *Cal. Salis. MSS.*, vol. xi, pp.92-93.
(6) *A.P.C.* (1600-1601), p.208.
(7) H.M.C. *Cal. Salis. MSS.*, vol. xi, pp.135, 160, 329; vol. xii, p.172. He later sold the said goods for £400, declaring when challenged that they represented a part of the £1500 promised him by Sir Gelly at the time of his marriage, of which only £500 had been paid. He also mentioned that nothing had come of the promises of great preferment made to him by Meyrick, and generally regretted his association with him (P.R.O. E112/146/85).

In this course he was followed by Sir George Devereux, who later uninhibitedly appealed to Cecil, "I beseech you to pity me in sending me something to supply my present want".[1] A few local people may have been ready to relieve their feelings by chastising individuals who spoke ill of the Earl.[2] But by the end of the very month of the revolt Sir Richard Lewkenor could write to Cecil, "I find it both throughout Wales and the Marches thereof that the people thereof are generally very quiet, without any stirs, mutinies, or spreaders of rumours or news . . . The Earl of Essex was greatest in South Wales . . . I assure you the fall of the Earl, in those parts where he was greatest, is not grieved at, because I do generally hear that he was (and the rather by Sir Gelly Meyrick his means) often very chargeable and burdensome unto them; and Sir Gelly Meyrick himself lived by such oppression and overruling over them that they do not only rejoice at his fall but curse him bitterly".[3]

This may have been so. Yet the broader history of our times has frequently revealed that it is only in the aftermath of his passing that the tag "tyrant" is pinned on the hero, when his erstwhile dependants, often snug in a new palm, enthusiastically maul the dead hand that formerly had fed them. Like Perrot in Parliament, Essex had all the makings of a leader. From the March and from north Wales he did draw a fair amount of support.[4] The south-west at the crucial time remained indifferent. To attribute this either to loyalty to the Tudor dynasty or to the hurried and precipitate events of the revolt, is to ignore the self-centred apathy to external affairs that was the hallmark of this region throughout this period and beyond.[5]

A month before the Armada of 1588 the deputy-lieutenants of

(1) H.M.C. *Cal. Salis. MSS.*, vol. xv, p.85.
(2) This, at least, was the impression of Richard Bathoe, a native of the county then a cleric in Dublin, arising out of an assault allegedly perpetrated upon his person by Thomas Adams, gentleman, Hugh Powell, Lucy Meyrick, and Elizabeth Adams, wife of Nicholas Adams, esquire, with others, at Pembroke (P.R.O. St. Ch. 5/A41/40).
(3) H.M.C. *Cal. Salis. MSS.*, vol. xi, p.81.
(4) *Vide*, for example, David Mathew, *op. cit.*, pp.348-358; A. H. Dodd, "North Wales in the Essex Revolt", *E.H.R.*, vol. lix (1944), pp.348-370; *id.*, "The Earl of Essex's Faction in North Wales *circa* 1593-1601", *N.L.W. Journal*, vol. vi (1949-1950), pp.190-191.
(5) For "Watson's Plot", described as an afterblow of the Essex conspiracy and allegedly involving south-west Wales gentlemen, at the time of the Stuart succession, *vide* A. H. Dodd, "Wales and the Scottish Succession", *T.H.C.S.* (1937), pp.214 *et seq.* Evidence of complicity from this region depends, to a great extent, upon interpretation of depositions of known conspirators.

Carmarthenshire wrote to the Council that it was only with the greatest difficulty that they could persuade the inhabitants to provide arms and munitions.[1] Two years later complaint was made of the deputy-lieutenants of Pembrokeshire that they "are by reason of their great occasions of business continually absent from their charge of lieutenancy, whereby that county remaineth destitute and unprovided of any sufficiently authorised to call together the bands and forces in the case of need for the defence of those parts, especially in these doubtful times".[2] In 1599 Sir John Wogan reported on his county's attitude towards the possibility of foreign invasion, "We are very careless and more backward; most people imagine there will never be any such matter". He himself affirmed, "I would sooner spend my living and life also than the enemy should possess any part of her Majesty's dominions", but rather spoiled the effect of this by saying, in another letter written the same day in response to instructions to see the county's defences put in readiness, that he would do his part but "let every man do the like according to his ability, there being many in this shire far better able than myself".[3] Some force, apparently, had been raised, but then it transpired that "the gentlemen of the country do fear lest the same be drawn from thence to serve in other parts of the realm".[4] Accordingly, Pembrokeshire, in common with Anglesey, presumably on account of their peculiarly vulnerable locations, was "forborne from foreign services according to the suit made in that behalf":[5] a privilege of which it was not slow to take advantage. When the county was instructed to send one hundred and fifty men to Bristol for service in Ireland the deputy-lieutenants failed to comply and drew upon their heads in no un-

---

(1) *C.S.P.Dom.* (1581-1590), vol ccxi, no. 44.
(2) *A.P.C.* (1590), p.248. The letter continues: "Forasmuch as this service is of importance and craveth expedition, and that we cannot at this present think on any in the same shire so fit for the supply of those wants", Sir William Herbert of Swansea, Sir Edward Stradling, Thomas Carne and Thomas Mansell, esquires, all from Glamorgan, were called upon to perform the duties of deputy-lieutenants in Pembrokeshire for the time being. So much for a county where eighty-five gentlemen had in 1584 signed the Instrument of Association (P.R.O. S.P.12/ 174/14), and containing Milford Haven, the first-named of those harbours "aptest for the enemy to land in" in a 1572 list of these (H.M.C. *Cal. Salis. MSS.*, vol. ii, p.42).
(3) *C.S.P.Dom.* (1598-1601), vol. cclxxi, nos. 136, 137.
(4) *A.P.C.* (1591-1592), p.32.
(5) *Ibid.* (1597-1598), p.301. *Cf.* 1 Edward III, st.2., c.5, by which men could be taken from their county only to meet invasion (*vide* C. G. Cruickshank, *Elizabeth's Army*, p.4).

certain terms the wrath of the Privy Council.[1] Next year, complaint was received from Carmarthenshire of the "backwardness and great undutifulness of divers gentlemen and others in the execution of her Majesty's service".[2] Haverfordwest, where many of the troops *en route* for Ireland were victualled, caused the Council to "marvel very much of so many as ran away from that place, that there are two only apprehended".[3] In Cardiganshire there flourished "a general and common abuse . . . when there is any occasion to levy men that the tallest and fittest persons for service do withdraw themselves and go out of the country".[4] And even when local men did take it upon themselves to conduct investigations into matters of national moment, it seems to have been the threat of invasion *via* Milford directly threatening themselves that motivated such fearful diligence.[5]

The special circumstances of the Irish route, and Elizabethan authorities' general difficulties in securing local co-operation in such matters, modify the immediate significance of this impression. But attitudes of this kind did not bode well for the success of financial exactions under the Stuarts, and especially the momentous levies of Charles I. Demands for money for the royal service were met with as great evasion as were requirements of a more physical nature; and the reaction in this region, far from objection founded upon principle, was largely one of excuse backed by dishonesty and prevarication.[6] To the subsidy of 1623, for instance, the sheriffs and justices of Pembroke, Cardigan and Carmarthen counties alike failed not only to levy their contribution but even to offer any explanation

---

(1) "This inconsiderate dealing of yours in a matter so highly concerning her Majesty's service . . . may breed that prejudice to her Majesty's service as, if you should be called to a strict accompt, you could hardly answer the same . . . This present occasion is such as no excuse is to be admitted, and your indiscretion apparent to send unto us excuses at the very instant when the men should have been ready at the port" to be embarked (*ibid.* (1599-1600), p.65). Carmarthenshire, called upon to send one hundred men, also defaulted and received equally harsh rebuke (*ibid.*, p.66).
(2) *Ibid.*, p.269.
(3) *Ibid.*, p.760.
(4) *Ibid.* (1600-1601), p.382.
(5) For instance, the examination of John Kethin before John Gronowe, mayor of Tenby (P.R.O. S.P.12/271/136(1)i), and that of Daniel Gibbon and Edward Reade before Sir John Wogan, George Owen and Alban Stepney (*ibid.*, /135(1)). The latter relates the capture of the examinees by pirates off Corunna and their questioning by several renegade Englishmen as to whether Milford and Tenby were fortified, the distance from Tenby to Haverfordwest and to Carmarthen, the quality of the roads and the general state of the country.
(6) In marked contrast to the spirit of Perrot's speech, *supra*, p.106.

for their omission.[1] The levy of 1626-1627 upon coastal shires and towns, which furnished the immediate precedent for the ship-money demands of the 1630s, drew at first from the justices of Pembrokeshire in August the observation that "it had ministered no small comfort to their hearts if, by course of Parliament, this supply had been added to their former burden".[2] But by the following month they ascribed their inability "to do what they intended" to "the justices of county Cardigan having refused to join on equal terms in furnishing a pinnace for his Majesty's service".[3] Meanwhile from Carmarthenshire the justices reported that the people "were ready to supply his Majesty's wants according to the usual and ancient custom".[4] Yet in the following year the lack of response from all three shires earned them the exasperated warning that "so great a neglect of the commands of this Board, especially iterated as aforesaid by several letters, is not to be passed by without censure and punishment".[5] Declarations of willingness to contribute were accompanied by interminable permutations of worn excuses: decay in local estates, present disability, the hazard of conveying the money to London, the fall in the prices of wool and cattle.[6] In one collection in Cardiganshire in 1627 there were 174 defaulters.[7] In the same year, when the official reply of the commissioners for the loan in Carmarthenshire announced "with all cheerful and dutiful hearts" the readiness of the subsidy-men to contribute,[8] one collector alone returned a list of forty people who "refused to pay the moiety of the loan moneys by them promised".[9]

The main burden for the collection of ship-money from 1634 to 1640 fell upon the sheriffs, who, besieged by the epistolary insistence of the Privy Council, can hardly have found comfortable their revived importance in local administration. The three shires reflect some of the features of the general reaction to these levies: objections to the rate imposed, or a simply negative response. In 1635 the local

(1) *A.P.C.* (1621-1623), p.409.
(2) *C.S.P.Dom.* (1625-1626), vol. xxxiii, no. 57. 8 August 1626.
(3) *Ibid.*, vol. xxxvi, no. 19. 19 September 1626.
(4) *Ibid.*, vol. xxxv, no. 97. 15 September 1626.
(5) *A.P.C.* (1627-1628), p.114. It was here directed that the money be used for fortifying Milford Haven, on which subject, wrote Perrot, "there is a coldness, I will
not say a carelessness" in the locality (P.R.O. S.P.16/92/31).
(6) *C.S.P.Dom.* (1627-1628), vol. liv, no. 74; vol. lxxix, no. 44; *ibid.* (1619-1623),
vol. cxxxii, no. 23; vol. cxxxi, no. 62.
(7) P.R.O. S.P.16/68/47.
(8) P.R.O. S.P.16/54/54.
(9) P.R.O. S.P.16/55/85.

officials of Haverfordwest failed to meet in time to decide on a mutually acceptable assessment for that town, and then protested against their eventual assessment at £65 10s.[1] In 1637 Richard Price, sheriff of Cardiganshire, petitioned the Council that "endeavouring to levy the ship-money, he tried by all fair and gentle means, but could not receive one penny, so that he was compelled to distrain oxen, kine, horses, sheep, household stuff and implements of husbandry, the which petitioner can get no money for, nor any man to offer for them one penny, though often set at sale".[2] But it is difficult to discern in this the type of opposition which has been recognised in Somerset, in the form of "a close-knit and elusive conspiracy . . . given organisation by clever minds and powerful hands".[3] Prominent men might object to the sheriff on behalf of their locality against their "proportion of the charge, and their desire that it may be abated to that same proportion which they bear in all public charges", suggesting reasons for the sheriff to tender to the Council.[4] But in August 1637 Sir John Stepney reported for Pembrokeshire that the difficulty he had experienced in collecting arrears was "in respect of men's poverty and not otherwise", though in October he had still not delivered these arrears.[5] By and large the explanations offered for delay in delivering money remained the same as before: distance from London, local poverty, in one instance the accidental death by drowning of the Pembrokeshire sheriff.[6] Even as late as 1640 the Carmarthenshire escheator explained to the Council "why the ship-money has not been returned; it is the slackness of some few. The most part having already been paid, the residue will be recovered on the getting in of this harvest".[7] That the persistent demands for ship-money represented in the seventeenth century an unacceptable form of permanent taxation is obvious; that they aroused increasing antipathy is evident.[8] But

(1) *C.S.P.Dom.* (1635), vol. ccciv, no. 80.
(2) *Ibid.* (1637-1638), vol. ccclxxvi, no. 141.
(3) T. G. Barnes, *Somerset, 1625-1640*, p.209.
(4) *C.S.P.Dom.* (1635), vol. ccxcviii, no. 32: Sir John Lewis and ten others to Hector Phillips, pleading that the rate for Cardiganshire "was ever but half the rate for counties Pembroke and Carmarthen".
(5) *Ibid.* (1637), vol. ccclxvi, no. 45; vol. ccclxix, no. 43.
(6) *Ibid.* (1639), vol. ccccxx, no. 73; *ibid.* (1637-1638), vol. ccclxxxi, no. 70; vol. ccclxxxv, no. 59; *ibid.* (1636-1637), vol. cccxxxiii, no. 12. The increasing difficulties of ship-money collection and the multipying of excuses of the kind noted, are further illustrated in the Carmarthenshire collectors' letters: *vide* P.R.O. S.P.16/347/25; /349/1; /350/5; /379/50.
(7) *C.S.P.Dom.* (1640), vol. cccclxvi, no. 33.
(8) *Vide infra*, Appendix A.

that this antipathy, expressed in this region simply in familiar reluctance to co-operate, implied any broader principle or gave rise to consolidated opposition, cannot be shown.

Statistical analyses of participants in the conflict between King and Parliament can obscure attitudes arising out of irresponsibility, indifference or parochial preoccupation.[1] Usefully to separate cavalier sheep from roundhead goats requires recognition of the many who fit into neither fold. As regards those involved *ex officio*, the most distinguished member for this region in the Long Parliament, John Vaughan of Trawsgoed, made relatively frequent contributions on the opposition side to parliamentary business, including the proceedings against Strafford, but was absent from the final division on that bill of attainder,[2] and has been described as "much concerned about the royal cause" in the war itself.[3] Apart from Sir Hugh Owen, roused only by anxiety for his constituency of Pembroke in view of the Irish crisis, and by some dubious concern for his "servant", John Poyer,[4] no other local representative participated to any significant degree in the development of events at the centre. At home, of the three members from Pembrokeshire two, Owen and Wogan, in company with Richard Phillips of Picton, reported in highly-coloured terms to the Earl of Stamford in November 1642 their efforts to defend "the only towns of consequence in this county";[5] but this region's military endeavour was not to be led by them. The third, Sir John Stepney, was later dealt with by the Committee for Compounding in company with Sir Thomas Tomkins of Hereford, neither having been in arms, and Stepney, as it appeared, having been captured at Hereford because he was there seeking a pass when the town was taken.[6] Moreover, the commissioners entrusted by the Parliament with securing the paying

---

(1) Particularly D. Brunton and D. H. Pennington, *Members of the Long Parliament*, *passim.* "To divide members of the House of Commons into two parties, labelled 'Royalist' and 'Parliamentarian', and then to treat all members of the two groups as statistically equivalent, is misleading . . . [and discounts] the marginal turncoat on either side who had no principles at all" (C. Hill, *Puritanism and Revolution*, p.17).
(2) A. H. Dodd, "Wales in the Parliaments of Charles I", part ii, *T.H.C.S.* (1946-1947), pp.59-96, esp. p.73.
(3) It must be said that the evidence discussed by Professor J. Gwynn Williams ("Sir John Vaughan of Trawscoed, 1603-1674", *loc. cit.*) in support of this assertion seems to indicate scant positive and some dubious activity by Vaughan in the period of the war itself.
(4) Dodd, *op. cit.*, p.80.
(5) *L.J.*, vol. v, p.441.
(6) *Cal. Comm. Comp.*, vol. ii, pp.1035-1036.

of fines by royalists do not appear to have operated with a marked degree of increased efficiency in comparison with their earlier counterparts under the monarchy.[1]

Apart from this, evidence from the papers of the Committee for Compounding against "delinquents" such as Thomas Phillips of Llanelli, Rowland Morgan of Llangendeirne, Anthony Morgan, John Evans, Samuel Hughes, George Okeley and others,[2] is at least as explicible in terms of local rivalries and jealousies as of positive royalist views on the part of those so accused. Several of those to whom such views and activities were attributed in a list of 8 March 1648 eventually escaped with unexpectedly light penalties. Sir Rice Rudd of Aberglasney, "a Commissioner of Array, and very active for the King", and fined at £581 12s. 7d., soon secured the abatement of his fine by £500 "on settling £50 a year out of St. Peter's rectory, Carmarthen, on the minister there"—a rectory apparently worth £110 a year.[3] Information against Henry Middleton of Llanarthney, at first similar to that against Rudd, was soon modified, and the accused described as "useful to the Parliament forces, and only continued at his habitation and appeared amongst the revolters for special reasons, by advice of a well-affected person".[4] Middleton was fined at £120; John Lloyd of Ffrŵd, Carmarthenshire, described by the same informers as "very violent in promoting the King's service, persecuting Parliament's friends, some of them to the death and was constantly in arms for the King", was fined at £56.[5] Ostensibly geared to the assessed values of delinquents' estates, these fines, with their repeated adjustments, may equally reflect the doubtful reliability of the central committee's local *aides*, One of the three compilers of the list of 8 March was Ralph Grundy, who was later

---

(1) Similar excuses were offered as had been tendered then, with the additions of the plague in Pembrokeshire and Carmarthen, and the misguided loyalty of "the inferior people" who "will not offend their landlords, come what may". "Affairs of importance requiring our attendance" were pleaded; and the central committee was driven to "sharply hint of your carelessness in the service" (*ibid.*, vol. i, p.61, pp.222, 391-392, 571-572, 600, 614, 618, 639, 714). *Cf.* the central Committee for Plundered Ministers' "lack of faith in the Committee of Carmarthen" (T. Richards, *History of the Puritan Movement in Wales*, pp.42-43).
(2) *Cal. Comm. Comp.*, vol. iii, pp.1825-1826. Allegations often included "plundering".
(3) *Ibid.*, p.1827. *Cf.* Dodd, *Studies in Stuart Wales*, pp.132, 144: "The nucleus of the Carmarthenshire committee [of 1647] consisted of ex-Cavaliers (including most of the governing families) who had negotiated the surrender of the county in October, 1645"—including Rudd, and other "West Wales weathercocks".
(4) *Cal. Comm. Comp.*, *loc. cit.*
(5) *Ibid.*, *loc. cit.*, and vol. i, p.443.

to write to the Committee for Petitions, "that at the beginning of the Parliament he was the only person in Carmarthenshire that acted for them . . . for which he was plundered, his brother murdered, and himself condemned to death as a traitor":[1] a statement suggestive of the degree of altruism to be expected of its author. There were certainly some, such as William Gwynn who fought at Edgehill, Sir Henry Vaughan of Derwydd at Naseby,[2] or Thomas Wogan, who signed the royal death warrant and won honourable mention in parliamentary despatches,[3] of whose positive participation and sentiments there can be little doubt. But for the majority of local gentlemen who, unlike Sir John Meyrick and Rowland Laugharne,[4] had no direct personal attachment to either side, the call to arms evoked small access of political thinking or activity.

For of the sixteen gentlemen of Pembrokeshire to whom in 1642 Parliament entrusted the calling out of the militia to prevent the executing of the royalist Commission of Array, all but three in 1643, after the Earl of Carbery had taken Tenby and Haverfordwest for the King, signed a pledge "to the utmost of our power and endeavour speedily to reduce the same to his Majesty's obedience".[5] In 1644 John Vaughan wrote to Colonel Herbert Price that the south-west counties were "likely to yield themselves to the first danger, or to fall in with the first protection, being very impotent for resistance in themselves".[6] The local Welsh emerge as sufficiently unenthusiastic for either cause to merit the contemporary observation, "The Welsh care not for fighting but upon passage, and scarce then either, except

(1) H.M.C. *Cal. Portland MSS*, vol. i, p.661. In March 1633 Grundy's father, Hugh, had mortgaged his capital messuage in Llangendeirne to a Bristol goldsmith in £500 (N.L.W. Muddlescombe, 2120). Hugh Grundy had been prosecuted in Star Chamber by the Vaughan family; his son was "a man with more than one axe to grind and many old debts to pay" (T. Richards, in *A History of Carmarthenshire* (ed. Sir. J. E. Lloyd), vol. ii, p.135.)
(2) For a royalist song mentioning Sir Henry, *vide* D. Lleufer Thomas, "Iscennen and Golden Grove", *loc. cit.*, p.124.
(3) "Captain Wogan (a member of the House who behaved himself so gallantly against the enemy in Wales)," *etc.* (John Rushworth, *Historical Collections*, pt. iv, p.1121.)
(4) Meyrick, nephew of Sir Gelly, emulated his uncle's service to the house of Essex with service as adjutant-general to the third Earl, to whom Laugharne had been a page (J. F. Rees, *Studies in Welsh History*, pp.95-96).
(5) J. R. Phillips, *The Civil War in Wales and the Marches*, vol. ii, pp.4, 84-85. Phillips suggests that some of the signatures to the second of these documents were forged, mentioning in particular that of Sir Hugh Owen. Yet it was John Vaughan's opinion, privately conveyed by letter to Colonel Price, that Owen would be ready to deal with the royalist forces and "may prove of great use" (*ibid.*, p.157).
(6) Quoted in *Arch. Camb.* (1853), pp.63-64.

they have a good opportunity. For the Welsh have always been observed to be cowards and seldom act but upon advantage".[1] Though Carbery had initially gained prompt control of the region for the King, the early months of 1644 saw Rowland Laugharne secure the fall of Pill fort for Parliament after no more than token resistance by the royalist garrison; the evacuation of Haverfordwest by royalist gentlemen who apparently mistook a frightened herd of cattle for the approaching enemy; the fall of Tenby;[2] the abandoning of Carew Castle; and finally the voluntary surrender of Carmarthen at the approach of Laugharne, the townsmen promising loyalty to Parliament if no harm were done to them. When in 1644-1645 Sir Charles Gerrard moved in on him, Laugharne in his turn was driven helter-skelter from Kidwelly, Carmarthen, Newcastle Emlyn, Cardigan and Haverfordwest, but once this intruder had departed he encountered little difficulty in recovering his position.[3]

Interpretations of the events of the Civil War, and the conduct and attitudes of those involved, are, clearly, greatly subject to the bias inherent in evidence drawn from pamphlet and newspaper accounts published for purposes of political propaganda.[4] But the vacillations of this region are more convincingly explained in terms of personal animosities and local insularity than of genuine changes in political conviction and commitment. John Poyer, in one of his answers to Parliament's repeated demands for his surrender on terms in 1648, stated that he and his troops required payment in full for their charges, costs and arrears: "this granted, we are willing to

(1) Phillips, *op. cit.*, vol. ii, p.354. A. L. Leach (*History of the Civil War in Pembrokeshire*, pp.34-35) argues that in Pembrokeshire active participation in the war was virtually confined to the Englishry.
(2) When the town and castle of Tenby fell again on 1 June 1648 twenty-one officers were taken prisoner, and one report commented that "the town and castle was able to have held out ten weeks longer, having food sufficient . . . " (Rushworth, *op. cit.*, pt. iv, p.1142).
(3) The recapture of Cardigan seems to have involved some intensified military activity, but Leach's account of this, as of some other incidents (*op. cit.*, pp.95-98), is based on conflicting pamphlet and newspaper reports, and the presence of Gerrard thereat is doubtful. The ebb and flow of royalist fortunes in this region in this period otherwise coincides directly with the absence and presence of Gerrard and his forces.
(4) *Vide*, for instance, "A True Relation of the Routing of His Majesty's Forces in Pembroke" (*Thomason Tracts*, B.M. E42.13); "A True Relation of the Proceedings of Colonel Laugharne" (*ibid.*, E42.19); "News from Wales" (*ibid.*, E147.4); "The Welshman's Jubilee" (*ibid.*, E136.16); "The Welshman's Prave Resolution" (*ibid.*, E149.33); "The Welshman's Public Recantation" (*ibid.*, E129.20); "The Welshman's Postures" (*ibid.*, E89.3); "The Welshman's Propositions" (*ibid.*, E346.15): many of these devoted to mocking Welsh ignorance and inconstancy.

surrender Castle and all; if not, we are resolved, with the assistance
of the Almighty, to hold the Castle for the King and Parliament,
according to the covenant by us taken . . . Our trust is not in the arm
of flesh, but our hope standeth in the name of the Lord . . . We have
bestowed our time to good purpose at last to be proclaimed traitors
and rebels for demanding our own; and no more but what yourself
and those mercenaries desire that you have brought to murder us".[1]
Laugharne's own switch of allegiance, following hard upon Poyer's
defection if less dishonourably motivated and contradictorily expressed, owed much to the overruling of his local jurisdiction by the
central authority for whose victory he had ostensibly been fighting.
His letter to Horton, who replaced him as commander-in-chief, was
brief and peremptory: "I desire you would let me know by what
power you first came and would remain in the counties of my
association . . . I should gladly be satisfied in these particulars, otherwise your perseverance in these affronts to myself and the soldiery
and the country will not be without some difficulty. Sir, if you please
to withdraw your forces out of this country, it may be a special means
to prevent several inconveniences, besides the necessary resolutions
which may otherwise be forced, upon, Sir, your obedient servant,
Rowland Laugharne".[2]

The opinion of a writer from Carmarthen at the time of the
Restoration as to the "true character and deportment for these
eighteen years last past of the principal gentry within the counties of
Carmarthen, Pembroke and Cardigan"[3] seems, accordingly, to
have been grounded as much upon fact as upon prejudice. Carbery,
the royalist commander, had been enough of a friend of Cromwell's
to receive from him a gift of deer for the park at Golden Grove.[4]
Roger Lort was "of any principle or religion to acquire wealth";[5]
as for Sampson Lort, "any government, religion or office will suit
him so it carries some lucre along with it". In Sir John Stepney, "the

---

(1) Rushworth, *op. cit.*, pt. iv, p.1034. The suggestion that the forces of the New
Model Army, recruited in a manner overriding local jurisdictions, were mercenaries, was, of course, one that they themselves had found it necessary to refute
(*vide* the "Declaration" of June 1647, printed in Rushworth, *op. cit.*, pt. iv,
pp.564-570).
(2) Phillips, *op. cit.*, vol. ii, p.362.
(3) N.L.W. Llanstephan, 120, 145. The writer signed himself "O. P. Maridunensis".
(4) As the shelterer and patron of the royalist cleric, Jeremy Taylor, his conduct
becomes even more ambiguous.
(5) *Cf.* Lort's earlier efforts to secure the right of wreck along his stretch of coastline
(P.R.O. S.P.16/189/26); also, the committee career of the "ambodextrous Lorts"
(Dodd, *op. cit.*, pp.118, 123, 144, 153).

habit of ease hath made his disposition not very inclinable to be very industrious to his own or the public affairs of his country".[1] Sir Walter Lloyd "contents himself within the walls of his house". Sir Francis Lloyd "seems to love his private ease above the public affairs of his country". James Lewis was "loved for doing no wrong more than for doing any good, his body being a lazy instrument of so good a mind". John Vaughan was "one that upon fits will talk loud for monarchy, but scrupulous to wet his finger to advance it".[2] Harry Vaughan would do "anything for money"; James Phillips was "one that had the fortune to be in with all times but thrived with none". Instances such as John Barlow, a consistent royalist, were so rare that "he was rather a pattern for the gentry of the country to wonder at than in hopes to be imitated by them". One concludes that the gentry would have preferred to imitate the sphinx-like attitude of Sir Hugh Owen, who was "so habituated to reservedness that it is thought he cannot now extricate himself if he would from it". Throughout the writer's tone is not of condemnation and denunciation of political opponents but of contempt for the nonentities he saw everywhere about him.

In 1655 Thomas Dring compiled his *Catalogue of the Lords, Knights and Gentlemen who have compounded for their Estates*. The list is generally incomplete, but it reveals an interesting distribution of known committed royalists in Wales. Out of eighty-eight gentlemen listed from the twelve shires and Monmouthshire, sixty-one came from the four counties of Denbigh, Flint, Glamorgan and Monmouth. The three shires of south-west Wales supplied together only eleven. Yet of the 344 Welsh officers who laid claim to the £60,000 granted by the Crown after the Restoration for the relief "of many worthy persons brought into great distress by their fidelity", the greatest number from a single shire hailed from Carmarthenshire with seventy-six, though Pembrokeshire, with twenty-four, and Cardiganshire, with four, were below the average.[3] This conflict of evidence can only suggest that in this region "ambidexterity" was not confined to the Lorts; that in the Civil War and Interregnum principle here played a minor role in the making of decisions; and

(1) Having offered to represent Haverfordwest in Parliament free of charge, he was driven to borrow money from its corporation.
(2) Circumspection is, perhaps, understandable in one who had recently invested heavily in land (*cf. supra*, p.41).
(3) *A List of Officers claiming to the Sixty Thousand Pounds, etc.* (1663). The publication of this list was intended to discover how many of the claimants were fraudulent; it was suspected that many were so.

that in matters of serious political moment the men of this region
were immature and unaware.

3. THE PROVINCE

To judge from his own career and from his known fondness for
Aristotle, Sir James Perrot may have subscribed to the view that man
is by nature a political animal. In 1569 the mayor of Haverfordwest,
in an action brought against him by three denizens of that town,
made a statement to the following effect. Francis Laugharne, acting
in his capacity as high sheriff of Pembrokeshire, had attempted to
arrest in Haverfordwest a follower of Sir John Perrot's. The accused
called his friends to his assistance. The sheriff, and others with him,
"being sore hurt and wounded by the said servants of Sir John Perrot
and their friends", retired into a nearby house and "kept themselves
close with the doors shut fast upon them for the safeguard of their
lives, and nonetheless the said servants of Sir John Perrot continued
still in raging manner about the doors of the said house where the
said sheriff then remained and called him out with loud words and
talk of defiance, whereby it appeared that they intended with great
violence to pull him out of the said house and then further to maim
and murder him". The mayor attempted in the Queen's name to
pacify them, but to no effect, until Perrot arrived in person and
suggested that the mayor and justices of the peace that were present
should come to the town hall and examine the cause of the riot. This
they did; and once there, discovered that the only witnesses available
for examination were Perrot's men. Sir John persuaded the mayor to
take down his servants' depositions, and the next day, before the
Justices of Assize, declared that these represented an unbiassed view
of the incident. The mayor managed to rebut this, but Perrot
promptly contrived to obtain a further dozen depositions from men
not strictly his servants but, for various reasons, favourably disposed
towards him, and produced these before the jury examining the
affair. The mayor encountered the greatest difficulty in showing that
these, too, were partial testimonies; and in his efforts on behalf of
Laugharne exposed himself to allegations of favouritism and corrupt
dealing, which Perrot, ever ready to cause "trouble, vexation and
expenses", was not slow to impute.[1]

---

(1) P.R.O. St. Ch. 6/2/T21A. The point of the liberties of Haverfordwest was not
    raised against Laugharne as it was against Wogan in similar circumstances
    (*vide infra*, p.165).

Whether Laugharne was in the right, or whether Perrot; whether
the mayor was seeking to draw a veil over his own malpractices;
how far the situation arose out of non-recognition of the Pembrokeshire sheriff's authority within Haverfordwest: these questions may
here be set aside. The present significance of this incident lies in the
admission of the mayor, favouring Laugharne, that the latter was
backed by allies, and in his frequent references to Perrot's servants.
Here, incidentally revealed, are "parties" of a kind. In this is epito-
mised the nature of politics in south-west Wales: petty politics,
founded upon faction, led by men to whom family tradition and
material circumstances had lent a natural authority accepted without
much question by their tenants and kinsfolk, in whom the terms
respectively of "retainer" and "patron" take on fresh meaning.
Frequently the litigation of the time discloses the importance of such
relationships. It was the servants and relations of Robert Williams
who, ignoring official attempts at reconciling the parties, were
alleged to have sought to chastise Humphrey Lloyd of Llandeilo
Talybont for seducing Williams's wife.[1] In 1600 David Lloyd of
Abermâd, supposed to bear "mortal and causeless hatred and
malice unto divers gentlemen of your Highness's said county" of
Cardigan, was alleged to depend for its expression upon his sons and
tenants and to have "received them into [his] house and there hath
and doth harbour and maintain, encourage and commend them and
their wicked practices and enterprises, who were and are continually
ready at the commandment of the said David Lloyd to commit and
perpetrate any lewd action".[2] The bill in the suit which followed
the election of a coroner at Carmarthen similarly discloses cliques and
"parties" on both sides. It described how David Lloyd Griffith,
disqualified from that office upon his appointment as sheriff, conspired with Walter Vaughan of Golden Grove to elect a new coroner
from among their "own people or friends"; how Sir Thomas Jones
of Abermarlais and others got to know of it, and on the appointed
day packed the hall with their supporters; and how thereupon the

(1) P.R.O. St. Ch. 5/L25/10.
(2) P.R.O. St. Ch. 5/P29/21. The dispute with Thomas Price, plaintiff in the present
suit, seems to have arisen over the possession of a messuage in Llanilar (P.R.O.
E112/59/24). If the repeated references to Lloyd's retainers were calculated to
show contravention of the statute, Lloyd in his answer did not deny this aspect.
He demurred firstly that the case should be heard before the Council in the
Marches, secondly that in the alleged riot he was the provoked party. *Vide*
P.R O. St. Ch. 5/L34/4, for other disputes between Lloyd, Price and others.

sheriff and his followers, "in close and covert manner", withdrew
to the castle and there elected one Harry Lloyd, "a man unlearned,
unskilful and one of small ability or wealth".[1]

When the men of Sir John Perrot and the Earl of Worcester's
servants clashed in London over a quarrel between their respective
masters, the Privy Council ordered them "to forget all private and
old grudges".[2] Further armed affrays by Perrot and his men, involving Thomas Catharne, and William Phillips and his associates,
and other disturbances by Edward Vaughan, John Wogan, Francis
Laugharne and Sir Thomas Perrot, drew the attention of the Privy
Council to these factions.[3] Their conduct abroad seems to have
improved.[4] At home, meanwhile, circumstances were easier;
groupings in Pembrokeshire in particular became firm, often indicating the lasting influence of earlier quarrels. The families of Phillips
of Picton, Barlow of Slebech, Wyrriott of Orielton, Laugharne of
St. Bride's, Stepney of Prendergast and Owen of Henllys, tended to
oppose the Perrot preponderance;[5] the Wogans of Wiston and
Boulston, and the Bowens of Pentre Evan generally supported it.
In Carmarthenshire Jones of Abermarlais lent further weight to the
Perrot group.[6] The opposition, born as it appears in the case of
Barlow of Perrot's inquiry into concealed lands in 1559 which
threatened much of the Slebech property,[7] sustained in 1566 in the
Great Sessions and beyond when Barlow sued Perrot for debt,[8]
and continued in 1570 when Perrot was declared to have impressed

(1) P.R.O. St. Ch. 5/J2/17.
(2) A.P.C. (1552-1554), pp. 388-389.
(3) Ibid. (1556-1558), pp.333, 354, 386, 390; (1558-1570), pp.55, 149; (1578-1580),
    p.384.
(4) Particularly after about 1580, to judge from the incidence of such occurrences in
    the records of the Privy Council.
(5) Phillips, Barlow and Owen had been amongst those who, with the Devereux
    and Rowland Meyrick, formed a "powerful coalition of clergy and laity" against
    Bishop Ferrar (Glanmor Williams, "The Protestant Experiment in the Diocese
    of St. David's", part ii, B.B.C.S., vol. xvi (1954), p.42; vide infra, p.176). The oc-
    casional elasticity of these associations, however, is shown in 1589 when Stepney
    joined Thomas Perrot in pleading the cause of Jenkin Davids, arrested by Sir
    John Wogan on instructions from the Privy Council for illegal purchases of salt
    (B.M. Add. MSS. 12507, f.221.)
(6) Dennis Rowghane, the Irish priest, in his colourful denunciations of Perrot,
    linked Wogan's and Jones's names with his as "the only men to bring Sir John
    Perrot's wicked purposes to pass, as to receive the King of Spain's navy into
    Milford Haven" (H.M.C. Cal. Salis. MSS., vol. iv, p.117). Perrot had been Sir
    Thomas's ward (P.R.O. E210/D.9714). The alliance with Wogan was not
    uniformly close: vide infra, p.165.
(7) J. Phillips, History of Pembrokeshire, pp.437-438.
(8) P.R.O. C3/12/9, ff.1-4.

men for service in Ireland because "they had not served his turn in juries or inquests, or displeased him in any other matter, or depended upon any gentleman with whom he was offended",[1] brought matters to a head with the parliamentary election of 1571 in Haverfordwest. The mayor, John Voyle, and the sheriff, Edmund Harries, both Perrot men, supported John Garnons; the opposition put up Alban Stepney. The sheriff was alleged to have exerted threats and physical force in order to prevent Stepney's supporters from casting their votes for him, answering that the latter was ineligible for election being neither a burgess of the town nor resident within it.[2] The court found that Harries had falsified his return and, concurring in judgement with the plaintiff's bill, fined the sheriff £200.[3]

Both Voyle and Harries were related by marriage to Perrot's associates, Voyle's wife being the daughter of James Bowen of Pentre Evan and Harries being Voyle's son-in-law. But simple ties of kinship should not be over-emphasised in this connection. The leading families were linked together by an intricate pattern of marriages. Among the leading opponents of the Perrot faction may be counted William Phillips of Picton, who was married to Perrot's half-sister, Jan, the daughters of which union becoming the wives of George Owen and Alban Stepney. Owen Laugharne, father of Francis, formed an alliance with the Wyrriotts, implacable enemies of Perrot, through marrying Katherine, daughter of Henry Wyrriott; yet his grandson, Roland, married Sir John's daughter, Lettice, and his father, David, had married Sir John Wogan's sister.[4] The ties of kinship were loosening; often, at this level, they represent little more than an added bond between those whom similar quarrels had thrown together. It is the breakdown, rather than the persistence, of "an organisation of society for legal purposes by kindreds and families"[5] that contributed to the disorderly nature of these "political" relationships. Antagonism towards Perrot had many causes,[6] and transcended county boundaries. In 1581 Griffith Rice of Newton

(1) P.R.O. S.P.12/172/124.
(2) P.R.O. St. Ch. 5/S31/16; /S79/34. The case is fully described in J. E. Neale, *The Elizabethan House of Commons*, pp.255-260. *Vide supra*, p.95.
(3) B.M. Harleian, 2143, f.30.
(4) Dwnn, *op. cit.*, vol. i, pp.73, 133, 165.
(5) F. W. Maitland, "The Laws of Wales: the Kindred and the Blood-Feud", *Collected Papers* (ed. H. A. L. Fisher), vol. i, p.208.
(6) For instance, P.R.O. St. Ch. 5/P50/21: an exchange of lands between Sir John and Morgan Phillips of Picton resulted in allegations of fraudulent dealing and lawsuits before the Council in the Marches and Star Chamber.

in Carmarthenshire and Sir John were bound in £1,000 "for themselves, their friends and servants on each side ... upon consideration of a certain quarrel like to have grown between" them.[1] With Perrot's passing, sensational estimates of the extent of his oppression were put forward;[2] the jackals fell upon his property;[3] and "political" groupings became more fluid. Barlows and Laugharnes joined Thomas and James Perrot under the aegis of the Earl of Essex. New quarrels could revive old hostilities;[4] they could also bring into alliance families formerly hostile towards one another.[5] But this diversity did not change the nature of "political" sentiment nor the significance of faction in this region.[6]

It seems, accordingly, that the dominance of one outstanding personality produced some temporary degree of stability in the distribution of "political" forces, which thereafter dissolved. Feuds sometimes reached the proportions of a vendetta, with "persons of wealth and quality, as it is said",[7] involved in alleged attempts "to blind the eyes of justice", in cases of alleged murders of kinsfolk and of other offences.[8] Attitudes of this kind remained paramount throughout this period, prohibiting the growth of a broader and

---

(1) *A.P.C.* (1581-1582), p.88.
(2) B.M. Lansdowne 72, f.4: a list of forty-five gentlemen, including the Wogans, whom Perrot "hath greatly impoverished and undone" by "continual suits, quarrels and vexations at law", to the extent of over £5,000.
(3) *A.P.C.* (1591-1592), p.445. The Council, having heard that Thomas Williams of Ystradffin, sheriff of Carmarthenshire, had upon hearing of Sir John's conviction "caused your undersheriff to seize upon all his goods at Laugharne ... and do offer to carry away and oppose [*sic*] the same to sale without sufficient warrant in that behalf directed unto you", did "much marvel thereat" and instructed Williams only to compile an inventory of the estate.
(4) For example, P.R.O. St. Ch. 8/308/15: Phillips family opposed to the Wogans over the wardship of James, stepson of John Phillips of Picton; P.R.O. St. Ch. 8/290/6: Alban Stepney and George Owen in association against William Warren of Trewern; P.R.O. St. Ch. 8/75/1: Wogans against Barlows over a matter of poaching; N.L.W. Slebech 3199: Phillips, Stepney and Canon against Barlow. George Barlow recorded (*ibid.*, 3151) "how the said Alban Stepney, upon his blessing, charged his son, John Stepney, to be a perpetual enemy to me and my children".
(5) P.R.O. St. Ch. 8/188/3: Stepney and Wogan combined against Griffith Jones of Longridge.
(6) In his opposition to Sir Thomas Canon in 1605 Sir James Perrot could still look for support to Henry White, Nicholas Adams, Thomas Lloyd and Devereux Barret, described as "those least affected to Canon and therefore most to be trusted" (H.M.C. *Cal. Salis. MSS.*, vol. xvii, p.555).
(7) *A.P.C.* (1613-1614), p.109.
(8) *Ibid.* (Rice Gwyn against James Price of Gogerddan); and P.R.O. St. Ch. 8/194/15, 8/239/2, 5/V5/20: for disputes involving Lloyd of Ynyshir, Morgan Jones of Llandeilo, Sir John Vaughan of Golden Grove, with their kinsmen, servants and "alliesmen".

more profound political awareness and maturity. Major-General Laugharne's observation in 1646 concerning certain individuals, that they were "so wholly taken up with prosecution of private malice they can spare no thoughts for the public good",[1] has a more general application. Yet it was to local gentry such as these that the duty of preserving law and order in their community had perforce to be entrusted by the central government.

---

[1] H.M.C. *Portland MSS.*, vol. i, p.338. The individuals concerned were Lort and Elliott, who had denounced Poyer.

CHAPTER FOUR
Public Order

1. INSTRUMENTS.

Shortly before the Act of Union of 1536, the Reformation Parliament passed an "Act for making Justices of the Peace in Wales"[1]—a title which implies that that office was a new one in the country. George Owen states categorically that "before the said statute of Henry VIII we in Wales had no such officers".[2] That it was an innovation has, however, been questioned, on the grounds partly of Owen's own suggestion elsewhere that in Haverfordwest the mayor had earlier executed similar functions, and partly of Kidwelly's charter of 1444 which had placed the borough in the charge of "trustees" whose powers corresponded, to some degree, with those of justices of the peace.[3] If particular boroughs enjoyed exceptional privileges, Welshmen elsewhere certainly participated significantly in local administration. The lesser offices of *rhaglaw*, *rhingyll* or reeve, themselves representing some continuation of pre-conquest institutions,[4] together with that of "serjeant of the peace" with its duties of carrying official messages, arrest, distraint and collecting fines:[5] these appear necessarily to have been occupied by native Welshmen. Even the position of sheriff, "entrusted by the king with the administration of the county in all its aspects", had, in some counties at least of the principality, been held "for many years before 1536 . . . by leading local landowners".[6] In view of this, it has been held that for the Welsh gentry the Act of 1536 was, as regards local administration, "a measure which advanced and

---

(1) 27 Henry VIII, c.5.
(2) Owen, *The Description of Penbrokshire*, vol. iii, p.53.
(3) T. H. Lewis, "The Justice of the Peace in Wales", *T.H.C.S.* (1943-1944), pp. 120-123.
(4) *Vide* William Rees, *South Wales and the March*, pp.92-103.
(5) The exact relation between the native *cais* and the later *custodes* or *servientes pacis* is not wholly clear. Rees (*op. cit.*, p.103) suggests some distinction between them in their post-conquest functioning; to R. Stewart-Brown (*The Serjeants of the Peace in Medieval England and Wales*, p.45) the office "looks more like an imposition upon a conquered race than an ancient customary obligation". At all events, neither the status nor the authority of these officials corresponded with those of the English justices of the peace.
(6) W. Ogwen Williams, *Calendar of the Caernarvonshire Quarter Sessions Records*, vol. i, pp. xlvi-xlvii.

confirmed the claims which they had, to a large extent, already established";[1] and, with even greater emphasis, that in the period 1282-1485 "the holding of office was a major factor in the growth of the gentry class".[2]

But whether or not these interpretations are well-founded; and whether the Tudors created the significance of the office of justice of the peace, or simply inherited its potential:[3] the fact remains that generally that office grew in importance in the sixteenth century to a degree which made it "the backbone of county officialdom",[4] in a form quite distinct from the executive functions performed by Welshmen in the pre-Union period. Apart from all transformations at the centre of government, this growth in the influence and authority of the magistracy constitutes in itself, at least as far as Wales is concerned, a measure of political and administrative revolution. But the introduction of new public offices, with their emancipatory implications, was not instructively accompanied by a wholesale abolition of old institutions in a comprehensive process of administrative reform, integrating public with royal administration. Crown offices persisted. In 1541 Sir Thomas Jones was appointed surveyor and receiver of the castle, manor and lordship of Narberth, governor and keeper of the castle and of its forests and chases, and "leader of the manrede", with fees of £5 6s. 8d. a year, and with similar functions in Coetrath and Tenby worth £4 12s. 3d.[5] William Herbert succeeded Sir William Thomas as keeper and captain of Aberystwyth and Carmarthen castles, a situation carrying an emolument of twelve-pence a day *plus* £20 a year.[6] Rees and Edward Mansell held the offices of chamberlain and chancellor of South Wales, steward of the Pembrokeshire Crown

(1) *Ibid.*, p.lviii.
(2) Glyn Roberts, "Wales and England: Antipathy and Sympathy, 1282-1485", *Welsh History Review*, vol. i, no. 4 (1963), p.387.
(3) Dr. G. R. Elton would "warn one against the sort of rhapsodies common on this subject" by Tudor enthusiasts (*The Tudor Constitution*, p.453, note 1); Professor T. G. Barnes considers that "the Tudors inherited an institution little more powerful or useful than it had been under the last Plantagenets and with their peculiar genius transformed it into the foundation of royal power in the shires" (*op. cit.*, p.40). Acceptance of this latter view would again cast Welsh "apprenticeship" in coincidence with English in this sphere in this period.
(4) W. B. Willcox, *Gloucestershire, 1590-1640*, p.55.
(5) *L.P.H.VIII*, vol. xviii, pt. i (1543), no. 476(9). In 1554 Jones and his son Henry added to these the posts of lieutenant of Llandovery castle and "steward, receiver and 'penkysarid' with the nomination of all other officers" in Llandovery, Perfedd and Hirfryn (*C.P.R.* (Philip and Mary), vol. ii, p.62).
(6) *L.P.H.VIII*, vol. xviii, pt. i (1543), no. 623 (71).

lands, steward of five Brecknock lordships and gatekeeper of two Brecknock castles, "with the accustomed wages and fees and power to appoint all such officers under them as shall seem necessary".[1] For his zeal in discovering that the office "has been withdrawn and concealed from the Crown" and his willingness to farm it at an annual rent of £6 13s. 4d. instead of the former twenty shillings, John Gwynne was leased the "office of constable or *ragler* [*sic*]" in all the commotes of Cardiganshire for 21 years in 1562.[2] The office of *rhaglaw* provoked lawsuits over its tenure by interested parties in Cardiganshire;[3] the profits of the same office in Cardiganshire were the subject of a Star Chamber suit in 1579.[4] Four local gentlemen clashed with Sir Thomas Perrot over the stewardship and "court keepership" of Cilgerran in 1594,[5] the complainant's father having in his day been a great collector of Crown offices.[6] Stewardships with the right to hold courts, both on the estates of the Earl of Essex and in the form of Crown offices claimed by his followers and dependants, provoked several disputes at law.[7]

There arises, accordingly, the question of how far the nature of local public administration was distinguished from royal, in the minds of local gentry.[8] The oath taken by the sheriff,[9] for instance, would not have prevented some confusion. It was to the Crown that he pledged allegiance, and the property of the Crown clearly fell within his charge. He swore to "do the Queen's profit in all things that belongeth to you to do by way of your office . . . You shall truly keep the Queen's right and all that belongeth to the Crown . . . Whensoever you shall have knowledge that the Queen's right or the rights of her Crown be concealed or withdrawn, be it in land, rent, franchises or suits or any other thing, you shall do your true power to make them to be restored to the Queen again".[10] Before

---

(1) *C.P.R.* (Philip and Mary), vol. ii, p.61.
(2) *Ibid.* (Elizabeth), vol. ii, p.266.
(3) For example, P.R.O. E112/59/9; /59/11.
(4) P.R.O. St. Ch. 5/J15/13.
(5) P.R.O. E112/62/15. The four were John Garnons, Robert Vaughan, James Morris and John Lloyd, gentlemen.
(6) For example, *C.P.R.* (Philip and Mary), vol. iii, p.485; *ibid.* (Elizabeth), vol. i, p.45.
(7) P.R.O. E112/145/40; /145/43; 146/65.
(8) For different reasons, Mr. Ogwen Williams has argued that "it could scarcely have been realised at the time that a political and administrative revolution took place in Wales between 1536 and 1542" (W. Ogwen Williams, *op. cit.*, p.lviii).
(9) Since Union, of course, appointed annually, whereas previously, as George Owen noted for Pembrokeshire, "by patent for term of life" (*op. cit.*, vol. i, p.156).
(10) P.R.O. E199/59/2.

taking his oath, the sheriff was required to find sureties in £300 for
his good behaviour in office;[1] after being sworn, he was empowered
to appoint bailiffs who in their oaths undertook always to be at his
commandment.[2] Neither circumstance was calculated to remind
him of his diminished importance in local administration. Further,
for the public, like the royal, official there was often an immediate
cash return. A justice of the peace was allowed four shillings a day
for his attendance at quarter-sessions.[3] In 1631 the muster-master
in Pembrokeshire could received up to £30.[4] The profits of the
Admiralty in the three shires amounted in 1632 to £85 18s. 6d., of
which one half went to the Crown, one quarter to the vice-admiral
and one quarter to his under-officers.[5] In 1602 the sheriff of Cardiganshire was receiving a fee of £5.[6] Finally, to wield any form of
authority was to acquire some degree of social eminence and a
means to public immunity and private gain.

These superficial incentives stimulated some local eagerness to
serve. In 1584 Edward Mansell approached Serjeant Puckering on
behalf of Henry Morgan, who desired to be "put in the commission
of the peace in Carmarthenshire", and of his son-in-law, Walter
Rice, "to affurther him as far further as our skills shall serve to direct
him".[7] George Devereux combined in the same letter an appeal to
Puckering for release from a summons for debt with a request that
"a couple of my kind" be made justices of the peace in Cardiganshire;[8] his nephew Essex's patronage, compensating in assiduity
for its lack of altruism,[9] found no lack of clients. Sir John Wogan
regarded Cecil's intention to appoint him *custos rotulorum* of Pembrokeshire in 1601 as "a favour which I hold in great estimation".[10]
The attractions of the magistracy much exceeded those of lieuten-

(1) George Devereux found his in Staffordshire in 1581, and Thomas Revell his in
     Ludlow in 1583 (P.R.O. E199/59/2, 3). That Revell found his in Ludlow suggests
     that this condition could without too much difficulty be circumvented.
(2) An example of a bailiff's oath containing such an avowal is to be seen in N.L.W.
     Wales 19/25/7.
(3) Lewis, *op. cit.*, p.126.
(4) *C.S.P. Dom.* (1629-1631), vol. clxxxiii, no. 21.
(5) *Ibid.* (1631-1633), vol. ccxx, no. 57.
(6) John Doderidge, *The History of the Ancient and Modern Estate of the Principality
     of Wales*, p.72.
(7) B.M. Harleian 6993, f.64.
(8) *Ibid.*, f.109. The two concerned were David Lloyd ap Rhydderch and David
     Lloyd of Abermâd. Devereux later wrote again on behalf of John Stedman, that
     he should be restored to the commission of the peace following his year as sheriff
     (*ibid.* 286, f.246).
(9) *Vide supra*, pp.114-116.
(10) H.M.C. *Cal. Salis. MSS.*, vol. xi, p.164.

nancy. "Since I have been a deputy-lieutenant", complained Wogan, in the same letter to Cecil, "I have spent above £1,000, which is great for a man of so small a living". The shrievalty, too, would appear to have declined in popularity. Oliver Lloyd wrote to Sir Thomas Hoby to seek his recommendation for that office in Cardiganshire in 1566.[1] But in 1635 Lord Carbery wrote from Golden Grove for the "relief of his cousin Rowland Gwynn from being sheriff of Carmarthenshire".[2] But other positions remained inviting. Although it was "the poorest place in England [sic], not worth ten shillings besides the poor fee of £10 a year", Thomas Middleton informed Burghley of his desire that "my brother, who lives near the place, may be appointed to the controllership of customs at Milford."[3] When about thirty horses were to be sent in 1599 to Essex in Ireland from the three shires, James Perrot, eager, it seems, to re-establish the name of Perrot in the public service, wrote to the Earl, "I crave I may have the charge" of them.[4] If the great opportunities of Court preferment, such as the appointing, after much supplication, of Sir John Vaughan as Comptroller of the Prince's Household,[5] were few, there were available plenty of local positions, such as that of muster-master in Carmarthenshire,[6] or town-clerk of Kidwelly;[7] and men were prepared to compete for them.

However, public offices were, of course, vastly different from those under the Crown which they may, to the unsophisticated, have resembled. Moreover, for all the efforts of such as Lambarde,[8] the

---

(1) *C.S.P.Dom.* (1547-1580), vol. xxxix, no. 87.
(2) H.M.C. *Eleventh Report*, Appendix, Part vii (Bridgewater Trust MSS.), p.148. *Cf.* Miss J. S. Wilson, "Sheriffs' Rolls of the Sixteenth and Seventeenth Centuries", *E.H.R.*, vol. xlvii (1932), p.39: "The office was generally regarded as a great burden and all possible means were used to escape it".
(3) P.R.O. S.P.12/261/18.
(4) H.M.C. *Cal. Salis. MSS.*, vol. ix, p.54.
(5) For example, Vaughan to Somerset, October 1614 (*C.S.P.Dom.* (1611-1618), vol. lxxviii, no. 42). His pride in this position emerges in his ostentatious signing of himself as its holder even in matters of a purely local nature (for example, N.L.W. Derwydd 688).
(6) If he were to be deprived of this office after fourteen years' service James Reade "should be greatly disappointed and disabled in his poor means of living" (*A.P.C.* (1600-1601), p.429).
(7) The absence of Richard Herbert from the town on legal business gave William Davis the chance of purchasing the office, previously Vaughan's, from the local townsmen for £10 (*C.S.P.Dom.* (1629-1631), vol. cxlix, no. 80; vol. cli, no. 4).
(8) Lambarde, seeking to outline the several functions of the justice of the peace according to statute, defined that officer's purpose as being "to suppress injurious force and violence moved against the person, his goods or possessions . . . not every contention, suit and disagreement of minds" (*Eirenarcha*, pp.7-9).

obligations of public office were frequently ill-defined, with the duties of different officials overlapping to a disconcerting degree. Certain features were clear enough. It was obviously the province of justices of the peace, for instance, to investigate such matters as the allegations of Alice Jordan in Carmarthenshire that people other than she were responsible for her husband's poisoning—a problem upon which the guidance of the Privy Council was both solicited and forthcoming.[1] Similarly, when William Reece, a carpenter, stole wheat from Elizabeth Lloyd of Pentre Evan, the case fell within the competence of the Pembrokeshire justices of the peace.[2] There were other, social as distinct from judicial, matters which were theirs to consider. In 1628 an increased influx of Irish immigrants constituted a subject of scandal and concern in Pembrokeshire, and the local justices earned themselves the applause and support of the Privy Council by providing the unwanted arrivals with shipping and packing them off home.[3] So it was with ensuring that trade, particularly that of wool, was properly conducted,[4] and with measures for the relief of the poor.[5] In 1631 Alban Owen, George Owen and Thomas Warren, all justices of the peace, gave instructions to the petty constables of Cemais for the well-ordering and training of youths in trades, the correcting of masters who dealt badly with their apprentices, and the apprehending and reforming of rogues and vagabonds, themselves supervising the discharge of these duties.[6]

But there were other matters with which justices of the peace, almost unreasonably,[7] found themselves expected to be concerned.

---

(1) *Trans. Carms. Antiq. Soc.*, vol. xi, p.48.
(2) N.L.W. Bronwydd 338.
(3) *C.S.P.Dom.* (1628-1629), vol. cxix, no. 18; vol. cxl, no. 56; vol. cxliv, no. 62; *A.P.C.* (1628-1629), p.419. It was stated that "the owners of barks make much gain by transporting them for three shillings apiece for young and old".
(4) *C.S.P.Dom.* (1629-1631), vol. clxiv, no. 19 (*cf. supra*, p.90).
(5) P.R.O. S.P.16/286/63.
(6) N.L.W. Bronwydd 339.
(7) From the mid-fourteenth century "the issue of separate commissions of array . . . [and] the loss of the justices' military duties left the way open for their development as administrators of economic legislation and as criminal law judges" (B. H. Putnam, *Proceedings before the Justices of the Peace in the Fourteenth and Fifteenth Centuries*, p.xxviii). In the sixteenth century justices were increasingly required to inquire into and punish offences against statutes relating to the keeping of arms and the taking of musters (for example, 4 & 5 Philip and Mary, c. 2, 3); and to assist lords lieutenant and their deputies. But it was "the large discretionary power of the Privy Council in matters pertaining to military affairs [that] led in practice to the extensive use of the justices in all matters pertaining to national defence" (C. A. Beard, *The Office of Justice of the Peace*, p.112).

When in 1570 the Council in the Marches found the returns of local commissioners "for the furniture of armour and weapons and the preparation of horses and geldings to be ready for the service of her Majesty" to be highly unsatisfactory, it was the justices of the peace who were required to "pay to the persons subscribed who appeared before this Council £3 6s. 8d. each towards their charges", and "at their next sitting to make serious inquiry and advertise the Council of the ability of every person of lands of £20 yearly upwards".[1] They, again, were held responsible for the maintenance of troops passing to and from Ireland;[2] dealing with troops driven by foul weather into Milford;[3] paying coat and conduct money to men sent for service in Ireland.[4] Indeed, affairs concerning the defence of the realm were committed not only to deputy-lieutenants but to officials of all descriptions. From 1546, when Fulk Pigott, searcher of Milford, himself pressed the Privy Council for some ordnance to defend the haven,[5] the letters of the central authority were sent to justices of the peace, local mayors, and minor officials and private individuals, whether resident or not within the shires to which their attention was directed, and sheriffs alike in this connection.

For the position of the sheriff was not unlike that of the justice of the peace. Whereas in his oath he promised specifically to concern himself with the capturing of criminals, the maintaining of "true religion", the returning of "reasonable and due issues" to the Crown, and similar matters, he was also indiscriminately bound to "assist or defend all jurisdictions, privileges, and pre-eminences and authorities granted or belonging to the Queen's Highness, her heirs and successors, or united and annexed to the imperial crown of this realm".[6] Thus to matters which were obviously his responsibility,

(1) R. Flenley, The Register of the Council in the Marches of Wales, 1569-1591, pp.72-73.
(2) For example, A.P.C. (1575-1577), p.154. When Sir William Drury passed through Pembrokeshire with 350 men the justices were instructed to provide him with 220 quarters of corn "to be levied there in such places as are most convenient and nearest to the sea-coast", to see the same carried cheaply to the appropriate harbours and the officers there instructed to let it pass, "foreseeing nevertheless that by the providing of this quantity there be no great scarcities bred nor the prices raised to the injury of the poor there", no more than the specified quantity of corn to be let through—altogether a formidable task.
(3) Ibid. (1599-1600), p.730. The justices were instructed to see that these men were sent home again and their coats taken from them, this injunction being so strict as to imply common abuse in this.
(4) Ibid. (1598-1599), p.303.
(5) Ibid. (1542-1547), p.385.
(6) P.R.O. E199/59/2; as sworn by John Price of Gogerddan, 1581.

such as the custody of criminals after they had been captured,[1] supervising the securing of jurymen,[2] running elections, or even reporting the general temper of his locality in times of national stress,[3] were added the tasks, in association with one or two justices, of seeing that "the laws for the true and sufficient tanning of leather"[4] were properly observed, that markets were sufficiently supplied with grain in time of dearth,[5] investigating the misappropriating of butter and other victuals intended for troops in Ireland,[6] and, inevitably, supervising the armour in their counties.[7] For if quantity of correspondence and other documents is any guide, the central authority's main concern was with this last. It was vital that in this distant and vulnerable region armed men should be readily available to deal with the ever-present threat of invasion. All the way down the official scale the same concern was called for. Local mayors were obliged, over and above the controlling of the affairs of their boroughs in normal times and in circumstances of domestic emergency such as dearth of corn,[8] to have ships and victuals ready for the transporting of men and horses for Ireland,[9] to see to the board and lodging of such troops,[10] to prosecute deserters with their aiders and abettors,[11] and even to extend their jurisdiction out to sea to stay suspected ships.[12]

To this uncertainty as to the exact functions of each official may be added another factor: the cornering of offices in a relatively small

---

(1) *A.P.C.* (1575-1580), p.227: an instruction to the sheriff of Pembrokeshire to deliver up two Frenchmen held by him on charges of piracy, who "as their Lordships are informed are very well acquainted with the coast of Ireland". Conditions of custody were sometimes hazardous for the prisoner: witness the indictment in 1597 of Roger Price, keeper of Cardigan gaol, before the Great Sessions for "evasion and negligence" when five prisoners died whilst in his charge, as he said "from a visitation of God" (P.R.O. Wales 7/7).
(2) N.L.W. Haverfordwest Corporation Records, 207: the sheriff of Haverfordwest instructed to summon "forty-eight good and lawful men" to the town hall for this purpose.
(3) H.M.C. *Cal. Salis. MSS.*, vol. xvii, p.485: Alban Stepney, following the Gunpowder Plot, confidently reports Pembrokeshire to be "filled with most faithful subjects".
(4) Flenley, *op. cit.*, pp. 123-126.
(5) *C.S.P.Dom.* (1581-1590), vol. cxci, no. 11.
(6) Flenley, *op. cit.*, pp.108-109.
(7) *Ibid.*, p.60.
(8) N.L.W. Haverfordwest Corporation Records, 234.
(9) *C.S.P.Dom.* (1598-1601), vol. cclxx, no. 25.
(10) *A.P.C.* (1599-1600), p.758.
(11) *Ibid.* (1600-1601), p. 182: "We do understand that divers persons do buy of these soldiers their armour and other furniture, and some others do help to hide the soldiers, whereby they do escape and run away".
(12) *Ibid.* (1542-1547), p.121.

number of hands. In 1573-1574 there were twenty-four justices of
the peace listed for Pembrokeshire.[1] In 1575, when each sheriff was
asked to declare the distribution of justices in the hundreds of each
county, it was reported that only nine were resident in Pembrokeshire,[2] a postscript being added that as "it were convenient in my
opinion that as there are seven hundreds in the shire there should be
fourteen justices of the peace resident . . . I have . . . put down the
names of six of the aptest gentlemen of this shire . . . The fathers of
most of them have been justices and they are of the best credit in the
county". It was stated that "there dwell not continually any justices
of the peace in the hundreds of Dewsland or Cemais". Two lived in
Carmarthenshire, another in Radnorshire and a fourth in county
Brecknock. Carmarthenshire, which boasted twenty-nine justices in
the *liber pacis*, had seventeen resident; Cardiganshire, eight as opposed
to twenty-three. A comment on sheriffs in Wales in 1572 read: "The
use hath been to make strangers, that hath neither lands nor goods
in the country, sheriffs in Wales, and they lie in ale-houses and live
of the spoil of the country, or else take £100 of a polling undersheriff for the office and never come there".[3] Of those who were
resident, the 1566 sheriff of Carmarthenshire, Thomas Vaughan of
Penbre Court, was the son of the 1557 sheriff, married the daughter
of the 1543 sheriff, and served again in 1570; the sheriff of 1577 and
1592, Thomas ap Rhys Williams of Ystradffin, was the son of the
1549 sheriff who had also served in 1562, and brother-in-law of the
1575 sheriff, his widow marrying Sir George Devereux who was
sheriff of Cardiganshire in 1583 and 1610, of Carmarthenshire in
1581, of Pembrokeshire in 1580, and of county Brecknock in
1582.[4] In Pembrokeshire, Griffith White of Henllan served as
sheriff in 1561, 1570 and 1581, was an uncle of the sheriff of 1588,
and fathered that of 1592; whilst John Wogan of Boulston was
himself sheriff in 1574, 1584 and 1598.[5]

The effects of such a concentration, in view of the ill-definition
and demanding nature of the responsibilities of these offices, might

(1) B. M. Egerton, 2345, f.43.
(2) B.M. Stowe, 570, f.79. The Pembrokeshire return was made by Perrot, to whom
the Council's letters were addressed, although the sheriff in that year was John
Barlow of Slebech. The unsatisfactory nature of a procedure whereby a local
potentate could nominate so many men for the magistracy, is self-evident.
(3) P.R.O. S.P. 12/235/18.
(4) *Trans. Carms. Antiq. Soc.*, vol. iii, pp.33-34; corrected from James Allen, *Notes on
the Sheriffs of Pembrokeshire, passim;* P.R.O. *Lists of Sheriffs.*
(5) Allen, *op. cit.*, pp.10, 13, 14, 16, 21.

have been mitigated if the men concerned had been well-prepared and adequate. This was not so. Quite apart from the fact that men were appointed in Wales who in their material means would have been in England considered far from "sufficient", in education and training they were equally unqualified. At least 299[1] separate individuals served, from amongst the local gentry, as sheriffs or justices of the peace in the three shires between 1540 and 1640. Of these, sixty-five had been educated at a University, and forty at one of the Inns of Court.[2] Twenty-four had been educated at both a university and one of the Inns; eighty-one, or approximately 27 per cent, had attended one or the other. Nor does criticism end there. There are some grounds for believing that men who had received some training were sometimes, at least, set aside in favour of their less instructed neighbours. David Lloyd Griffith of Ystradcorrwg, who was twice sheriff of Carmarthenshire, a justice of the peace and a member of the quorum, appears to have attended neither University nor Inn of Court; Nicholas Adams, scholar of Jesus College and barrister-at-law of the Middle Temple, was never sheriff and, though a justice of the peace for Pembrokeshire, is not recorded as having been a member of the quorum.[3] George, Morgan and Roger Walter of Haverfordwest all matriculated from the Queen's College, Oxford, two in 1596 and the third in 1598; their father had attended the Middle Temple. Yet none of these appears to have held major office in the shire's local administration. Some awareness of the need to be educated appears to have developed.[4] The later members of

(1) Before 1558 and after 1603 the names of justices of the peace were entered on the dorse of the Patent Rolls (P.R.O. C66). During Elizabeth's reign they were recorded separately in *Libri Pacis*, many of which are missing; moreover, the Patent Rolls lists for the reigns of Edward VI and Philip and Mary do not include the Welsh shires. This figure, though as complete as may be, is therefore tentative. Moreover, exact identification of individuals registered at the Universities or the Inns of Court is often difficult, owing to problems of duplication of nomenclature and non-statement of place of origin, as well as occasionally doubtful attribution in the published Registers (for sources, *vide infra*, p.194).

(2) *Cf.* Yorkshire from 1625 to 1640, where of 161 gentlemen in higher county offices (sheriffs, deputy-lieutenants, justices of the peace) 60 had been educated at both University and one of the Inns of Court, 30 at University only and 32 at an Inn of Court only (J. T. Cliffe, *op. cit.*, p.328). It has been estimated that in the early seventeenth century "in general over half of the prominent land-holders who served as lords-lieutenant or their deputies had received some University training", and that "the same conditions prevailed in the education of the justices of the peace" (M. H. Curtis, *Oxford and Cambridge in Transition, 1558-1642*, p.59, citing Professor J. H. Hexter). But *cf. infra*, pp.195-196.

(3) It must, again, be pointed out that identification of members of the quorum depends upon the reliability of clerks, often demonstrably suspect in this.

(4) For expansion of this, *vide infra*, pp.194 *et seq.*

the family of Gwyn of Glanbrân went to the Middle Temple.
John Mortimer, sheriff of Cardiganshire in 1576, sent his son to
Oxford, as did Rice Phillips of Rushmoor, a Carmarthenshire
justice of the peace. But it may be significant that it was his second
son whom Griffith Lloyd of the Forest sent to Gray's Inn, which
suggests that education may have been considered necessary chiefly
for those who would have to make their own way in the world, and
perhaps not so much for those who would inherit leading positions.
At all events, the growth in the realisation of its value did not come
early enough to have much practical effect in the administrative
sphere during this period.

There was some tendency, particularly at first, to appoint men of
proven ability in those areas where they might have been expected
to exercise the influence of example. Rowland Meyrick, formerly of
St. David's and by this time Bishop of Bangor, and Walter, Viscount
Hereford, later Earl of Essex, were perhaps expected to act in some
supervisory capacity in Pembrokeshire in 1564.[1] Again, prominent
local men were appointed, possibly as a hard core, to be justices of
the peace in all three shires: men like Sir James Williams of Pant-
howell, who also served as sheriff in all three counties in his turn,
Sir John Perrot, Sir Thomas Jones of Abermarlais and—a rare
instance where ability outweighed lack of means—Thomas Phaer.
Lewis Gwynne, chancellor of St. David's, earned comparable administrative distinction. But in 1566 Sir Henry Jones was dropped
from the list of Pembrokeshire justices of the peace, which suggests
that this was not a uniform practice; although other considerations
might merit dismissal. After the Essex revolt Sir George Devereux
lost his place on the commission of the peace; yet by 1610 this
sycophant had been reinstated.[2] Administrative talent was certainly lacking: on the Council in the Marches, it has been observed
that "it was only in the last two years of Elizabeth's reign that a
substantial number of Welshmen entered the Council".[3] Of the
one hundred members of the Council listed by Dr. Penry Williams,
only five were from south-west Wales.[4]

(1) P.R.O. C66/998/156.   (2) P.R.O. C66/1822.
(3) Penry Williams, *The Council in the Marches of Wales under Elizabeth*, p.145.
(4) *Ibid.*, pp.342-361. They were John and Richard Price of Gogerddan, Sir John
    Perrot and Sir Thomas Jones of Abermarlais. The fifth, Sir John Vaughan,
    originally of Whitland in Carmarthenshire, became a London lawyer, Master
    of Chancery and Requests, and served as sheriff. The other Welsh counties
    were represented by another twelve members. Under James I "the proportion
    of Welsh members was steadily growing at the expense of the Border members"
    (A. H. Dodd, "Wales's Parliamentary Apprenticeship", *op. cit.*, p.56).

With relatively few men, and these for the most part in-sufficiently prepared, called to a service that was far from clearly defined, and with the central authority apparently concerned rather with preserving intact the frontiers of the realm than with what went on within those frontiers, the prospect for law and order was not bright. To supplement local machinery in the judicial sphere there were the courts of Great Sessions. There were occasions when the guidance of the Justices of Assize was sought by diffident local officials. In 1592 Edward Dounlee wrote direct to Serjeant Puckering to obtain bail for Jane Lloyd and Anne Delahay, both indicted for treason but now, apparently, submissive and repentant, because "no justice of the peace in the county will adventure [this] without especial warrant from you".[1] But there are also indications of hostility towards, and resentment of, such outside interference. In response to Richard Atkins's[2] warning that he should guard a prisoner with the utmost care, George Devereux wrote to Puckering in 1584, "Rather than Mr. Atkins should have his pleasure therein I had rather spend £40. If you will not be angry I will a little cross him; he is his own hostler already, and I mean he shall be his own caterer and cook if you command me not the contrary".[3] Walter Vaughan of Golden Grove, having strenuously denied proved charges of accepting bribes, returning a partial jury and staying the execution of a convicted murderer, revealed that his main objection to the unfavourable verdict was "that I shall submit to all these points in open Sessions at Carmarthen, to the end Mr. Atkins may glory over me and I be utterly discredited".[4]

The most violent antipathy towards the Assize Justices was expressed by George Barlow in 1619, who, having been fined £155 for neglecting his duties as sheriff,[5] affirmed that he "did behave himself in the exercise of the same office more to his Majesty's benefit than any of his Majesty's sheriffs of the same county before him, and

(1) B.M. Harleian 6998, f.1. Cf. infra, p.186.
(2) A Justice of Assize on the south-west Wales circuit, attitudes towards whom were also conditioned by faction-allegiance (vide Penry Williams, op. cit., pp.282-283).
(3) B.M. Harleian 6993, f.63. Devereux found the duties of sheriff rather inconvenient. He urged that the next Sessions be held at Cardigan, "for that my prison is so far off if it be appointed in any place else I shall hardly have carriage for the same, and also the time of the year will as like be so hot that no victuals will be kept sweet".
(4) Ibid., 7002, f.6; also f.3, and ibid., 6994, ff.3, 11, 12, 13, 15, 48, 62. Vide supra, p.115. Vaughan's fine for these offences was, at least as first appointed, extremely heavy: £500 and half a year's imprisonment (ibid., 2143, f.34b.)
(5) C.S.P.Dom. (1611-1618), vol. ciii, no. 97.

yet to the contentment of the whole county, preferring the public service before his private suits of great importance". He went on to point out that "whereas the Justices of Assize . . . have their allowance for their diet and entertainment of his Majesty, yet it is an ordinary thing with them to exact the same also of the sheriff for the time being, every of the Sessions continuing by the space of a week at the least, whereby some sheriffs . . . have been utterly undone, and others greatly weakened in their estates and impoverished". He attributed his own misfortunes to his resolution in "not giving your said Justices their diets";[1] other, more accommodating, sheriffs had had their "failures . . . to carry out their official duties" ignored, although these included "the escapes of notorious felons and other foul faults". Mr. Daston, one of the Justices, had married one of his daughters into one of the principal families of the district, and members of that family were, in consequence, unjustly favoured in any suits in which they might happen to be engaged. The fines against Barlow were, he claimed, the direct result of the personal prejudice of the Justices against him, which had expressed itself further in the favouring of his opponents in lawsuits, and which, unless redress were forthcoming, was likely to "make all men of worth withdraw their desire to do his Majesty's service".[2]

These examples themselves prove no more than individual prejudice. But the question remains of how effective the courts of Great Sessions were in administering English law in the regions of Wales. No student of local government in this period can fail to observe the frequent gulf between the neatness of governmental intention as embodied in statutes and the confusion often resulting from their application at the local level. The convenience, from the point of view of the central government, with which the twelve shires of Wales were grouped into four circuits was not matched, from the point of view of prospective litigants, by the seasons in which the

---

(1) Which involved a significant outlay, to judge from the acceptance by the two Justices riding the western circuit in June 1600 "of Mr. Sheriff, a piece of roasting beef, a goose, a pig, a leg of mutton, 2 capons, 2 joints of veal, a partridge, 2 quails, a duck, a dish of peas, artichokes, ½ a lamb, 2 rabbits, 2 chickens, and 6 small birds, a tart, a custard, and a heronshaw, for Wednesday's dinner" (W. D. Cooper (ed.), "The Expenses of the Judges of Assize", *Camden Miscellany*, vol. iv (1859), p.40). The cost of entertaining the south-west Wales circuit Justices certainly seems to have increased phenomenally, from £3 18s. 2d. for the diet of the one Justice and his horses in Haverfordwest in 1568, to nearly £40 for the two Sessions of 1615 for two Justices (B. G. Charles, "Haverfordwest Accounts, 1563-1620", *N.L.W. Journal*, vol. ix., pt. ii (1955), pp.168-169).

(2) N.L.W. Slebech 3221.

Great Sessions were actually held and the duration of their sittings. George Owen, despite his anxiety to show that these were, second only to Star Chamber, the most efficient lawcourts in the kingdom, noted this and several other weaknesses;[1] and his observations concerning Welsh lawcourts in general contain some ambiguous implications. By his flattering references to them, he appeared eager to attract litigation to the Great Sessions and to the Council in the Marches, but for all his criticisms of lesser courts[2] he insisted that the latter performed a useful function in hearing certain kinds of "small actions" with which, because of the excessive delays and fees that would there be involved, the Great Sessions should not be troubled. Partly because "most of the poorer sort of people . . . seldom useth any money", and partly because of the seasonal fluctuation in the availability of money at this social level, "one man will be indebted £10 to ten several men or more, and to one man, specially to the mercer, you shall find 300 debtors";[3] such pleas should be brought before the "base courts". But the extant Plea Rolls of the Great Sessions contain a great many suits of this very nature. In 1561 John Vaughan of Carmarthen brought seven such actions against yeomen.[4] In Cardiganshire in 1606, apart from a handful of suits concerning trespass upon the case, assault or perjury, the Great Sessions were almost entirely occupied with pleas of debt in some shape or form.[5] The nature of the plea might vary from arrears of rent to Alban Stepney's action against two yeomen in 1585 for their failure to deliver as contracted barrels of coal to the value of sixty shillings;[6] the litigants might range from leading merchants such as Humphrey Toy or John Voyle[7] to minor husbandmen. Basically, the character of a great many of the actions

---

(1) Chiefly, certain defects in procedure, and a tendency to undervalue stolen goods owing to the existence of the death penalty for "the theft of anything above the value of twelve pence". For Owen's discussion of the Great Sessions, vide the Description of Penbrokshire, vol. iii, pp.43 et seq.
(2) Ibid., esp. pp.70-91.
(3) Ibid., pp.83-84.
(4) N.L.W. Wales 19/21/17-22. A detailed analysis of the records of the Great Sessions, now conveniently housed at N.L.W., is needed. The following conclusions, relating to civil actions between parties, are based on an examination of a sample of the extant Plea Rolls. Pleas of the Crown were enrolled in the Calendar Rolls, of which five for south-west Wales are extant (Wales 7/6, 7, 8, 9, 10): two for Cardiganshire, three for Pembrokeshire.
(5) N.L.W. Wales 18/60. Actions for debt could, of course, arise from a variety of causes, such as failure to perform the condition of a bond.
(6) N.L.W. Wales 25/48/9.
(7) N.L.W. Wales 18/3; /18/16.

fought here remains of the type described by Owen. Secondly, because "most of the country is champion"[1] there arose "many actions of trespass" through the straying of animals. These, again, were frequently brought before the Great Sessions.[2]

There are, accordingly, some grounds for believing that the Great Sessions were used excessively for petty matters; and that Owen was indirectly concerned to try to release some of their limited time for more significant business. Others of his criticisms of the hundred courts have some bearing elsewhere. At the hundred courts "shall you see divers petty-gentlemen that can do much among the meanest sort of people, commonly maintain matters openly in court and embrace the jurors to pass with their friend or client".[3] Yet at the Great Sessions in Pembrokeshire in 1584 Maurice Canon appears to have played the part of attorney in thirty-nine actions in addition to his own suit;[4] others acted likewise. In the details of his discussion Owen is often not the most reliable of guides. Occasionally he is misleading, as in his insistence that "King Henry VIII utterly abolished the Welsh Laws";[5] occasionally he contradicts himself, as in following the statement that "the hundred courts are always held before the deputy-sheriff" with concern for "the ease of the sheriff and his deputy from posting every day in the week to one hundred or other to keep those obscure, disordered courts".[6] But the implications of his argument seem in tune with the evidence: that the Great Sessions, burdened with petty suits, with ridiculous actions,[7] with insufficient time at their disposal, were not fulfilling their intended function; and that the base courts, dominated by local gentry often unversed in English law, and exercising a frequently

---

(1) Owen, *op. cit.*, p.85.
(2) For examples, *vide supra*, p.73.
(3) Owen, *op. cit.*, p.72.
(4) N.L.W. Wales 25/48. His own suit was against John Scourfield of New Moat for recovery of a debt of ten guineas.
(5) Owen, *op. cit.*, p.91. By 27 Henry VIII, c.26, the Lord Chancellor was to appoint commissioners to inquire into "all and singular laws, usages and customs used within the said dominion and country of Wales" and report to the Privy Council which should, as it might see fit, recommend any of these to "stand and be of full strength, virtue and effect and shall be forever inviolably observed, had, used, and executed in the same shires as if this Act had never been had or made". The outcome of this clause is not known.
(6) Owen, *op. cit.*, pp.71, 73-74.
(7) For instance, actions for slander, as when Miles ab Ievan and his wife sued a Llanrhian spinster for saying, "Jenett Miles is a thief for she has stolen my kerchief"; or Thomas Mansell's objection to Morris Bowen of Llechdwnni's remark that such a liar as he should have his "ears cropped and to preach in the pillory" (N.L.W. Wales 25/8/5; 19/56/27).

self-appointed right to "hold cognizance of plea"[1] between parties,
were exceeding theirs. The well-fed Justices of Assize do not appear
to have provided an adequate counterbalance, if any is to be found,
to the power of those gentry who, partly from force of circumstances and partly from their own choice, were called to govern
their localities.[2]

2. ADMINISTRATION.

Detailed conclusions as to the efficiency of the day-to-day working
of local government cannot be drawn from the evidence at present
available for this region. Too often one is left only with the testimonies of interested parties, given in the course of lawsuits, as to
abuses or inadequacies on the part of local officials. Tasks quietly
and properly performed may well have left no trace. One can do
no more than note this probability, and thereafter consider the
implications of the information that does remain.

If local officials were conscientious, their work cannot have been
easy. Occasionally a sheriff might fall victim to a prisoner's guile or
his own gullibility, as when Griffith Lloyd, sheriff of Carmarthenshire, accepted the promise of David Phillips, outlawed for debt,
that he would appear at the proper time to answer his charge, and,
when Phillips, failing to do so, instead "lurked in secret places", had
to pay the debt himself.[3] William Vaughan, accused of having
attempted, when sheriff, to manipulate the course of justice, protested that he had merely tried to recover a debt of £40 due to him
for wheat[4]—a questionable explanation, perhaps, but a possible one.
In 1587 the deputy-lieutenants at Haverfordwest, viewing the
musters there, suffered such abuse at the hands of Hugh Gwynne
that they were forced to "give over their intended service at that
time for fear of further dangers which by the said Gwynne's disorders were likely to ensue"; for Gwynne considered himself to
have been grievously wronged by these officials in their other
capacity as justices of the peace, and to have reason for saying, "As
for you, I care not for you, neither do I crave your goodwills; you

(1) Owen, *op. cit.*, p.86.
(2) W. Ll. Williams ("The King's Court of Great Sessions in Wales", *Y Cymmrodor*,
    vol. xxvi (1916), p.38) quotes a 1641 comment on the Great Sessions: "How little
    the presence of two Justices that be practitioners of law at Westminster will avail,
    to whom the Gentry can make their own access and application".
(3) *A.P.C.* (1580-1581), p.278.
(4) P.R.O. E112/146/113.

have done the worst you can against me already, and that which you have done you have done without authority".[1]

Even if events such as these did take place in accordance with the versions here recounted, it could be said that individual officials endowed with greater intelligence and foresight—and, in the case of the deputy-lieutenants, greater valour—might have acquitted themselves more creditably. But Gwynne's alleged refusal to recognise his adversaries' authority is interesting, for it does not stand alone. James Prydderch of Hawksbrook, a justice of the peace, claimed that he was the victim of assaults by several gentlemen because they held him personally responsible for fines and amercements imposed upon them at a court baron, and also in order to rescue men pressed for service in Ireland and to defeat other attempted arrests, succeeding so well that no officer in the county dared take punitive measures against them.[2] Thomas Phaer, when searcher of Milford, reported that he had seized thirty-two cotton frises from two merchants at Carmarthen, and heard them say, "If one or two of these searchers were hanged there would never come more any searcher to the country"; and that the mayor and other leading townsmen assisted the recalcitrant merchants in their resistance to him.[3] John Elyot of Earwear alleged similar circumstances met by him in Tenby.[4] Accounts such as these may not be strictly true; they may simply represent attempts by officials to conceal their own inadequacies or their abuse of their offices. But if nothing else, they do suggest that poor relations often existed between office-holders and those with whom they had to deal. There is little point in multiplying such instances, which involved the deputies and juries[5] necessary to the work of sheriffs and magistrates, deputy-lieutenants apparently anxious to replenish local stocks of munitions and armour,[6] and

---

(1) N.L.W. Haverfordwest Corporation Records, 207a, 201, 201a, 202a, 203.
(2) P.R.O. St. Ch. 5/P57/7; St. Ch. 8/21/10.
(3) P.R.O. E159/336/167.
(4) P.R.O. E159/331/31b.
(5) For example, P.R.O. St. Ch. 5/L27/37 (deputy-bailiffs); St. Ch. 5/B33/17 (deputy-lieutenants' deputy); St. Ch. 5/J6/7 (constable); St. Ch. 5/P44/36 (petty-constable acting for commissioners for musters); St. Ch. 5/L15/32 (deputy-sheriff); E112/62/12 (jury). Welsh juries were frequently indicted in Star Chamber for returning false verdicts, and often committed (for example, B.M. Harleian 2143, ff.9b, 10, 14).
(6) P.R.O. St. Ch. 5/A30/18: Sir Thomas Jones, Carmarthenshire deputy-lieutenant, alleged by local residents to have levied extortionate sums for unnecessary armour; cf., at a later date, Sir James Perrot's views on the state of Welsh munitions (vide supra, p.106).

customs men applying royal proclamations against the "transportation of sheeps' wools out of his majesty's kingdom" which more
than once provoked indignant protests from traders.[1]

Two cases involving Thomas Lloyd of Llanstephan illustrate the
difficulties encountered by local officials. The substance of the first
was that Lloyd, as sheriff, was required to execute a process against
Sir John Perrot; that, being apprehensive of the likely peril attendant
upon this, he took a large body of sympathisers with him, but to no
avail; that he found himself sued, having failed to achieve his object,
in the court of Common Pleas for proceeding "in disordered manner".[2] In the second William Davies, who succeeded Lloyd as
sheriff in 1580, attempted to execute an Exchequer writ of *fierfacias*
and to distrain on goods to the value of £131 13s. 6d. on Lloyd's
estate; endeavouring to do this by driving away cattle, he and his
assistants were attacked by Lloyd's followers, who effected a rescue;
and when Davies, showing his writ, arrested one of these, Lloyd's
men "with their weapons drawn and ready to strike at the said
sheriff . . . said that they should die before one of their number
should be so stayed, and so, for fear of further inconvenience, the
said sheriff was fain to let him go". According to nine witnesses
there had been no previous quarrel between the two principals.[3]
There may be little truth in either tale as it stands; yet the contrast
is certainly sharp between the timid Thomas Lloyd as public servant
and the valiant Thomas Lloyd as defender of his private rights.

Insofar as private individuals tended to object to the activities,
whether disinterested or otherwise, of local officials, they reflect
objections arising out of the jealously guarded immunities and privileges of boroughs.[4] The safeguarding of what was, in his view, his
right to have the maces carried before him in Old Carmarthen had
added spirit to the mayor of New Carmarthen's defiance of the
Devereux;[5] and this attitude was a common one. In Cardigan in
1605 Griffith ap Rhydderch and John Revell claimed that, while
attempting to collect the tolls on fairs and markets which had been

---

(1) *A.P.C.* (1615-1616), p.185; *ibid.* (1621-1623), p.72; *C.S.P.Dom.* (1619-1623),
     vol. cxxii, no. 130.
(2) *A.P.C.* (1578-1580), pp.140, 352.
(3) P.R.O. E134/22 Eliz./E13.
(4) For the formal incorporation of Pembroke, with extensive powers of self-govern-
     ment independent of the jurisdiction of the county officials, *vide* H. Owen (ed.)
     Calendar of Public Records relating to Pembrokeshire, vol. iii, pp. xiv, 211-216.
(5) *L.P.H.VIII*, vol. xv (1540), no. 427; vol. xvii (1542), no. 53(ii); vol. xxi, pt. i
     (1546), no. 970(30); and *vide supra*, p.113, note 3.

demised to them, they were prevented by the mayor on the grounds that Cardigan was a town corporate, had been so since the time of Edward II, and conducted its affairs in accordance with letters patent granted to it by Richard II.[1] The ship *Elizabeth* of Orkney, brought by pirates into Milford in 1587, involved Sir John Wogan in interminable exchanges with the Scottish ambassador. He was told to recover her cargo and to apprehend her spoilers. Many of these dwelt in the towns of Haverfordwest and Carmarthen, and the mayors there would not yield to Wogan's authority nor allow him to carry out arrests within their liberties, he having no warrant to compel them by force.[2] In 1627 the deputy-lieutenants of Pembrokeshire informed the Council that because they had no power to levy men in Haverfordwest and other corporations they were obliged to impress men whom they were "both sorry and ashamed to present" in order to make up the numbers required.[3] Robert Record, attempting to execute a process for wrongful intrusion on one Griffith Howell within the liberties of Tenby, secured a writ of *non omittas* directed to the sheriff to order the mayor and bailiffs of Tenby to carry out Howell's arrest, and claimed that even so he was prevented by about forty people and, on appealing to the mayor, was himself arrested and clapped in irons in the town gaol.[4] Personal friendship might secure the assistance of borough officials;[5] without it, county officials were often at a disadvantage in executing their duties as the servants either of the central administration or of the judiciary. Hostility between townsfolk and country gentlemen has, too, its social aspect, reaching its peak in Kidwelly where, according to John Cade, "a discord and dissention" between them had the result that "suddenly the country gentlemen betrayed the town and townsmen and with violence suddenly entered upon them

---

(1) P.R.O. E112/145/37.
(2) H.M.C. *Cal. Salis. MSS.*, vol. iii, pp.394, 405-407; vol. iv, pp.62-63. Wogan, harassed on all sides, complained to Archibald Douglas, the ambassador, "I have gotten in dealing with this commission many enemies in the country, gentlemen of good account and others . . . Truly, that salt has cost me already, one way and other, as good as £200". John Vaughan, customer of Milford, who was also concerned, was more vitriolic: "From Scots, Irish and bloody-minded 'wiffes' the Lord deliver me!" he wrote to Burghley (*ibid.*, vol. vi, p.449).
(3) P.R.O. S.P.16/75/37.
(4) P.R.O. E112/62/6.
(5) *Vide supra*, p.129. For some description of the development of an oligarchic structure in borough administration, with power in the hands of the mayor and some close associates, *vide* M. E. Jones, "The Parliamentary Representation of Pembrokeshire", *op. cit.*, pp.35, 39.

and killed and spoiled the chiefest and most substantial of them, sacked the town and set fire to the most part thereof, whereby they overthrew the state and good order of the town and most utterly impoverished it".[1]

Apart from the hysterical tone of this last, the evidence concerning the practice of local government in this region might seem to suggest little more than the efforts of a passably diligent, if at times uncertain, officialdom whose functions could not, by certain individuals or groups, be easily reconciled with their view of their own liberties. But there remains a number of alleged incidents which cannot be accommodated by so uniform a collective interpretation. Of these, several illustrate no more than dogged hostility between certain litigants: additional evidence, perhaps, of feud and faction, but not necessarily of the quality of local administration. Typical of these is the prolonged antagonism between William Warren of Trewern and Alban Stepney, expressed in several lawsuits following the latter's term as sheriff in 1605.[2] Warren accused Stepney of having persecuted certain individuals, profited through distraining on goods, and of general misconduct, including drunkenness, in office; to which Stepney answered that in everything he had tried to do he had been armed with writs from the central authorities, and, providing explanations on each count, referred to his long career of public service and his education at Cambridge and the Inns of Court, calling Warren an "informer" who had long nursed a grudge against him and given vent to it in harassing litigation. David Lloyd of Abermâd was accused of corrupt distraint upon James Lewis;[3] he in turn accused Richard Price of Gogerddan and Morgan Lloyd, deputy-lieutenants of Cardiganshire, of making £3,300 for themselves out of the county's armour, and of extracting commorthau in a notable display of intimidation;[4] and the whole may be related to the feud between Prices and Lloyds in Cardiganshire.[5]

---

(1) B.M. Harleian, 5203.
(2) P.R.O. St. Ch. 8/257/9; /290/5, 8, 9; E112/151/33. *Cf. supra*, p.62, for further lawsuits between Stepney and Warren.
(3) P.R.O. E112/145/54; E178/4999.
(4) P.R.O. St. Ch. 5/L2/10. The defendants, urged on by their wives, were said to have gathered with their followers outside churches on Sundays, setting a basin on the stile and causing "a public and solemn declaration to be made that the people should give their benevolence . . . and that the said Richard Price and the rest of the justices would thank them for it", collecting by these means sums of £100 and more.
(5) *Vide supra*, p.130.

The allegations against Rees Prydderch, former sheriff of Carmarthenshire, of embezzlement of distrained goods and forgery of an inquisition, must be considered in the context of the tangled dispute over the castle and demesne of Laugharne, in the course of which they were made, which involved even more deeply Rees Phillips Scarfe of Lamphey in Pembrokeshire,[1] and which produced such oddities as the naming of Sir John Phillips in one instance as Prydderch's chief surety and in another as his son's assailant.[2] In the same bill in which Rhydderch William of Llandebie accused the Carmarthenshire deputy-sheriff, Walter Jones of Llandeilo, of various misdemeanours, he admitted already having failed to obtain on these matters a verdict acceptable to himself at both the Council in the Marches and the Great Sessions.[3] Likewise, when John Morgan Wolfe sued Alban Stepney in Star Chamber for wrongful distraint when sheriff of Carmarthenshire, the Exchequer court had already found for the defendant with costs on the same plea.[4] Such allegations cannot be accepted at their face value. They simply show litigants' tactics.

Equally predictably, in a number of lawsuits individuals were expressly alleged to have abused their official powers from motives of pride, avarice, intolerance, partisanship or self-interest.[5] No more than this can be said of such instances, except that, whatever the foundation of particular allegations, they at least suggest that officials were engaged in some activity in the name of the authority given them. But there are many cases in which officials were reproached with having done nothing at all. Rees Leonard, sheriff of Haverfordwest, and Thomas Canon, mayor there, were alleged to have failed both to execute warrants directed to them and to hold

(1) For the involvement of Prydderch, his wife and his son, *vide* P.R.O.St. Ch. 8/15/14; /248/17; 233/14; E112/151/36; E124/7/119; /9/124; 15/159-160b; /15/191; E126/1/258-262; *et plur. al.*
(2) P.R.O. E124/16/96; St. Ch. 8/231/2. Prydderch was evidently a formidable man: the sheriff of Carmarthenshire failed repeatedly to execute process of extent against him, and the sheriff of London confessed himself reluctant to try to arrest him unaided (E124/16/85-86b).
(3) P.R.O. St. Ch. 5/W58/30.
(4) P.R.O. E123/25/132b-133.
(5) For example, P.R.O. St. Ch. 5/L47/6 (John Birt, justice of the peace, "a corrupt and greedy mind insatiably set upon his own gain and lucre", accused of accepting bribes); St. Ch. 5/R20/33 (William Davies, sheriff, accused of violence and intimidation); St. Ch. 5/W69/22 (Hugh Owen, justice of the peace, whose answer was described by the court as "stuffed with unnecessary circumstances" (B.M. Harleian 2143, f.37) found to have favoured a neighbour over a "stranger" in a dispute over title despite directives to the contrary from the Justices of Assize).

persons already arrested.[1] Francis Laugharne, sheriff of Pembroke-shire, for no valid reason stayed the execution of Griffith Phillips, sentenced for wilful murder.[2] William Powell of Trimsaran was accused not only of having failed to arrest but also of having sheltered Morris Gwynne, a fugitive from justice.[3] The subsidy appears, not surprisingly, to have furnished particular occasion for neglect. The collector for Llanbadarn Fawr, "notwithstanding divers warrants . . . to him directed for the speedy execution thereof, hath been both negligent and careless therein and hath detained the said warrants in his custody without returning any answer thereof".[4] But other matters evoked no greater display of zeal. In 1556 the sheriff of Pembrokeshire, ordered to arrest four men, failed not only to do so but even to acknowledged the Council's letters.[5] Of the four com-missioners for piracy in Carmarthenshire in 1578, one was not available because he was "so busied with divers affairs", another had gone to London, and the remaining two shrank from proceeding alone.[6]

In social matters, lack of diligence could have regrettable conse-quences. The failure of the Pembrokeshire justices of the peace to deal with the annual payment of £48 towards the relief of the poor and a similar sum for maimed soldiers prompted a petition on behalf of these from John Phillips of Llanfyrnach in 1615; to which the justices replied that there were too many maimed soldiers for the money available to suffice to "give each of them a competent portion of maintenance", though as they were rapidly dying the problem would very likely soon solve itself.[7] Two such unfortu-nates were the subjects of individual intercession ten years later; in one instance two years elapsed before the Privy Council's instructions that the man should receive his pension were carried out.[8] When officials did attend at the scene of their responsibilities, failure in preparation could make the gesture futile. When a Spanish ship put in at Aberdovey in 1597 the deputy-lieutenants of Cardiganshire,

---

(1) P.R.O. St. Ch. 8/178/25(i); /201/3.
(2) *A.P.C.* (1577-1578), p.306; (1578-1580), p.55.
(3) P.R.O. St. Ch. 8/288/4.
(4) P.R.O. S.P.16/68/47; *cf.* N.L.W. Haverfordwest Corporation Records, 231: subsidy payments had been "returned with so loose a hand that half the last subsidy . . . is not received".
(5) *A.P.C.* (1554-1556), p.268.
(6) P.R.O. S.P.12/122/48.
(7) N.L.W. Bronwydd 380, 398, 399, 3329.
(8) *A.P.C.* (1623-1625), p.356; (1625-1626), p.69.

though present, had neither force nor ordnance available to do anything against her. They sent for the vice-admiral, who came at once, but he had no better success in obtaining shipping to attack the enemy by sea; and so they all stood powerless on the shore "and saw the sailing of the ship but could not resist it".[1]

To the contemporary central authorities, ultimately the bodies responsible, the outstanding and persistent weakness of local officialdom lay in its failure or reluctance to act. Occasionally they might lend an ear to suggestions that the commissioners for musters in the three shires had been found to "favour themselves in providing of armour and maintenance of horses to the evil example of others in those counties".[2] More often, they preferred to echo the attitude of the Justices of Assize towards Wyrriott's accusations against Sir John Perrot, in "no way to have the life of a gentleman of Sir John Perrot's quality generally to be sifted to his great discredit".[3] But time and again the Privy Council intimated its annoyance at the indifference of, for instance, deputy-lieutenants who failed to render "any due accompt" of the money and armour they were to have collected, so that special commissioners would have to be appointed to inquire into this.[4] Nor was such reproof a guarantee of improved activity. Justices of all three shires were in 1626 instructed to investigate exactly parallel suspicions, and were so tardy in doing so that eight months later they were admonished in the words, "This Board useth not to pass by so great neglect showed to their orders and directions without some more sharp reproof and censure".[5] Another seven months went by, until at last the Council was driven to call upon the most powerful names in the locality to take charge of the matter: Lord Vaughan, Baronet Phillips, Sir James Perrot, Sir John Lewis and others.[6]

The simple fact of the distance from the seat of central authority of people "dwelling in the county of Carmarthen, being one hundred and fourscore miles or near thereabouts distant from the city of

---

(1) *C.S.P.Dom.* (1595-1597), vol. cclxv, no. 15. Robert Jones, the muster master, declared that he had urged the officials to press men and attack the vessel in boats, "but they said they had no authority to levy her Majesty's subjects to risk their lives at sea on so dangerous a service" (*ibid.*, no. 77).
(2) *A.P.C.* (1580-1581), p.340.
(3) B.M. Lansdowne 72, ff.6-7.
(4) *A.P.C.* (1601-1604), p.25.
(5) *Ibid.* (1627), p.181.
(6) *Ibid.* (1627-1628), p.123.

Westminster"[1] could render that authority virtually impotent. Those people themselves on occasion gladly reminded judges of central courts of this circumstance.[2] Neither the judiciary nor the central administration, either in its secular or in its ecclesiastical aspect, can have needed such reminder. When in 1564 the Privy Council circularised the bishops of the dioceses of England and Wales, asking for information as to the attitudes of justices of the peace towards the established church, the only three for which no return at all was made were Bangor, St. Asaph and St. David's.[3] On his being appointed by the Lords of the Admiralty to be vice-admiral for south Wales, the Earl of Pembroke felt "bound to let them know that the King's service suffers much in those parts for want of a Judge and Registrar".[4] Justice Lewkenor, writing to Cecil concerning the defects in men, armour and munitions in Cardiganshire, said that he advised the local musterman that he "knew no course but to write to the sheriffs and justices of the peace of those counties to cause the trained bands to be made complete and supplied with arms; which he thought would do little good".[5] As Thomas Winter had suggested to the Spaniards, if they proposed to make a landing in Britain, "then I thought Milford Haven more convenient, being in parts where they could not be offended with the Queen's power".[6]

In this region, matters of justice or administration which the central authorities might consider pressing were seldom so regarded. The pursuivant who came with a warrant from Walsingham to arrest two Tenby men for consorting with pirates was reported by Thomas Perrot to Dr. Caesar, Judge of the Admiralty, as "a bad pursuivant" who "would not defer the matter" until the two "very honest and sufficient" men concerned had completed fresh voyages

---

(1) P.R.O. St. Ch. 8/239/10. *Cf.* Thomas Perrot's excuse to Walsingham that he had been unable to arrest one James Price because he lived in Carmarthenshire, forty miles away (*C.S.P.Dom.* (1581-1590), vol. clxxx, no. 20).
(2) For instance, Rees Prydderch informed the Exchequer Judges that "he cannot make perfect and direct answer to the same [bill] without perusing certain writings which are in the country about 180 miles distant from London...and that this short vacation they shall not have sufficient counsel in that part of the country to draw their answer to the said bill ... It is therefore ordered that the said defendants may take a commission to take their answers in the country" (P.R.O. E124/9/70b).
(3) The return for Llandaff was imprecise (W. R. Trimble, *The Catholic Laity in Elizabethan England, 1558-1603*, pp.24-26).
(4) *C.S.P.Dom.* (1631-1633), vol. clxxxix, no. 20.
(5) H.M.C. *Cal. Salis. MSS.*, vol. xi, pp.459-460.
(6) *Ibid.*, vol. xvii, p.513.

to Rochelle and to England and back respectively.[1] Alternatively, when pressure from the Council for discovery of a wrongdoer would brook no denial, a scapegoat might be found, such as John Kiste, who "taketh the matter wholly upon himself",[2] thereby abrogating the need for further investigation. Some men, indeed, were anxious that the Privy Council should know of a grand-juryman who was susceptible to bribery,[3] of a powerful local gentleman, for the moment in the ascendant, who might rely upon "extraordinary favour to be yielded him in his cause" against another, for the moment less popular, magnate,[4] of a coroner's having "impanelled and returned a very partial jury".[5] On occasion that body might be moved to order that a trial which "would not fall out to be indifferent within the counties of Cardigan and Montgomery" be held "in the next English county adjoining"[6]—this over half a century after Union; or again, that the trial of Rees Prydderch and John Scourfield for the murder of Lewis Watkyns should be held in Monmouthshire because of "some partiality and indirect dealing", and "because of their great friendship to many of the gentlemen and, namely, to the now sheriff" of Carmarthenshire the accused "were almost assured of all the favour which by their procurement could in that behalf be shewed them".[7] On the other hand, it was content that a suit concerning Sir John Perrot should be heard not before the Council in the Marches, of which Sir John was a member, but in Carmarthenshire, "for the avoidance of suspicion and partiality".[8] The Privy Council reiterated its determination that it "may not easily give credit to . . . complainants that do touch the credit of a sheriff of a county with suspicion of partial and wrongful proceeding".[9] Some corruption there may have been; it does not appear to have considered this its main problem. That which cast a blight on official souls was the sin of omission. Officials prepared to do something, however ill-advisedly

---

(1) B.M. Add. MSS. 12507, f.103.
(2) *Ibid.*, ff.119, 121.
(3) *C.S.P.Dom.* (1598-1601), vol. cclxviii, no. 109.
(4) *A.P.C.* (1591), p.218: John Barlow, ally of the powerful Devereux, against William Wogan.
(5) *Ibid.* (1595-1596), p.200.
(6) *Ibid.* (1590), p.399.
(7) *Ibid.* (1587-1588), pp.295, 377. It is noteworthy that Monmouthshire is here clearly held to be an English county.
(8) *Ibid.* (1580-1581), p.24.
(9) *Ibid.* (1599-1600), p.370.

or maladroitly, must be cherished; they served at least as reminders of the presence of government and the existence of English law. They were far more valuable than those nominal public servants who themselves cherished the title and renounced the deed.

For the very circumstances which frustrated closer supervision forced the central government to repose far greater confidence than it might otherwise have done in those very men whose devotion to duty was often questioned. If Thomas Perrot and Alban Stepney were prepared to tender to Dr. Caesar "our promise and assumption which we make for him by these lines under our handwriting" that Jenkin Davids was "both by reason of age and impotence" unable to travel to London to answer charges of having illegally purchased salt, and that they would themselves instead examine the matter and in due course send a representative;[1] or if Sir Francis Meyrick and George Owen would certify that Richard Tasker, though master of a ship and allegedly quite capable of transporting soldiers out of Ireland, was "both aged and sick and not able to make his repair" to London:[2] the Privy Council could do little other than allow them to proceed and rely upon their findings. A man like Sir Thomas Canon, prepared to devote his energies to the public service, might expect to be able to accommodate, and to win the gratitude of, his town;[3] and, though subjected to allegations of fraud and malpractice that may have been well-founded or may, again, have arisen out of local suspicion towards honest official dealing,[4] such a man could eventually rise to see his own interpretations of events

(1) B.M. Add. MSS. 12507, f.221. The charge was one of dealing with pirates (*cf.* *A.P.C.* (1587-1588), p.167).
(2) *A.P.C.* (1599-1600), p.338. In 1590 Sir Thomas Jones and other Carmarthenshire justices of the peace certified to the Scottish ambassador that "John Morys, mayor of Carmarthen, who has been commanded to appear at the suit of a Scotchman [*sic*], is not able to travel by reason of an accident" (H.M.C. *Cal. Salis. MSS.*, vol. iv, p.53).
(3) N.L.W. Bronwydd 3365. The corporation of Haverfordwest expressed to him their greatest appreciation of "your loving care of us and our country in freeing us of the £100 for the mises", and committed their other affairs "unto your accustomed care and good discretion".
(4) At a suggestion that he might alter the muster-books after their delivery to him, Canon waxed indignant, warning the corporation, "If it would move you to reap tares where you have sowed corn, let them not be discouraged that do willingly endeavour the good and reputation of the town" (N.L.W. Haverfordwest Corporation Records, 223). Elsewhere he was accused of being a "turbulent person", given to intimidating by threats of litigation those whom he would oppress, of using his office of Crown steward of Pembroke to his own profit, depriving tenants of their rights and liberties, and even fortifying the castle of Tenby in a manner that enabled him to conduct himself like a robber baron and that even hinted at treason (N.L.W. Slebech 3253).

outweigh those of ecclesiastical dignitaries,[1] and himself employed in commissions and company of the highest worth.[2] One so "rich and powerful and of great experience in suits of law"[3] could conduct himself virtually as he chose and still retain the central authorities' trust. It was upon such individuals that any kind of local administration in the last resort depended.

There was one activity above all in which are highlighted the opportunities and the hazards, the difficulties and the limitations, of these local officials. That activity was piracy.

3. PIRACY.

In the year 1541 an English merchant, Thomas Barnsby, complained to the Privy Council on behalf of two Bretons that they had been robbed by English pirates off the coast of St. David's and their goods sold to, amongst others, the chantor of the cathedral.[4] There followed a long period of collaboration between local inhabitants and spoilers of ships. There is little evidence that resident inhabitants of south-west Wales themselves actually conducted raids upon ships at sea. Theirs was a less spectacular role: that of pilot-fish to the marauding sharks. Among the latter may be counted names of some notoriety: John Callice, Luke Ward, Robert Hickes. The coastline, liberally sprinkled with discreet bays, and the trading route up the Bristol Channel, provided a fine hunting ground for such as these. With a market close at hand, far from the perturbed eye but uncertain arm of central government, they needed only the goodwill of local authority.

Such goodwill was forthcoming. Mayors and undersheriffs prepared to embezzle goods from ships driven by foul weather into

(1) Respectively, the Bishop of St. David's, whom he accused of preventing his renewal of the lease of Abergwili rectory (*C.S.P.Dom.* (1631-1633), vol. ccxxxi, nos. 6-7; (1633-1634), vol. ccxxxvii, nos. 75-76); and the Bishop of Chester, who strongly objected to Canon's investigation into his affairs (*ibid.* (1633-1634), vol. ccxxxvi, no. 32; vol. ccxxxvii, no. 78; vol. ccxxxviii, nos. 43, 71; vol. ccxxxix, nos. 77-78; vol. ccxliii, no. 3; (1634-1635), vol. cclxxx, no. 9). He also clashed with Sir James Perrot, upon whose jurisdiction as deputy vice-admiral he was alleged to have trespassed (*ibid.* (1631-1633), vol. cxciii, no. 8; vol. ccxxxiii, no. 45; vol. ccxxxiv, nos. 2, 41, 71). Perrot had long since spoken of him as his "professed enemy" (H.M.C. *Cal. Salis. MSS.*, vol. xvii, p.555).
(2) With Inigo Jones he joined the Commissioners for Pious Uses to see to the repairing of St. Paul's in 1634 (*C.S.P.Dom.* (1634-1635), vol. cclxvii, no.66).
(3) *Ibid.* (1631-1633), vol. ccxxxiii, no. 59.
(4) *L.P.H.VIII*, vol. xvi (1540-1541), no. 925.

their locality[1] were unlikely to cavil at other fortuitous sources of spoils. An occasional official might, after the operation had been completed and the cargo dispersed, report such activities to his superiors;[2] or the prospect of a reward might result in a surprised pirate's arrest.[3] Offsetting these occurrences, natives of Pembroke and Tenby appeared in pirate crews as far afield as the Kentish coast;[4] and it was not long before more illustrious names were to be found in piratical company. As early as 1553 Sir John Perrot was called upon to correct the misdemeanours of Philip ap Price, "whom he and others in that country supporteth", and to see his victims recompensed.[5] In 1556 Sir John Wogan was declared to have himself sold the goods of a Breton merchant whose ship had been brought by English merchants into Tenby.[6] With the vice-admiral and former sheriff so involved, little rectitude might be expected from lesser men.

Some evidence appears to suggest that there was, particularly in Pembrokeshire, a strong and effective organisation for trafficking with pirates, Perrot being its mainspring.[7] Certainly from 1564, when Sir John's failure to hold Thomas Cobham, whose capture of a Spanish vessel had evoked strong protests from Spain and jeopardised Elizabeth's foreign policy, earned him the rebuke of the Privy Council and lost his kinsman the deputy-vice-admiraltyship;[8] to 1579, when he was appointed to cruise along the coast of Ireland and act against pirates operating from the Scilly Isles:[9] his conduct with regard to piracy was repeatedly questioned. Most notably, perhaps, he was in 1577 informed that their Lordships "do not a

(1) The mayor of Pembroke and Arnold Butler, the undersheriff, were tagged the chief culprits in this by the commissioners John and Roger Barlow and Henry Wyrriott, Butler finding himself in the Fleet in consequence (*ibid.*, vol. xviii, pt.i (1543), nos. 190, 478, 513, 533, 568; *A.P.C.* (1542-1547), pp.89, 125, 128, 130, 135, 143). Yet by 1565 Butler was a commissioner for piracy (*ibid.* (1558-1570), p.285).
(2) Thus the mayor of Haverfordwest after the spoiling of a Portuguese carvel in 1546 (*L.P.H.VIII*, vol. xxi, pt. i (1546), no. 789; *A.P.C.* (1542-1547), p.414).
(3) For apprehending the pirate Cole in 1549 Rice ap Morgan and Philip Lower earned themselves £60 (*ibid.* (1547-1550), p.286; *C.S.P.Dom.* (1547-1580), vol. vii, no. 23 (ii, iii).
(4) Thomas Phillip and Hugh William of Pembroke and Frolike Young of Tenby with thirteen Englishmen raided a French ship at the Downs (*C.P.R.* (Edward VI), vol. iv (1550-1553), p.95).
(5) *A.P.C.* (1552-1554), p.251.
(6) *Ibid.* (1554-1556), p.358.
(7) Carys E. Hughes, "Wales and Piracy: a Study in Tudor Administration, 1500-1640", University of Wales unpublished M.A. thesis (1937), p.174.
(8) *A.P.C.* (1558-1570), p.148.
(9) *Ibid.* (1578-1580), p. 240.

little marvel at the negligence of such as are justices in those parts"
when Callice, "arriving lately at Milford, was lodged and horsed in
Haverfordwest, and being there known was suffered to escape", and
Edward Herbert, a former servant of Perrot's, "bearing himself bold
upon his countenance and others' thereabouts, hath in like case of
late brought into Milford a prize laden with wines, and having made
sale thereof hath also been suffered to depart and winked at", although they had "for a show and colour of justice . . . apprehended
some of the poorest and permitted the chiefest pirates to escape".[1]
Yet, with outside investigators such as Fabian Phillips proving unable
to elicit much information from Cardiff concerning pirates who
operated further west,[2] it was to Sir John that the Council continued
to direct its correspondence in these matters. He, making half a
dozen arrests here and reporting some traders with pirates there,[3]
maintained a passable semblance of retributive activity; until in
1578 Richard Vaughan of Whitland, "late vice-admiral under Sir
William Morgan", produced against Perrot a voluminous "book of
complaints", which was referred to Drs. Lewis and Dale of the
Admiralty for examination.

Vaughan's accusations,[4] couched in violent language, were calculated to reveal himself as the Admiralty's faithful servant defeated
in his efforts by Perrot, who, "making his lust a law in all things and
to all men", trafficked directly with pirates, conspired with them,
shielded them, and was highly susceptible to their bribes. But when
he came to call witnesses in support of these opinions, Vaughan's
case lost impact. The first, John Kiste, serjeant of the Admiralty,
stated categorically that none had been so active as had Sir John in
the cause of bringing pirates to justice, and recited numerous instances in support of this. Next, Lewis Michelett criticised Perrot
for having refused to set at liberty one Bernard Jordeyne on being
proferred a thousand French francs for this favour. James Gwynne
disclosed that Perrot's servants had, in fact, accepted this money,
and accordingly thought it disgraceful that Jordeyne had not been
released, and shocking that such thieves were so lacking in honour.

(1) *Ibid.* (1575-1577), p.267.
(2) *C.S.P.Dom.* (1547-1580), vol. cxii, no. 5. Of Orleton, Herefordshire, Phillips was
    Recorder of Carmarthen, second Justice of the Anglesey circuit and a member
    of the Council in the Marches (Penry Williams, *op. cit.*, pp.354-355).
(3) For some measures taken against pirates in this region, *vide C.S.P.Dom.* (1547-
    1580), vol. cxi, nos. 15, 16, 28, 36; vol. cxx, no. 77; vol. cxxii, no. 21; vol. cxxiii,
    no. 8; *Addenda* (1566-1579), vol. xxv, no. 70(iv).
(4) P.R O. S.P.12/124/12, 28, 31, 66, 67.

There were several more witnesses who, though not as disappointing to Vaughan as these three, could produce only unconvincing and ambiguous depositions. Perrot, in his turn, brought forward a more impressive array of witnesses, headed by John Kiste again, but supported by David Williams, a Fellow of the Middle Temple, and John Price of Gogerddan. Their evidence was largely non-committal. But by this time Sir John's expressions of outraged denial, his re-interpretation, in an entirely different light, of Vaughan's more factual allegations, and his flourishing of his special commission, under the Great Seal of the Admiralty, for the apprehending of pirates, which entitled him to supersede his accuser's authority, seemed far more convincing than the latter's embittered and un-confirmed protestations, especially when those upon whose support he may have relied had, for whatever reasons, left him.

Vaughan himself was not above suspicion. The four tardy com-missioners for piracy in Carmarthenshire in 1578,[1] whilst noting several minor purchasers of pirate goods, alleged him to have been in the habit of seizing the spoils of pirates to her Majesty's use and then selling them to his own profit: a suggestion supported by the association of his name with that of George Devereux as having openly consorted with Captains William Vaughan and William Beere in disposing of a French grain cargo forcibly appropriated by them.[2] More illuminating than the evidence in Vaughan's case, where the personal animosity of the two principals and the probable intimidation or misplaced loyalty of witnesses are unmistakeable, are the results of the inquiry conducted by the Bishop of St. David's, Francis Laugharne, the Pembrokeshire sheriff, and John Barlow, with the Carmarthenshire sheriff, Griffith Lloyd, again in 1578.[3] Examinations of thirty-four witnesses showed that, although many individuals had had dealings with pirates to the extent of a barrel of salt or a bushel of rye, only two acknowledged gentlemen were amongst them: John Butler of Laugharne, who "laded in a vessel of the burthen of twenty tons or thereabouts certain salt from Hickes, to what quantity they knew not"; and Richard Vaughan, who had purchased wine. Though Sir John Perrot was often mentioned, it was largely in connection with his activities as a suppressor of pirates. Only one witness hinted at nefarious conduct on his part. This was the respectable merchant Morgan Powell, who testified that Perrot's

---

(1) *Vide supra*, p.156.   (2) P.R.O. S.P.12/129/24.   (3) P.R.O. S.P.12/126/40.

men had confiscated from Roger ap Richard of Aberystwyth two boats laden with corn and salt acquired from Hickes, taken them to Carew and thence disposed of them, adding that Sir John had incarcerated Richard for his activities. Powell's most forthright revelation was that George Devereux had acted as middle man between him, his partner Griffith Dawes, and Hickes, in a matter of two hundred barrels of corn, all three later exporting these to Ireland.

The evidence as a whole suggests that dealings with pirates were essentially haphazard. The reports to which they occasionally gave rise are consistent rather with the general muteness of this region, occasionally broken either by personal animosity or sufficiently to placate the more insistent inquiries of the central authority, than with the existence of a powerful organisation. Though there remains around Perrot a strong aura of collaboration with them to the extent that he was not above turning a dishonest penny through pirates when he could, and would, if his interest so dictated, shield them, the evidence will not sustain Vaughan's picture of him as a kind of adult piratical Fagin. Indeed, his own report to the Privy Council in February 1577 that John Wogan of Wiston had traded butter, cheese and other foodstuffs for several tuns of wine with Edward Herbert and had defied the undersheriff sent to call him to answer for it,[1] simultaneously endangered his friendship with a family allied to him and incriminated his former servant. The Wogans were probably involved with pirates to much the same degree as was Perrot himself. Certainly Sir John Wogan of Boulston encountered great difficulties between 1588 and 1591 over his alleged share of the salt from the *Elizabeth* of Orkney and the plundered flyboat of George Paddy, in both of which affairs he was accused, with Thomas Canon, John Kiste and John Vaughan, of having assisted the pirates, and ordered to discover the culprits.[2] In 1597 his kinsman of Milton was the object of the injured recriminations of Hugh Butler who, as captain of the trained bands, claimed to have boarded a grounded Spanish vessel at Galtop only to be himself forestalled, wounded and driven off by Wogan and his men who made off with the booty.[3] Deference to an officer was no more conspicuous here than was consistent behaviour. Maurice Canon, protesting in 1576

(1) P.R.O. S.P. 12/111/37.
(2) H.M.C. *Cal. Salis. MSS.*, vol. iii, p.378; vol. xiii, pp.346-347, 386; *A.P.C.* (1590), p.104; (1590-1591), pp.58, 84, 146. *Vide supra*, p.153.
(3) *A.P.C.* (1597-1598), p.119.

against having been robbed at sea by the Englishman Phipson, appears in 1587 to have joined with Robert Toy, Edward Middleton, Griffith Howell and others, in buying up the cargo of a Frenchman brought by seven pirates into Carmarthen and Laugharne.[1]

So complete an individual reversal of behaviour came to be reflected in the attitude of the community in general. The heyday of the pirates' popularity passed with the turn of the century. If such great men as the Vaughans of Golden Grove could continue in 1627 to flirt furtively with Flemings,[2] the complaints voiced as early as 1593 by the inhabitants of Carmarthen[3] were by that time common opinion. In 1630 the sheriff and deputy-lieutenant of Pembrokeshire appealed to the Privy Council concerning a fifty-tonner from Biscay stationed at the mouth of Milford Haven, which was persecuting local merchants and threatened to prevent the region's accustomed trading at St. James's fair in Bristol.[4] By 1631 the protest had broadened to embrace all pirates who haunted the coast, and in particular the peril of the "Moors". It was implored that Milford Haven be fortified, as it had become "a receptacle for all rovers and robbers".[5] Another Biscayner in 1632, coupled with fear of raids by apparently Turkish pirates, brought prayers for a King's ship to guard Milford. This, when it arrived, was urged to greater efforts by Admiralty lords assailed with more complaints from local residents who, estimating the duration of the pirate plague at a conservative five years, drew fresh attention to the mischief done by it to their legitimate trade. Plumleigh found the islands around Lundy to be infested with pirates, but had small success against them.[6] Despairing of him, the local people begged for a commission out of the Admiralty authorising some of their own number to apprehend pirates on that coast. The first two names they proposed for that duty were those of Perrot and Wogan.[7]

Favoured by the complexion of local administration, the profitable

---

(1) *Ibid.* (1575-1577), p.102; (1587-1588), pp.44-45.
(2) *C.S.P.Dom.* (1627-1628), vol. lxxxvi, no. 2; vol. xciv, no. 92.
(3) *A.P.C.* (1593), p.401. They had contrived the arrest in Jersey of one Hellier Brock, who had sold in the Channel Islands what he had stolen from Carmarthen: an unacceptable reversal of procedure.
(4) *C.S.P.Dom.* (1629-1631), vol. clxx, no. 35.
(5) *Ibid.* (1631-1633), vol. cxcvii, no. 27.
(6) *Ibid.*, vol. ccxv, no. 47; vol. ccxxiii, no. 5; (1634-1635), vol. cclxxii, no. 1(ii).
(7) *Ibid.* (1634-1635), vol. cclxxii, no. 76. To the commissioning of Plumleigh was added the appointing of Evan Owen, the Admiralty officer for south Wales and third son of George Owen of Henllys, as a justice of the peace for Pembrokeshire (P.R.O. C66/2725).

intrigue of piracy had offered ample opportunity for the expression of the spirit of exclusiveness which here characterised public affairs. In this concern, as always, prominent personalities had clashed and combatted. And when matters went out of control, with those central powers which had been unable to intrude proving equally unable, when invited, to assist, it was to those local families into whose hands authority had been given, and whose members had wielded it so uncertainly, that their countrymen turned. For they were their natural leaders.

4. LAW.

The apparent litigiousness of Welshmen in the later sixteenth and the seventeenth centuries[1] is at variance with the foregoing portrait of local indifference to the forces of law and order. People who litigate may not respect the law: they may even abuse it, but they are, undoubtedly, aware of it. This appearance of litigiousness would appear to have two foundations. Firstly, some contemporary statements describe how local Welshmen "stand in fear (and our fears are not in vain) continually without intermission to be sued at the courts", largely because "the number of clerks and solicitors at the Council in the Marches have increased so exorbitantly, if not pro-digiously";[2] or how "poor David . . . [is] given so much to con-tention and strife that, without all respect of charges, he will up to London, though he go bare-legged by the way and carry his hosen on his neck (to save their feet from wearing) because he hath no change."[3] Such disparaging remarks may show prejudice on the part of commentators; they do not necessarily prove the existence of great numbers of litigants. Unflattering comments on the num-bers and conduct of lawyers are common enough in England in the seventeenth century.[4] Secondly, contemporary records at first sight

(1) "By the time Elizabeth came to the throne the English common law courts and the Crown's prerogative courts . . . were dealing with an ever increasing number of Welsh litigants; . . . little persuasion was necessary" (G. Dyfnallt Owen, *Elizabethan Wales*, p.169).
(2) W. Vaughan, *The Golden Fleece*, p.33.
(3) W. Harrison, *A Description of England* (ed. L. Withington), p.53. Harrison, mocking impecunious folly rather than litigiousness, noted the Welshman's refusal "to have his cause heard so near home" as Ludlow.
(4) "This is one of the great inconveniences in the land, that the number of lawyers are so great that they undo the country people and buy up all the lands that are to be sold" (Thomas Wilson, "The State of England", *op. cit.*, p.25). *Cf.*, too, George Wither's opinion in 1628 that lawyers should suffer the fate of the monasteries; and the view of *The Laws Discovery* (1653) of "the profession of our laws as epidemically evil" (C. Hill, *Intellectual Origins of the English Revo-lution*, pp.261-262); also, Sir Edward Hoby's comment in 1601 (*supra*, p.100).

appear to show that Welshmen were involved in a disproportionate number of cases in the lawcourts. But the number of suits contained in the records of different courts is in itself no guide to the number of different litigants involved. The device of bringing an action in one court in order to forestall, delay, or contrive the contradicting of, an order made in another, was frequently resorted to by experienced litigants. Less practised plaintiffs often presented their bills in the wrong courts and were ordered to others. Other individuals might use the law in the manner of their ancestors' use of the bludgeon, aiming to stun their antagonists with repeated blows: such men were, of course, not peculiar to Wales. In such ways was the business of the lawcourts increased, whilst those who made use of them multiplied, if at all, less speedily.

According to statistics compiled by Miss Elfreda Skelton,[1] in the last year of Elizabeth's reign an average of 4.0 cases *per* Welsh shire were heard in the court of Star Chamber, 17.0 for each of the border shires,[2] and 17.1 for each shire of England. Dr. Penry Williams has taken these figures as evidence that the Council in the Marches, most of whose legal records have been lost, was "taking off the shoulders of Star Chamber many of those cases with which it might otherwise have been burdened".[3] Now the Council in the Marches was at least as accessible to litigants from the border as to Welshmen. Dr. Williams concludes from this that the Council, "while doing its work with reasonable success in Wales, was meeting with less success and with some distrust in the border shires."[4] He adduces evidence to show that the Council provoked opposition, some of it fierce, in the border shires owing to what was regarded as its interference in established liberties there, but explains that in Wales, where its jurisdiction was less hampered by such considerations, the Council's authority was more easily imposed and more capable of direct administration.[5]

These views are open to objection. On a point of detail, the suggestion[6] that the degree of co-operation between locality and Council was commensurate with the number of members from each

---

(1) As quoted in Penry Williams, *op. cit.*, p.215.
(2) Monmouthshire, Gloucestershire, Worcestershire, Herefordshire and Shropshire.
(3) *Ibid.*, p.216.
(4) *Ibid.*, *loc. cit.*
(5) *Ibid.*, pp.181-204.
(6) *Ibid.*, p.204.

locality who served on the Council seems, if tenable for the border shires, curious when applied to Wales.[1] More broadly, the contention that Welsh litigants brought proportionately more of their suits to the Council than did border litigants is based largely on surmise; whereas there is evidence that, at least where Star Chamber was concerned, far fewer men *per* Welsh shire litigated than *per* English shire, border or otherwise. Aspects of evidence presented elsewhere by Dr. Williams tend to further this latter view. He has calculated[2] that during the reign of Elizabeth the four shires of Glamorgan, Monmouth, Denbigh and Montgomery sent to Star Chamber 573 out of the total of 1,031 suits presented there which can with certainty be ascribed to individual Welsh shires. He explains this, in part, by pointing out that "on the whole the Star Chamber was more popular with the shires nearer London, as one might expect".[3] Reasonable though this seems, one reflects that Ludlow, too, was tolerably accessible to these same shires; more so, in fact, than to many other shires, especially those of south-west Wales.

That the Council was, at certain stages of its existence, particularly busy, seems possible. Dr. Williams has noted that "in 1594 it was 2,000 cases behind", and that "its frequent complaint was of too many cases"[4]—though George Owen, when he wrote, seems to have been unaware of this.[5] Elsewhere, Dr. Williams has argued that "towards the end of 1605 the Westminster courts began to gain support from the gentry of the English border shires"; that opposition from the border, led by Sir Herbert Croft and John Hoskyns, the Hereford county and borough members of parliament, contrived the pressing of a bill in Parliament for the removal of the four border shires from the jurisdiction of the Council in the Marches, and ultimately the issuing of fresh instructions, almost to this effect, to that Council; and that only the personal intervention of James I in November 1608 procured for the Council the restoration in the following May of its jurisdiction over these four shires.[6] Yet he

(1) Cf. *supra*, p.145.
(2) *Id.*, "The Star Chamber and the Council in the Marches of Wales, 1558-1603", *B.B.C.S.*, vol. xvi (1956), p.297.
(3) *Ibid.*, p.296.
(4) *Ibid.*, p.294.
(5) Owen, *op. cit.*, vol. iii, p.23: "There is great speed made in trial of all causes", referring to the Council in the Marches.
(6) Penry Williams, "The Attack on the Council in the Marches, 1603-1642", *T.H.C.S.* (1961), pp.3-6. The border shires are here four owing to the excluding of Monmouthshire. This "attack" represents, of course, an aspect of the contemporary opposition of the common lawyers to the prerogative courts.

has shown that in 1608-1609 (that is, in a year when the Council's jurisdiction over the four border shires was depleted) "it heard 1,350 cases from the four Marcher shires alone, and in the following year the figure rose to 3,376".[1] This, at a time when the Council had lost its criminal jurisdiction in the English shires and had its civil jurisdiction restricted to "cases of debt and trespass when the sums involved were not above £10", would seem to support one of the charges levelled against it, that its presence on the border "encouraged frivolous and unnecessary litigation".[2] Such litigation would appear to have come largely from the border shires themselves. In times of greater harmony the number of cases brought from those shires before the Council would have been very much greater.

Dr. Williams has shown the extent to which the Council depended for its income upon fines. At the time of this first "attack" from the border shires, this income fell from £2,311 8s. 4d. in 1602-1603 to £1,140 18s. 4d. in 1604-1605, and to £683 3s. 4d. in 1606-1607.[3] In other words, during the period of opposition from, and presumably withdrawal of litigation by, the border shires, the Council's income from fines fell by seventy *per cent*. Even when allowance is made for the fact that the same period saw the Council deprived of its jurisdiction over sexual offences in Wales—which seem, admittedly, to have been remarkably numerous[4]—it appears clear that the Council must have handled proportionately far more criminal cases from the border than from Welsh shires. When Dr. Williams later remarks that the Westminster lawyers who supported the Marcher opposition to the Council did so "mainly because its authority threatened their incomes" one feels more inclined to agree than when he accounts for these same lawyers' ignoring of Wales "because they had no jurisdiction there". Equally possibly, prospects there were insufficiently inviting to excite their interests. "Admittedly", says Dr. Williams, "the parliamentary bill of 1597 did make proposals about Wales, largely with a view to replacing the great sessions with the Westminster courts. But thereafter the dispute turned entirely about the exemption of the English shires".[5] Why

(1) *Id.*, "The Star Chamber and the Council in the Marches", *op. cit.*, p.294.
(2) *Id.*, "The Attack on the Council in the Marches", *op. cit.*, pp.5,10.
(3) *Ibid.*, p.5.
(4) Though the problem of bastardy "was common to every county in England" (W. B. Willcox, *op. cit.*, p.67).
(5) Williams, "The Attack on the Council in the Marches", *op. cit.*, p.12.

was this clause in the bill not pressed? Could it not have been because the Welsh aspect of the matter was not, relatively at least, worth pressing? because, too, the Welsh gentry, by and large, might not have joined with the Westminster lawyers in their campaign as the border gentry did, since their attitude towards the Council was one not of opposition but of indifference? Even as late as 1641, with the Council, its authority diminished and discredited, the victim of a final, concerted "attack", it was "a group of Marcher gentry led by Sir Thomas Myddelton" who paid, in part at least, the expenses of the Commons emissary sent "to search the Ludlow records on behalf of the Welsh shires", to free them from the Council's burdensome—or inadequate—governance.[1]

One further comment must be made. Miss Skelton's statistics, as quoted above, show that the border shires were responsible on the average for as many cases brought in Star Chamber as was the average English county: in the last year of Elizabeth's reign, 17.0 for the former, 17.1 for the latter. If the border shires were also the source of the greater part of the litigation conducted before the Council in the Marches, it would appear that it was the men of those shires who were excessively litigious. But whilst an average figure for four shires in reasonable geographical proximity to one another may be acceptable, a single figure for all the shires of England is, in this context, misleading. It seems likely that if the border shires are allowed to have conducted much of their litigation before the Council of the Marches, then the total amount of litigation brought from them before different courts would be comparable with the quantity brought from counties adjacent to London before the Westminster courts; or at least, the disparity would not be so excessive as to be unaccountable.

As Dr. Williams recognises, it is difficult to form a satisfactory picture of the relations with Wales of the Council in the Marches.[2] To query his conclusions in this regard is largely to meet surmise with surmise. He has shown that the activities of the Council in the border shires provoked resentment and antagonism there. No comparable reaction appears to have come from Wales. It does not seem to have been satisfactorily shown that Welshmen fully made up in the Council in the Marches for the litigation they failed to bring else-

(1) *Ibid.*, p.18.
(2) *Id., The Council in the Marches of Wales*, p.195.

where.[1] Increased litigiousness may well be a sign not of increased lawlessness but of a growing awareness of the power and usefulness of the law. It would be indiscreet, on the basis of the foregoing discussion, to generalise for the whole of Wales. But it would seem that in south-west Wales, and particularly in Pembrokeshire and Cardiganshire, which shires yielded, apart from Anglesey, the least number of Star Chamber suits of all the Welsh shires in Elizabeth's reign, there was little such awareness. Despite the "exciting vistas of new legal careers which the Union opened up for ambitious Welshmen of all degrees",[2] it is those who "were stubbornly adhering to customary habits"[3] that remain to constitute one's most lasting impression of this scene.

In Ireland in this period "there be many wide countries . . . which the laws of England were never established in, nor any acknowledgement of subjection made; and also even in those which are subdued and seem to acknowledge subjection, yet the same Brehon law is practised among themselves".[4] In England during the Civil War, disenchantment with lawyers prompted the Levellers to propose that far more business be left to local courts, and to insist upon lay assessors; and even Coke, in his *Compleat Copyholder*, "said that the lord (and presumably his steward as well) 'is not tied to the strict forms of the common law, for he is a chancellor in his court' ".[5] The popularity of hundred and other courts presided over by local gentry in Wales has already been noted.[6] There are, moreover, several instances of gentry acting as arbitrators in disputes of various kinds, usually involving title to land;[7] submission to arbitration was sometimes pleaded in bar to an action at law.[8] In England, to

---

(1) Likewise, that the apparent revival in the quantity of the Council's business in the 1630s arose rather out of a genuine increase in litigation than from its own manipulation of its procedure in order to increase its income from fines (*vide id.*, "The Activity of the Council in the Marches under the Early Stuarts", *Welsh History Review* (1961), pp.133-160).
(2) T. Jones Pierce, "The Law of Wales—the Last Phase", *T.H.C.S.* (1963), p.26.
(3) *Ibid.*, p.25.
(4) Henry Morley (ed.), "Edmund Spenser's View of the State of Ireland", *Ireland under Elizabeth and James I*, p.40. *Cf.* T. Birch, *Memoirs of the Reign of Queen Elizabeth*, vol. i, p.336: "The course of justice, common to the whole realm, had made very small progress in that county of Northumberland" (report of Sir William Bowes, 1595.)
(5) C. Hill, *op. cit.*, p.260.
(6) *Vide supra*, p.149.
(7) For instance, N.L.W. Bronwydd 1127, 1267, 857, 782, 741, 1007; Dynevor B/211, 662; Slebech 4079; Crosswood I.6, 8, 47, 65.
(8) For instance, P.R.O. E112/59/25; /151/64.

submit disputes to the award of arbitrators was a fairly common practice. No form of direct appeal or review of an award was possible; hence, the arbitrator was in no sense bound to observe the rules of the common law.[1] In Chancery, on the other hand, it was normal procedure to commission lay gentlemen to arbitrate between disputants, who were often persuaded "to execute penal bonds or recognizances in substantial sums to conform to any award the referees might make".[2] In Wales, there is some evidence, most notably from the beginning of this period,[3] but also from a later contemporary diary,[4] of the surviving influence and relevance of Welsh law in the settling of disputes. The available evidence is in itself quite insufficient to support a view that the practical application of Welsh law at this time was widespread, or that Welshmen, insofar as they did not litigate in accordance with the forms of English law, relied instead upon this alternative. Positively to argue this on the basis of analogy, comparison and suggestion alone, would be reprehensible. But the suspicion remains that the "last phase" of the law of Wales may, if obscure, have been more protracted than can now effectively be proved: at least in the sense of the persistence of important and coherent local variants, if not in that of an integrated *corpus* of legal doctrine.

---

(1) For information on this point I am indebted to Mr. Brian Simpson.
(2) J. P. Dawson, *A History of Lay Judges*, p.165.
(3) The "Llwyn Gwyn" case discussed by Professor Jones Pierce (*op.cit.*, pp.7-32).
(4) H. Owen (ed.), "The Diary of Bulkeley of Dronwy, 1630-1636", *Transactions of the Anglesey Antiquarian Society* (1937), pp. 52, 57, 59, 64, 70, etc..

CHAPTER FIVE

Religion and Society

1. CHURCH

The laodicean attitude of local government officials towards their general duties in this region may have effectively concealed some reluctance on the part of the local people to abandon the Roman faith at the behest of the central government. Recently, Mr. J. M. Cleary has argued that there was a significant degree of "Catholic resistance in Wales";[1] evidence discussed by Mr. Emyr Gwynne Jones to some extent supports this view.[2] Tenable though it may be for some parts of Wales, especially Flintshire and the eastern regions, neither historian has found much confirmation for it in the south-west. Mr. Jones recognises a lack of evidence for Cardiganshire—and, for that matter, county Brecknock—in the sixteenth century, though he finds it hard to believe that Catholicism was dead there.[3] Mr. Cleary, in his list of the students from the Welsh dioceses and Hereford at the continental seminaries between 1568 and 1603, notes a total of about one hundred, but only five from St. David's;[4] moreover, his arguments concerning the Barlow family are not uniformly convincing.[5]

But at the time of the Henrician Reformation, William Barlow,

---

(1) J. M. Cleary, "The Catholic Resistance in Wales, 1568-1678", *Blackfriars*, vol. xxxviii (1957), pp.111-125; "The Catholic Recusancy of the Barlow Family of Slebech in Pembrokeshire", *The Newman Association (Cardiff Circle), Paper i* (1956); "A Checklist of Welsh Students at the Seminaries", *ibid., Paper ii* (1958).
(2) E. G. Jones, *Cymru a'r Hen Ffydd, passim*.
(3) *Ibid.*, p.37.
(4) Cleary, *op. cit.*, pp.15-23. The five named are Lewis Barlow of Slebech, Erasmus Saunders of Tenby, Morgan Thomas, William Watts and Charles Floyd. *Vide* also a reference to one seventeenth-century *alumnus* of the grammar school at Carmarthen who "went overseas to become a priest" (A. C. F. Beales, *Education under Penalty*, p.265).
(5) Cleary, *op. cit.* Of William Barlow he is critical because he married a young nun (p.7). His opinion that John Barlow was "the only considerable recusant among the Pembrokeshire gentry" (p.10) is based largely upon John Birt's questionable evidence (*vide supra*, p.117).His similar view of George Barlow derives from Sir James Perrot's report (*vide infra*. p.192), and, more convincingly, from Barlow's own manuscript (Cardiff Free Library MS. 497), which he dedicated to his grandson "in unity of the Catholic church with your outwardly inclination thereunto, wherein I am much joyed, for *extra ecclesia non est salus*". Some sympathy towards Rome, rather than positive activity, is proved on the part of the Barlows.

Bishop of St. David's, faced with accusations of his having em-
bezzled church goods, accounted for these in terms of his neighbours' dislike of his "continual preaching and setting forth the King's
articles to the reproach of superstition and idolatry, which, with
blasphemy and delusion of the King's subjects, have been here
shamefully supported".[1] He drew attention to the persistent use of
images in his diocese, in particular a taper at Haverfordwest and
another at Cardigan, and the continued celebration of such feasts as
St. David's Day and Innocents' Day in the Romish manner, with
the preaching of an "ungodly disguised sermon". He had done his
best to prevent the worshipping of a "piece of old rotten timber",[2]
and hoped that the people would soon be rescued from "Popish
delusions, and erudition be planted even in Wales".[3] In bringing
this pious wish to pass he appears to have had the active support of
his brothers John and Thomas, dean and prebendary of Westbury
respectively, and Roger, who, together with Sir Thomas Jones of
Abermarlais, made some attempt to incriminate George Constantine
for heresy.[4] Behind the ink-cloud of these endeavours, the brothers
were able to secure for themselves much ecclesiastical property and
the goodwill of the Devereux family, whose acquisition of the manor
of Lamphey was made possible by its alienation by Barlow:[5] an
alliance of families which marked the instability of those Romish
tendencies previously suspected in the Devereux,[6] and which
contributed in no small measure to the confusion of the next bishop,
Ferrar.

When the mayor and corporation of New Carmarthen took the
cleric, Nicholas Byford, to court for persisting in saying mass and
observing holy days,[7] a measure of sincerity may be allowed both
sides. But so ingenuous an attitude was rare in this diocese. The same
cathedral chapter that was accused of misappropriating a sum of
ninety pounds intended for the repair of the fabric of the cathedral,[8]

---

(1) *L.P.H.VIII*, vol. xii, pt. i (1537), no. 830.
(2) *Ibid.*, vol. xiii, pt. i (1538), no. 634.
(3) *Ibid.*, vol. xiii, pt. ii (1538), no. 111.
(4) *Ibid.*, vol. xiv, pt. ii (1539), no. 400; *Archaeologia*, vol. xxiii, p.56.
(5) *L.P.H.VIII*, vol. xxi, pt. ii (1546-1547), no. 332(86). *Vide supra*, p.113, and *infra*,
p.176, note 1. Lamphey was one of the diocese's richest possessions.
(6) Lord Ferrers's son was in 1546 examined before the Privy Council "of creeping
to the Cross. Holy water, and namely of a new sort of *Confiteor*", and Sir John
Olde, his chaplain, of being "a man of a light disposition concerning matters of
religion" (*A.P.C.* (1542-1547), pp.401, 479).
(7) P.R.O. C1/1094/28.
(8) P.R.O. C1/1071/55-58.

met the efforts of Robert Ferrar to re-organise the diocese with outright antagonism. Their leaders were Thomas Young, the precentor, and Rowland Meyrick, father of the second Earl of Essex's household steward. Their allies were the Devereux and the Barlows, whom Ferrar had estranged in turn, the latter by challenging their claims to the farm of the prebend of Brawdy and the lease of Monkton and by accusing them of with-holding tithes that ought to have come to the Bishop from Carew, and the former by seeking to recover Lamphey;[1] and other gentlemen, notably Griffith Dwnn, town clerk of Carmarthen, and Thomas John Thomas ap Harry, whose motives are less clear.[2] After many squabbles, Ferrar was charged by his chapter in fifty-six articles on five main counts: abuse of authority, maintenance of superstition, covetousness, wilful negligence and folly.[3] The Bishop was imprisoned and remained in custody until his martyrdom in Mary's reign. His chief accuser, Meyrick, proceeded to the office of a commissioner and the see of Bangor; and his leading lay opponents remained dubious in their spiritual leanings[4] and, for the moment, prosperous in their temporal affairs. Already the mood was emerging that drew from Bishop Richard Davies the comment, "There is so much greed in the world today for land and property, gold and silver and wealth, that rarely is there found one with his mind on God and his promises".[5]

It seems an appropriate comment. Few gentlemen from southwest Wales were indicted under Mary or in the first years of Elizabeth's reign on religious grounds. John Vaughan of Carmarthen was pardoned in 1554 and again in 1559; Sir Thomas Jones of Abermarlais, who had offended in 1553, also appears to have experienced too hasty a conversion, for his son Henry required a similar pardon in 1559. Half a dozen gentlemen from Carmarthenshire and Pembrokeshire figure in the company of Rowland

---

(1) Glanmor Williams, "The Protestant Experiment in the Diocese of St. David's", pt. ii, *B.B.C.S.*, vol. xvi (1954), p.41.
(2) H.M.C. *Cal. Salis. MSS.*, vol. xiii, p.32. Professor Williams (*op. cit.*, p.42, citing B.M. Harleian 420) describes Dwnn as mayor of the town.
(3) John Foxe, *Acts and Monuments*, vol. vii, pp.4-9; *vide* Williams, *loc. cit.*
(4) For example, Valentine Thomas's comment on the second Earl of Essex: "The Earl of Essex is a Catholic and . . . it is good policy for him to conceal his religion so that both Puritans and Protestants might be drawn to take his part" (P.R.O. S.P.12/278/64). In March 1590 "a newsletter reported that the puritans 'hoped well' of Essex" (P. Collinson, *The Elizabethan Puritan Movement*, p.444).
(5) Translated, from the foreword to William Salesbury's *Testament Newydd* (1567) as quoted in B. B. Thomas, *Braslun o Hanes Economaidd Cymru*, p.66.

Meyrick in this connection under Mary;[1] when her sister succeeded to the throne, twenty from the three shires sought and were
granted pardon.[2] Their offence cannot have been great, and they
appeared anxious to conform. By 1570 Richard Davies could report
that there was not "any person of any manner of degree within my
diocese within contempt of religion now established in the realm or
obstinately refuseth the Church's common prayers or receiving of the
sacraments at usual times", though he added, "I perceive a great
number to be slow and cold in the service of God; some careless of
any religion; and some that wish the Romish religion again".[3] But
if the duty of defeating apathy with inspiration devolves primarily
upon a community's spiritual leaders, here their example was dulled
by venality. Despite Bishop Davies's prestige as a scholar, the reality
of several of his suspected misdemeanours is unmistakeable.[4] His
comments on the condition of his diocese often suggest both
genuine frustration and an uneasy conscience, which, combined with
the opposition of his colleagues and the greater readiness of the
gentry to imitate his faults than to co-operate in his reforms, goaded
him to belabour them with words. In his report of 1570[5] he noted
the reluctance of sheriffs to arrest wrongdoers and their willingness
to allow others to purchase pardons. He deduced that "of this
default of sheriffs and abuse of the writ *de excommunicato capiendo*
cometh it also to pass that some priests in the diocese have remained
a whole twelvemonth together incorrigible, some in fornication and
some, against all injunctions to the contrary, taking upon them to
serve three, four, yea even five, cures, but never one aright; being
supported by gentlemen, farmers of the said churches and cures,
who do procure the favour of the sheriff, so as they neither regard

---

(1) *C.P.R.* (Mary), vol. i (1553-1554), pp. 410-468; vol. ii (1554-1555), p. 357. As
well as Jones and Vaughan there were John Bowen of Trefloyn, Griffith Higgon
of Carmarthen, David Vaughan of Kidwelly and Rhydderch David ap Rice of
Llanwrda.
(2) They included such prominent men as Sir John Perrot, who, though the recipient
of several grants under letters patent at this time, refused to serve on a commission
for purging heretics (*cf.* his alleged anti-Catholic attitude *supra*, p.97, note 6);
William Owen of Cemais; Walter Vaughan of Penbre; Thomas Phaer of
Cilgerran; Rhydderch Gwyn of Llanfair-ar-y-bryn; John Lloyd of Cilgwyn;
Sir John Vaughan of Whitland; *etc.* (*ibid.* (Elizabeth), vol. i, pp.149-246).
(3) P.R.O. S.P.12/66/26.
(4) Glanmor Williams, *Bywyd ac Amserau'r Esgob Richard Davies*, pp.54-55.
Amongst other things, he had given church livings and offices to his sons long
before they were sufficiently advanced either in years or in learning to take charge
of them.
(5) P.R.O. S.P.12/66/26(i).

any interdiction nor can be brought to observe any good order".

He enlarged upon this theme upon the occasion of the funeral of Walter, Earl of Essex, at Carmarthen in 1576. He criticised those set in authority in general, and locally so in particular; "Where they were put in trust and made officers in the commonwealth they have not judged rightly, meaning between party and party, but dealt partially and corruptly against law and conscience . . . They never think of any reckoning to be made how they behaved themselves in authority . . . but contrarily and unreasonably walk after the pleasures and riches of this world, apply all their powers to further and continue the kingdom of Antichrist, defend papistry and idolatry, pilgrimages to wells and blind chapels . . . Here would I wish that the justices of the peace with us in Wales should receive admonition and learning . . . They have altogether applied their authority and office to pyll and poll the country and to beggar their poor neighbours; to perform that which Isaiah the prophet says, 'You dress your houses with the goods of the poor'. How think you what it is to commit authority to such men? Is it any better than to commit a sword to a madman's hand? Would to God the manners and conditions of all justices of the peace and sheriffs in Wales were as well-known to her Highness's Council as they be in the country amongst their neighbours".[1]

It was to this malevolence on the part of local officials, coupled with the failure of lay farmers of benefices to see that adequate maintenance was allowed incumbents and proper attention paid to the church buildings within their charge, that Davies attributed the ruinous state of many churches and the parlous spiritual condition of their parishioners, ministered unto as they were by "a priest that shall come thither galloping from another parish, which for such pains shall have 40s. a year, 4 marks, or £4 at the best". Only direct intervention by the Privy Council could, in his view, remedy matters.[2] But Marmaduke Middleton, Davies's successor at St. David's, indicated a culprit nearer home. His report of 1583[3] began by echoing his predecessor's opinion, indicating little popery but considerable "atheism", a disturbing lack of qualified preachers, and

(1) Richard Davies, *A Funeral Sermon, etc.* (1577), no pag.
(2) P.R.O. S.P.12/66/26(i). The Council persisted with its accustomed expedients: it continued to address to men like Sir John Perrot and Sir Henry Jones its instructions to lend assistance to the Bishop in eradicating clerical misdemeanours (*A.P.C.* (1581-1582), p.142.)
(3) P.R.O. S.P.12/162/29.

with the people much given to vicious living. He continued by suggesting that Davies had been in a far better position to carry out reforms than was he, the former being "not only Bishop, Counsellor[1] and of the peace, but held in his own hands the Chancellorship, having *in commendam* two parsonages, one prebend and a vicarage, and (as his brother-in-law doth affirm) yet he never gave any living within his own gift nor admitted any to any other man's gift without consideration; alleging he could not otherwise have lived". The greater part of this, Middleton's first report, was taken up with expostulations as to his own poverty and pleas for relief. In his report on the state of the diocese, however, made in the same year and shortly after his appointment,[2] he described matters in greater detail. Poverty again furnished the main theme of his discussion; because of it "the poor clergy are kept continually in beggarly estate" and "religion condemned through the baseness of the clergy". For this there were three explanations, according to the nature of separate advowsons. In cases of "rectories and vicarages in the gift of lay patrons [they] are (most of them) either bought with great sums of money, to the utter undoing of the incumbent, or leased, to the patron or some of his men, the incumbent constrained to serve another cure". With this, Davies would doubtless have agreed. With "the rectories and vicarages in her Majesty's gift" the clergy themselves appear to have been held at least partly to blame, for "simony hath been so common a custom with them that they are neither afraid nor yet ashamed to make public bargains thereof". Thirdly, there were the "rectories and vicarages in the late Bishop's gift [which] are in the same estate, the best of them possessed with unlearned men and leased and advowsoned to such as were about the late Bishop and his friends, and the incumbent of that which is worth *per annum* £30 glad to take £6 13s. 4d., and some less". Middleton, indeed, held his predecessor responsible for much of the evil which he saw in his diocese, sparing him neither direct allegation nor innuendo.[3]

Verbal attacks unsupported by detailed evidence would carry little weight, especially in view of Davies's distinction and Middleton's later discomfiture. But the latter appended to his report an unusally detailed schedule, itemising benefices in the diocese with their

---

(1) *I.e.*, of the Council in the Marches, of which all the Welsh bishops were members *ex officio*—including, presumably, Middleton himself.
(2) P.R.O. S.P.12/165/1.
(3) For instance, "the people . . . already condemn me for my uprightness, wherewith they have not been heretofore acquainted" (P.R.O. S.P.12/162/29).

patrons, their annual values, their incumbents and whether or not these last were resident, together with their qualifications in education and in preaching ability. It appears from this that if the clergy of the diocese were inadequate, the fault lay as much with the former Bishop as with lay farmers of livings. Middleton listed a total of 298 benefices with their patrons.[1] These patrons may be classified in six groups: the Bishop himself; the Church, meaning such bodies as the cathedral chapter and individual clerics; the Crown; lay noblemen, such as the Earl of Essex, and outside bodies, such as All Souls College, Oxford; the parishioners of single parishes; and local gentlemen. The number of benefices attributed to each of these groups of patrons was, respectively: 91; 49; 76; 24; 4; 54. In other words, the Bishop was himself responsible for a considerably greater number of benefices than was any other single group. Clerical authorities were collectively responsible for nearly one half of the total number of benefices.

In the matter of residence or non-residence of incumbents, Middleton's schedule produces the following results. Of the Bishop's 91 benefices, 67 had resident incumbents; the Church had 18 out of 49; the Crown, 41 out of 76; external laymen and groups, 14 out of 24; parishioners, 4 out of 4; and local gentry, 29 out of 54. Percentage readings for these figures show 75%, 37%, 54%, 58%, 100% and 54% resident respectively. One quarter of the Bishop's benefices were therefore without a resident incumbent. But perhaps more revealing than this simple proportion is the fact that local gentlemen were responsible for only 25 benefices which lacked a resident incumbent: one more than the Bishop himself, or 8.4% of the total.[2]

One more calculation sheds further light on the conscientiousness of different patrons. Middleton classified the various incumbents into six types: those who were both graduates and "preachers"; those who preached but were not graduates; those who were graduates but did not preach; those who were neither, but had, presumably, some qualities distinguishing them from the last two groups, namely those who were "simply" learned, and those who

---

(1) This total includes only those benefices listed as having a patron, and excludes separate cures stated to be attached to such benefices.
(2) Middleton's schedule, the basis of these calculations, may not generally include benefices lacking both a known patron and an incumbent, though one or two such are included; nor have there here been included the 142 rectories, vicarages and chapels served by 85 curates separately listed by Middleton, apart from this schedule of patrons.

were "meanly" so. The different groups of patrons had presented
to livings the following representatives of each type:[1]

QUALIFI-CATION	BISHOP	CHURCH	CROWN	EXTERNALS	PARISH	LOCAL GENTRY
G-P	1	1	4	2[2]		1
N-G P		2				
N-P G	6	3	4	2	1	5
N-G N-P	1	2				
"Simply"	10	5	12	3	1	8
Totals	18	13	20	7	2	14

Local gentry had thus presented only one graduate fewer than had the
Bishop, and only four fewer of men who were at all qualified for
livings, the Crown having performed better than the Bishop on
both counts.

These calculations do not correspond with Middleton's own
statement of forty graduates resident in his diocese including fourteen preachers: a consideration which may shed some doubt on the
accuracy of his recital.[3] Even so, the diocese was evidently sadly
lacking in capable clergymen.[4] It seems, on the available evidence,
that the responsibility for this lay as much with the spiritual leaders
of the community as with its leading lay members. For all his heat
against Davies, Middleton's own conduct, though he advocated and
appears to have tried to carry out some reforms, provoked the
advancing of "many articles of foul and bad behaviour" against
him;[5] and he ultimately responded to these with a violent outburst,
addressed directly to the Queen, against many individuals, including

(1) In the "Qualifications" column the symbols represent the initial letters for the
    classes of incumbents itemised above, with "G" indicating "Graduate", "P"
    "Preacher", "N" "Non" and "Simply" "Simply learned". Totals are of all those
    rated better than "meanly learned", Middleton's largest single category.
(2) Both by the Earl of Essex.
(3) Middleton's account differs, too, on several points of detail from that of Davies.
    The latter, for instance, closed his 1570 report with a list of "cursal prebends",
    of which he says, "Some of them are worth 26s. 8d. a year, some 40s., the best
    53s. 4d.". All such prebends noted by Middleton are assessed by him at £4 a year,
    which he later suggests may be an overestimate. *Vide* also *infra*, p.183.
(4) In contrast, the *Liber Cleri* for 1585 showed for the diocese of Lincoln 399
    graduates out of 1285 clergy. Of preachers in 1592/3 other dioceses showed:
    Gloucester 84, against 169 non-preachers; Chester 172, against 213; Ely 79,
    against 38; York 207, against 372 (A. Tindal Hart, *The Country Clergy, 1558-1660*,
    pp.26, 30).
(5) P.R.O. S.P.12/230/78; /190/40; *A.P.C.* (1586-1587), p.250; (1589-1590), p.379.

several local gentlemen, who, he said, hated him for his opposition
to their avaricious and traitorous proceedings. Chief amongst them
was Alban Stepney, whose hopes of being Registrar and Receiver
of St. David's had been nullified by Middleton; and Sir John Perrot,
who "divers times solicited the Bishop for all his temporalities in
exchange, or at least for the stewardship of the lands, which he sought
for to have command of a great number of men". These two, related by marriage[1] and foiled in their ambitions, had, said
Middleton, headed a body of men "evil-affected in religion",
drunkards, rioters and pluralist priests, to concoct these "odious and
scandalous libels" against him.[2] Likewise accused were Sir Thomas
Perrot and John Morgan Wolfe of Whitland. Middleton was
eventually deprived. Whilst his allegations need not be accepted at
their face value, it remains true that an irresponsible bishop with
some reforming ideas blamed the irresponsibility of the gentry for
his failures. The gentry, on the other hand, blamed him. That lay
impropriation[3] was a significant factor affecting the ability of the
Church to perform its task is not in dispute.[4] But as important a
consideration was the general poverty, both material and spiritual,
of the diocese, and particularly of those who had official charge of its
affairs.[5]

In 1596 in Pembrokeshire, according to a report transcribed by
George Owen's unflagging pen,[6] of 95 rectories and vicarages
listed with their patrons 47 were in the Crown's gift, 28 in gentlemen's gift, and only eleven in the Bishop's gift, the remaining nine
having as patrons "other spiritual men". Seven benefices are here
noted which were omitted by Middleton in 1583, six of these being

(1) Middleton's explanation of an alleged partnership between Stepney and Perrot
in terms of their connection through marriage is inconsistent with their known
antipathy towards each other on other occasions, and with the fact of Stepney's
marriages in turn to the daughters of Thomas Catharne of Prendergast and William
Phillips of Picton, two declared opponents of Perrot. Here faction seems again
to have governed kinship.
(2) H.M.C. Cal. Salis. MSS., vol. iv, pp.279-281. The recital includes an account of
an attempted murder of the Bishop in his cathedral in curiously familiar circumstances.
(3) I have used this term broadly, to indicate all lay control over ecclesiastical
patronage and profits.
(4) For the struggle over the alleged collegiate church of Llanddewi Brefi and its
implications, vide Glanmor Williams, "Richard Davies, Bishop of St. David's,
1561-1581", T.H.C.S. (1948), p.163.
(5) In 1592 the Bishop of St. David's was fined one thousand marks and imprisoned
during the Queen's pleasure, for forging the will of Sir James Whitney (B.M.
Harleian 2143, f.41b).
(6) George Owen, The Taylors Cussion, pt. i, pp.103-106.

in the Crown's gift. Considered according to the categories, and in comparison with the conclusions, drawn from the 1583 report, the patronage of thirteen benefices may be said to have changed hands from one group to another. Of these, the Bishop had lost six: three to the Cathedral canons and three to the Crown. The Crown had gained seven and lost two. Five of the livings allocated by Middleton to lay gentlemen had changed hands within that group which, collectively, had made no gains. This report may suggest that Middleton's schedule had been carelessly compiled, though only in some of its details. Otherwise, it may be tentatively inferred from it that the Bishop may, in Pembrokeshire, have been patron to fewer livings than elsewhere in his diocese; that the direct influence of the Crown as patron was growing; and that what the Bishops construed as poverty may have been prompting them to surrender patronage, presumably for a price. At all events, Owen's report contains no further information as to the residence or non-residence of those presented by these patrons.

An inquisition on church lands, impropriations, preaching and related subjects in Pembrokeshire, taken in 1650,[1] reveals that out of 76 livings in the gift of laymen, 27 had preaching ministers who were approved by the commissioners. In 34 more, the ministers had been ejected and the profits sequestered, though for what cause was not specified. Only in fifteen was it stated that there was no minister, in some of these the reason being the recent death of the incumbent. Of livings formerly in the royal gift, sixteen were recognised as having preaching ministers and in another eight the minister had been ejected; in none was it stated that there had been no cleric at all. Two more livings had preaching ministers, the right of presentation being unspecified; and in four more with unspecified patrons, vacancies had arisen through the deaths of late incumbents. Where the gift remained in Church hands there was no great improvement upon the standards of the laity in this respect, at least from the commissioners' point of view. In Carew, St. David's and Whitchurch, Mathry, Lamphey and Warren[2] the ministers presented by the Bishop or by other ecclesiastics of the diocese were all ejected and the profits sequestered. In Slebech, where the living had been bestowed by Parliament on Colonel Horton's brigade "as

(1) Lambeth MS., 915.
(2) *Ibid.*, ff.117, 119, 123, 134, 141.

part of John Barlow's estate", there was still "no minister there".[1]
And although in such parishes as Bayvil, Nantgwyn, Newcastle
Emlyn and Mynachlog-ddu[2] the profits exceeded the stipends
allowed the ministers, the fact remains that, with gentlemen presenting, there were ministers there; the greatest difference between
profits and stipend was at Manorbier, in the gift of Christ's
College, Cambridge.[3]

It cannot be questioned that lay impropriation, with the clergy
too often getting "leavings, not livings",[4] was detrimental to the
welfare, the dignity and the effectiveness of the Church. In 1610 the
vicar of Tenby sued the farmers of his rectory for failing to pay him
his stipend of twenty marks a year, the defendants answering that
although an earlier incumbent had been entitled to an annual five
shillings out of the profits, this arrangement had lapsed and the present
vicar had no valid claim.[5] The vicar of Llanbadarn Fawr, a rectory
demised by Sir Henry Jones to his stepfather as a placatory gesture,[6]
protested that for three years he had received neither his stipend nor
the forty or fifty pounds which had been his share of the annual
issues.[7] From his indignation on both counts it is difficult to
tell whether Richard Evetts was more disturbed by the archdeacon
of St. David's failure to provide a curate for the chapel at Llanfihangel or by his reluctance to pay the farmer the subsidies and tithes
accruing therefrom and from Mydrim in Carmarthenshire.[8] John
North alleged that Anthony Rudd, Bishop of St. David's, had prevented and impeded North's nominee to the living of Llandysul,
for which interference the plaintiff felt entitled to damages of fifteen
pounds.[9] But the gentry as ecclesiastical patrons were not entirely
lacking in conscience. Thomas Price of Gogerddan appears to have
endeavoured in face of considerable opposition to ensure that

---

(1) *Ibid.*, f.175.
(2) *Ibid.*, ff.156, 159, 166, 169.
(3) *Ibid.*, f.144.
(4) C. Hill, *Economic Problems of the Church*, p.212.
(5) P.R.O. E112/151/35.
(6) T. Jones Pierce (ed.), *Clenennau Letters*, nos. 49, 50, 52, 55, 207-212, 214, 218,
    219, 221, 223, 229, 449, *et al. Vide supra*, p.30.
(7) P.R.O. E112/145/62.
(8) P.R.O. E112/59/48. Evetts, whose first name is variously given as "Richard"
    and "Thomas Nicholas", pleaded against the archdeacon's wrongful distraint
    in payment of tithes, and was compensated with the prebend of Llanddarog: an
    indication that in some judicial quarters lay impropriation could be deemed a
    fitting remedy for clerical absenteeism and misdemeanour (P.R.O. E123/26/
    323-323b).
(9) N.L.W. Wales 18/51.

services were held at Llansilin.[1] In 1637 Henry Vaughan of Cilcennin negotiated a lease of the rectory of Lledrod with a clause that the lessee should provide a literate man to perform divine service in the parish church every Sunday.[2] In 1641 his Carmarthenshire namesake made payments, *inter alia*, "to Sir Rees Lloyd, vicar of Llanelli, for his stipend for one year last past, £6 13s. 4d.; to the curate of Llannon and Llangennech, £6 13s. 4d.; to the curate of Penbre, £10"; and, significantly, "to the preachers, £10".[3] Sir John Perrot was at least anxious that the chancel and parsonage which he held at Robeston should be kept in good repair.[4] Thomas Price justified his refusal to pay the archdeacon of Cardigan his dues by arguing that these were intended to meet that dignitary's expenses on his annual visits to every parish, and as no such visits had been made for sixteen years there was no reason why he should be paid.[5] The intrusion of local laymen into ecclesiastical administration was no more responsible for the shortcomings of the religious life of this region than were the deficiencies of the clergy themselves, from the episcopate downwards.

If Bishops Davies and Middleton were self-exculpatory in their attitude towards the spiritual condition of their diocese, they were also somewhat premature in discounting recusancy therein.[6] In *circa* 1570 a list compiled by a supporter of Mary Stuart indicated many influential persons in England and Wales believed to be not only unwilling to conform with the established Church but prepared, on religious grounds, to act in the interests of the Queen of Scots.[7] Amongst the names of 37 knights described as "Catholics" from various English and Welsh shires was Sir Henry Jones of Carmarthenshire. Gentlemen described as "Catholics in Wales" numbered 68, together with five from Shropshire and 56 from Herefordshire grouped with them. In contrast with the distribution exhibited in the Exchequer Recusant Rolls,[8] the greatest concentration lay in the western shires of Wales: for north Wales Anglesey, Caernarvon-

(1) P.R.O. St. Ch. 5/P6/24.
(2) N.L.W. Crosswood 1.263.
(3) C.R.O. Cawdor, Box 1, no. 16.
(4) P.R.O. E210/D.9651.
(5) P.R.O. E112/151/40.
(6) Davies had again in 1577 certified that there were no recusants there (P.R.O. S.P.12/118/11(i)).
(7) *Catholic Record Society*, vol. xiii, pp.86-142.
(8) *Cf. infra*, p.190, note 2.

shire and Merioneth furnished 34 names, whereas only 14 were
ascribed to Denbighshire, Flintshire and Montgomeryshire. South
Wales yielded twenty names, some of doubtful identification, including three from Pembrokeshire and four from Carmarthenshire.
Those listed for Pembrokeshire were Thomas Catharne of Prendergast, William Phillips of Picton and George Wyrriott of Orielton;
for Carmarthenshire, Thomas and Richard Jones, sons of Sir Henry
of Abermarlais, Griffith Rice of Newton and James Vaughan of
Llangadog. The list's author was clearly optimistic in his estimate.
"Catholics" named therein are more numerous, and "heretics"
fewer, than other evidence warrants; moreover, there are generally
many inaccuracies in the association of names with counties. Another
list of 1582, listing sympathisers from amongst the peers and knights,
is much briefer and includes from Wales only Sir William
Herbert of Powys Castle. Even so, the Bishops' determinedly
negative reports seem, in the light of this and of other evidence, a
trifle sanguine.

In 1586 Rees Lewis expressed his disquiet that David William
Delahay, a gentleman of Llanegwad, who had not received communion for four years and whom he suspected of papist sympathies,
was likely to be made sheriff of Carmarthenshire owing to his
friendship with Griffith Vaughan of Trimsaran.[1] Five years later
rumour and the depositions of several witnesses tended to confirm
his misgivings. Delahay was reported to have been at some pains
secretly to contrive his son's christening according to Roman
Catholic rites. The child's nurse, by this account,[2] had travelled
on foot for two days with two companions to an outlandish church
in Glamorgan; delivered the baby to two others, themselves not
being permitted to enter the church; stood beneath the chancel
window "and heard a priest say service, but whether in Latin or in
English this deponent could not tell, but she is very sure it was not
in Welsh"; spent the night at "a gentleman's house", dined the next
day at the house of Philip Craddock, and slept that night at Morgan
Lloyd's house in Llandeilo Fawr. This incident gave rise to an inquiry
conducted by Edward Dounlee and Philip Williams, justices of the
peace, into recusancy. It transpired that the baptism had been conducted by Morgan Clynnog, a notorious recusant priest, who, with

---

(1) B.M. Harleian 6994, f.40.
(2) *Ibid.*, 6998, f.3: deposition of Gwenllian Evan of Llandovery.

another cleric also named Philip Williams,[1] had said several masses at the house of Jane Lloyd in Llandeilo, at Delahay's house in Llanegwad and at Thomas Bowen's house in Kidwelly. Bowen, who had some pretensions to gentility, denied this, as did his wife Sage, though she admitted her non-attendance at church. The other witnesses, for the most part poor country people, generally admitted their guilt, gave depositions similar in kind and differing only in detail, and were occasionally, like the witness John Williams, "heartily sorry for that which he did against the law and showeth it upon his knees with tears". Apart from Delahay and Jane Lloyd's son, David Williams, who denied all charges, the complicity of gentry[2] was not proved by this inquiry. Those who gave evidence knew nothing of the priests' background and, beyond the fact that masses had been said, could disclose little of importance to the investigators. They, accordingly, blamed all upon Hugh Lloyd of Llangendeirne, against whom other criminal charges were already pending.[3]

There is some suggestion here of deeper waters in which bigger fish may have hidden behind little ones with that success with which society's law belies nature's. There is no proof of this in the depositions. Thomas Bowen and his wife and Hugh Lloyd were all pardoned in 1594.[4] It was left to Griffith Gwilym and Rice Morgan of Llandeilo to bring an action against Morgan Jones, alleging that his previous conviction for recusancy at Carmarthen Great Sessions had done little to reform him.[5] The government was suspicious regarding this region. The Earl of Pembroke, President of the Council in the Marches, wrote to the Queen in 1593 that the inhabitants in the shires adjoining Milford Haven "are in religion generally ill-affected, as may appear by their use of popish pilgrimages, their harbouring of mass priests, their retaining of superstitious ceremonies and the increase of recusants".[6] The Privy Council shared his opinion, for it had already instructed fourteen local men "of whose

---

(1) Who had been named by Middleton in his allegations (*vide supra*, p.182). It seems likely that his gentle namesake may be identified with the associate of Perrot and of Essex (*vide supra*, p.117), in which case neither position of influence nor dubious activity on his part would be surprising. Dounlee, on the other hand, was known to hold anti-Catholic views (*vide supra*, p.97).
(2) There was no mention, for instance, of Morgan Jones, suspected by Sir John Vaughan of leading activity in the Llandeilo region (*vide supra*, p.133, note 8).
(3) B.M. Harleian 6998, ff.5-6, 8-13, 15, 16.
(4) P.R.O. S.P.12/248/48(iii).
(5) P.R.O. St. Ch. 5/G45/3.
(6) H.M.C. *Cal. Salis. MSS.*, vol.xiii, p.478.

soundness in religion, care and discretion we have good opinion" to examine the report "that there are divers sorts of people ... that do use to repair as well in the night season as other times of the day unto certain places where in times past there have been pilgrimages, images or offerings, continuing these superstitious uses in such sort as sometimes they assemble together in great numbers both of men and women, a thing intolerable to be permitted after so long time preaching of the gospel".[1] For all this, people accused outright remained either humble or slightly ludicrous, like Hugh David who had combined a lucrative trade in furtively saying masses for the souls of the dead with views openly aired upon the doubtful legitimacy of the birth of King Henry VII and the folly of entrusting the government of the kingdom to a woman:[2] thus exhibiting a quaint mixture of theological influences. Generally it required factors other than unorthodoxy in religion to provoke the leaders of this introspective society to play the judas on their neighbours.

Where strangers were involved reticence sometimes yielded. Cecil's letters of 1603 to Sir Thomas Jones, Sir James Perrot and Alban Stepney, to procure the arrests of a Harris, a Lloyd and a Vaughan, drew from them allegations against Thomas Hale who, born in Walthamstow, came to Carmarthenshire via Ireland, bought a house and land, and changed his name to Jerome Price to avoid detection.[3] The Bishop of St. David's expressed concern in 1611 that Robert Acton and his family had moved from England to settle in his diocese.[4] John Hayward's wife, Anna, was the occasion of discord in Haverfordwest and, nearly, of an international incident. Refusing to go to church, she claimed immunity as a "subject of the Archduke". The mayor and justices, ostensibly outraged by the presence of so blatant a recusant within their liberties, where, according to Sir James Perrot, "no recusant has been known since the Reformation", imprisoned her. This drew protests from the Spanish ambassador, and the local authorities were instructed to release her and molest her no further.[5] In the Exchequer Recusant Rolls the only Elizabethan representative of south-west Wales was Erasmus Saunders, who had arrived there from Norfolk by way of Brecknock, to own extensive properties in Carmarthenshire and Pem-

---

(1) *A.P.C.* (1591-1592), pp.544-545. (2) B.M. Harleian 6998, f.19.
(3) P.R.O. S.P.14/3/32. (4) P.R.O. S.P.14/67/1.
(5) *C.S.P.Dom.* (1619-1623), vol. cxix, nos. 15, 16; vol. cxxvii, no. 140; *A.P.C.*
(1619-1621), p.366; (1621-1623), p.305.

brokeshire and to marry Jennet Barret.[1]

Apart from these, recusant returns for this region take two forms. First, there were the returns made by local officials to the central authority; these include the Exchequer Recusant Rolls,[2] and the official returns of 1624[3] and 1625.[4] In 1607 four yeomen of Llandeilo Fawr were named in the Exchequer returns, together with two more of Llanddeusant, a weaver of Llanfihangel Aberbythych, the respective wives of a gentleman of Llandebie and another of Talley, and a spinster.[5] The 1624 return was more extensive. It included, from Llangathen parish in Carmarthenshire, Thomas David Williams, a gentleman said to be worth about five hundred pounds a year, and Jane, wife of Rees Williams, esquire, worth two hundred pounds a year; the wife of Rowland Lloyd of Llangendeirne, worth fifty pounds a year; two gentlemen of thirty pounds a year from Laugharne, with the wife of one of them; and three more, of uncertain estate, from Llanwinio; three gentlemen from Llanelli, one of whom was Robert Acton, the other two bearing English names; and from Llandeilo Fawr, Walter Lloyd, "gentleman, aged about forty years, and his wife for the like, whose estate is uncertain, who of long time hath been a noted recusant and a great seducer of the people". For Pembrokeshire, of the ten people named all but one were women, of whom two were stated to be married to gentlemen. In Cardiganshire "there is but one known papist . . . one Mr. Nicholas Lewis, who was born there and hath absented himself most commonly these two years". Except in the case of Walter Lloyd, all these were presented "for absenting themselves from their parish church contrary to the statute". Most were old and poor, many over sixty years of age, most well past forty; and women predominated. The 1625 return found 44 recusants in Carmarthenshire, of whom, apart from Robert Acton, three professed gentility and another six, gentle husbands. Pembrokeshire yielded fourteen, including one gentleman and his wife; and Cardiganshire now denied the existence of any. Again, widows, spinsters and occasional yeomen predominated.

In 1629 Katherine Vaughan of St. Issell's was fined £21 2s. 8d., and in 1637 further sums totalling £18 13s. 8d., for recusancy. On the former of these occasions Thomas Phillips of Llanwinio and Jane

---

(1) P.R.O. E377/1, 2, 4, 5, 8, 14, 15. *Vide* W. R. Trimble, *op. cit.*, p.212.
(2) P.R.O. E377/1-49.   (3) P.R.O. S.P.14/162/66.   (4) P.R.O. S.P.16/25/14.
(5) P.R.O. E377/15. The "gentlewomen's" fines were the same as the others'.

Williams of Llangathen, both included in the 1624 certificate, were again mentioned, the latter's fine being declared by 1631 to be recoverable from her husband.[1] In these there was some gentility of status and some persistence in the sin of omission, the more conspicuous in the context of 49 lists of recusants, 32 of which contained no entries at all for Wales, and in which Cardiganshire was never mentioned, Pembrokeshire only in connection with two individuals, and Carmarthenshire half a dozen times, thrice because Erasmus Saunders held property there and once more in order to clarify Jane Williams's position.[2] Certainly the Recusant Rolls, concerned only with those who owed fines for recusancy and not restricted to offenders of papist sympathies, cannot be considered an exhaustive index even to these; rather, "their bulk, or lack of it, may be an index to the intensity of official action against Catholics and separatists".[3] But if there was much recusant activity in this region the sheriffs, at least, were not anxious to disclose it.

Secondly, when, Mahomet-like, central authority came to this locality in the persons of its Justices of Assize, recusants were cited at the courts of Great Sessions. In Cardiganshire in 1595 Matilda, wife of Evan Griffith David of Llanfihangel Genau'r-glyn, was accused of "insulting behaviour in church"; and in 1600 John, Rice and Morgan Lloyd, all gentlemen of Llanbadarn Fawr, were cited for "illicit assemblies in church".[4] In Pembrokeshire, Stephen Barlow of Prendergast was in 1586 charged with "not coming to church";

(1) P.R.O. E377/36, 38, 44.
(2) The Pipe Series of Recusant Rolls (E377), better preserved and occasionally more complete than the apparent duplicates of the Chancellor's Series (E376), begin in 34 Elizabeth. For Wales the north-east shires provided the most frequent and the most copious entries. An examination of the first fifty rolls reveals entries in the following:

SHIRE	ROLL No. (E377/-)
Brecknock	14, 15, 18, 25, 29, 36, 38.
Carmarthen	2*, 5*, 8*, 15, 36, 38.
Caernarvon	2, 5, 8, 14, 15.
Denbigh	4, 8, 14, 15, 17, 18, 20, 21, 25, 29, 36, 38, 44.
Flint	1, 4, 5, 10, 14, 15, 17, 18, 21, 25, 29, 36, 44.
Glamorgan	1, 2, 5, 8, 14, 15, 21, 25, 36.
Montgomery	15, 21, 25.
Pembroke	1*, 2*, 4*, 5*, 8*, 15*, 36, 44.
Radnor	14.

Asterisks indicate entries relating exclusively to Erasmus Saunders. On one occasion (no. 8) Chester was included in the Roll with Wales.
(3) J. Anthony Williams, "Recusant Rolls", *History*, vol. 1 (1965), p.196.
(4) N.L.W. Wales 7/7.

and Richard Benson of Coedcanlas was described as a recusant in that and in the next year when he was joined by his sister. 1588 saw William Wediat of Jeffreston similarly described; and in 1595 Erasmus Saunders, together with two yeomen, was declared to have been "absent from church". In 1596 David Lloyd, gentleman, was said to have misbehaved in church; and seven years later John Barlow of Minwear, in company with two more yeomen, confessed to his absence therefrom:[1] as in 1603 did Owen Phillips of Narberth and David Morgan of Roch, both gentlemen, together with two spinsters. Rice Huet of Carew, John Lewis of Minwear, and the wife of Thomas Cole, with another widow, in 1605; Thomas Ffoomond of Molleston, with three husbandmen, in 1607: all these were described as recusants, those here named being gentlemen. Two yeomen and a spinster had misbehaved in church in 1609. But not until the 1620s did a significant number of recusants appear: fourteen in the spring of 1622, of whom three were gentlemen, and sixteen in the autumn, the previous year having produced another eight, none of these last being above yeoman status, though the 1622 spring Sessions had included the wives of the gentlemen Thomas Bowen of Trefloyn and Thomas Tooley of Arnoldshill.[2] In 1637 nineteen more were presented at the Great Sessions in Carmarthen. Amongst these were Walter Lloyd with his wife, and the wives of three other gentlemen, the remainder being yeomen, husbandmen or widows. Their offence was that of not having been to church for three months.[3]

All these may have been the flotsam on a dark tide of papist feeling. In themselves they amount to little more than a haphazard collection of unfortunates, representing some backsliders whose activities never prompted much reaction, either favourable or unfavourable; and many who were simply ignorant. There is a marked absence of the names of considerable gentry. Of course, men of influence in the locality, holding office, were scarcely likely to betray themselves; though the petition presented by the Commons to the King in 1626, listing "recusants, papists or justly suspected [persons] . . . in places of government and authority and trust" made fresh reference to "Rees Williams, a justice of the peace, his wife a convict recusant,

(1) N.L.W. Wales 7/9.
(2) N.L.W. Wales 7/10.
(3) *Trans. Carms. Antiq. Soc.*, vol. xi, p.36. The Calendar Rolls of the Carmarthen Great Sessions are not extant.

and his children popishly bred, as is informed", and also to "Morgan
Voyle, esquire, justice of the peace, his wife presented for not coming
to church, but whether she is a popish recusant is not known", and
to "John Warren, captain of the trained band, one of his sons suspected to be popishly affected".[1] But even Sir James Perrot, whose
integrity in this respect may be accepted,[2] could in 1627 report
little more than rumours and the vaguest of suspicions. He was
anxious to demonstrate that the vulnerability of Milford Haven "is
the more dangerous by dwelling or resorting of recusants and ill-
affected persons to those parts", but admitted that "for Pembrokeshire it hath not many recusants, and I know but of three widows
who are committed", adding, "but I suppose that divers do resort
unto them, and that they have intelligence with the recusants of
Monmouthshire". As for gentry, he could only indicate George
Barlow, emphasising that his father, uncle and brother were known
active Catholics, that he "himself when he lives in London doth
converse, diet and lodge" only in recusants' houses, that his servants[3] had been indicted for recusancy, and that he "faltered much"
when he took the oath of allegiance. Even he, however, was "not
an absolute recusant".[4] If Perrot could produce no more convincing material than this in support of his proposal that a watch be
kept on ports and bonds taken of shipmasters to carry no fleeing
recusants, it would be futile to inquire further. The Catholic resistance in south-west Wales was obscure if considerable, and in the
long term ineffective if tenacious.

Some of the foregoing evidence has a bearing upon opposition to
the established Church from another quarter. In 1551 Dafydd Llwyd
wrote to Griffith Dwnn:[5]

(1) J. Rushworth, *op. cit.*, pt. i, pp.393-400.
(2) As well as presenting his wife as a recusant he had in 1612 suggested to Salisbury
    that an *agent provocateur* sent to the border shires and to south Wales might
    produce results (*C.S.P.Dom.* (1611-1618), vol. lxviii, no. 75).
(3) Three of those named in 1624 were sisters from Slebech parish, tenants of
    Barlow's, all elderly and poor. In the official returns only minor branches of the
    Barlow family found any mention.
(4) P.R.O. S.P.16/88/23.
(5) D. J. Bowen (ed.), "Detholiad o Englynion Hiraeth am yr Hen Ffydd", *Efrydiau
    Catholig*, vol. vi (1954), p.5. An approximate translation reads:
        "I have a piece of the old religion
        One for this calls me a devil".
    It is, perhaps, noteworthy that Dwnn is addressed not for any papist sympathies
    of his but for his known patronage of poets and of learning:
        "Gruffydd, gawr dedwydd, gwr doeth—a graddawl,
        Perchen dysg a chyfoeth".

"Darn o'r hen ffydd sydd genni
Diawl un am hyn a fynn fi".

The author of *The Practice of Piety* and that work's popular versifier were both Carmarthenshire men.[1] If the old religion failed to inspire outspoken loyalty, Puritan attitudes, in whatever form, might have been expressed more energetically. If this was so, the court of High Commission failed to notice it.[2] Of the 74 Welshmen called before it, as recorded in the surviving Act Books,[3] fifteen came from the south-west, and half a dozen of these were gentry. Richard Parry of Llanfallteg allegedly disrupted a communion service by exclaiming, between the taking of the bread and the wine, "Some devil is in my knee"; further, having expressed the hope that the archdeacon of Carmarthen would be hanged, he promised that in the unlikely event of his becoming King there should be no more bishops in the land, and informed his rector, "I am a better preacher than thou, and I care not a straw for thee", thereby earning himself a heavy fine, which was later reduced.[4] However undignified this performance, it suggests some features, of anti-episcopalianism and concern for preaching, associated with Puritanism.[5] But others of this company may be otherwise accounted for. It seems possible that the charges against Sir James Price of Ynysmaengwyn, son of John Price of Gogerddan, arose as much from the antagonism of James Lewis[6] as from the grievous sins of the flesh which, with gleeful insinuations of divine retribution, have been laid at his door;[7] and that Henry Lort of Stackpole was similarly involved through a

---

(1) Though Lewis Bayly's descendants claimed him to have been of Scottish origin, of a family of Lanarkshire Baylys (*D.N.B.*).
(2) It must be emphasised that, despite its questionable constitutional position and apart from its use as a political instrument, the court of High Commission heard pleas arising from a great variety of causes; and "the really powerful forces fostering [its] evolution . . . were those aspects of its jurisdiction and procedure which caused suitors to prefer it to the regular ecclesiastical or common-law courts" (R. G. Usher, *The Rise and Fall of the High Commission*, p.89).
(3) Most of the Act Books, and many other documents belonging to the Registry of the Commission, have been lost, presumably destroyed by order of Parliament in the Civil War (Usher, *op. cit.*, p.367). Some survive, for the period 1633-1641, and the names of Welshmen therein contained have been listed by Dr. Thomas Richards (*Cymru a'r Uchel Gomisiwn, 1633-1640*, pp.141-144.)
(4) *Acts of the Court of High Commission*, vol. cclxi, ff.25, 72b, 138, 288b.
(5) In Dr. Richards's view, "It is a pity that Puritanism ever had to depend on the support of Richard Parry and his kind, those contemptible men who are a burden and a trial to the beginnings of every religious awakening" (*op. cit.*, p.51: my translation).
(6) *Acts of the Court of High Commission*, vol. cclxi, f.183.
(7) Richards, *op. cit.*, p.109.

quarrel over property with his neighbour, George Ellis.[1] Richard Jones of Llanllwni, who, arraigned with Henry Lloyd of Llan- dysul,[2] was the only Welshman to appeal to the delegates against his conviction by the High Commission, was acquitted by them. In John Lloyd of Ynyshir Dr. Richards again detects unnatural wrong- doings.[3] In none of these was there much indication of reforming zeal. The outstanding exception was John White of Tenby, with his scheme for using appropriated tithes to provide salaries for preachers, and, later, his leadership of the Committee for Plundered Minis- ters.[4] But if on the borders of Wales the life which had reluctantly left Catholicism sprang up afresh in new ideas, in the south-west religious enthusiasm generally slumbered more deeply and was not so easily disturbed.[5]

2. EDUCATION.

The lay leaders of this community were not all immobile squireens whose world had never extended beyond the boundaries of their estates. Between 1540 and 1640 at least 343 men from south-west Wales matriculated at the University of Oxford.[6] Of these, 132 were entered as the sons of gentry: a higher proportion than in England,[7] and another indication, perhaps, that in Wales a gentle- man was a less distinctive element in the social order. 143 were entered as "plebeians", and a further 39 as the sons of clergymen.[8] Of the gentry, at least fifty obtained degrees—again an unusually high proportion.[9] 33 proceeded from Oxford to the Inns of Court.

---

(1) *Acts of the Court of High Commission*, vol. cclxi, ff.38-39b. *Cf. supra.*, p.127.
(2) *Ibid.*, f.298; *C.S.P.Dom.* (1640-1641), vol. cccclxxiv, no. 90.
(3) *Acts of the Court of High Commission*, vol. cclxi, f.60b; Richards, *op. cit.*, p.131.
(4) *Cf. infra*, p.209..
(5) H. N. Brailsford's view that "Puritanism had not yet begun to penetrate Wales" (*The Levellers and the English Revolution*, p.7), seems, on this evidence for the south-west, broadly true.
(6) Except where otherwise stated, this discussion is based upon material from J. Foster, *Alumni Oxonienses*, Anthony á Wood, *Athenae Oxonienses*, John and J. A. Venn, *Alumni Cantabrigenses*, J. Foster, *Index Ecclesiasticus*, the published *Register of Admissions to the Middle Temple*, *Gray's Inn Admissions Register*, *Lincoln's Inn Admissions Register*, *Members of the Inner Temple*, *D.N.B.* and the *Dictionary of Welsh National Biography*. In most of these, apart from á Wood, the relevant information is as easily traced by the subject's name as by page references. *Cf. infra*, p. 216, note 1.
(7) *Cf.* A. L. Rowse, *The England of Elizabeth*, pp.520-521.
(8) The social status of 29 students is not given and has proved impossible to ascertain.
(9) In Somerset, of 52 laymen who matriculated at University and later served in local government between 1625 and 1640, only ten took a degree (T. G. Barnes, *op. cit.*, p.31).

At least 102 south-west Wales gentlemen were admitted to one of
the four leading Inns during this period: 34 at the Middle Temple,
of whom fifteen had previously been at Oxford; 26 at Gray's Inn,
nine of these coming from Oxford; 24 at the Inner Temple, of
whom five similarly; and eighteen at Lincoln's Inn, of whom seven
had been at Oxford.[1] There was not so much a steady increase
throughout the period as a distinct concentration, when the gentry
in particular reached a peak of attendance at Oxford, in the last years
of Elizabeth's reign, falling away at the Stuart succession before
recovering a little later. This trend was to some extent matched at
the Inns of Court, though the peak there was not reached so soon,
suggesting perhaps a passing fancy for some contact with legal
scholarship without the luxury of classical preliminaries, or possibly
accounted for by a sudden popularity of the Middle Temple in the
first decade of the seventeenth century, nearly equalled at Gray's Inn
between 1631 and 1640.[2] Some, though understandably not many,
elected to travel further eastwards to Cambridge. These numbered
thirty, of whom nine were either incorporated after graduation from
Oxford or had previously matriculated from an Oxford college. Of
the total, fourteen were gentry; two were the children of the
Bishops Richard Davies and Rowland Meyrick; and one, Robert
Devereux, was an Earl's son. Five of these gentlemen proceeded to
the Inns of Court, two being the brothers Henry and Thomas Jones
of Abermarlais, and another, David Edwards of Carmarthenshire,
whose two sons later followed him at Queen's, apparently the
favoured college of these Welshmen.

The quality of the education available at these several establish-
ments has recently been the subject of some controversy, particularly
as regards the activity of the Universities "in disseminating new
scientific discoveries and in training the experimental or new
philosophers".[3] Further, it has been argued that the traditional
system of legal education at the Inns of Court was in this period in
decline, with Readers and Benchers failing to honour their obli-

---

(1) The discrepancy between this total of 36 members of the Inns of Court previously
at Oxford and the total given earlier derives from my having tentatively identified
one or two, such as Walter Lloyd of Llanfair, Cardiganshire, and Richard Price
of Lampeter, with names recorded both in the *Alumni* and in the *Registers*,
without additional confirmation.
(2) *Vide infra*, Appendices B and C.
(3) M. H. Curtis, *op. cit.*, p.250. Dr. Curtis claims for the Universities a positive
contribution in this connection: a view disputed by Mr. Christopher Hill
(*Intellectual Origins of the English Revolution*, pp.301-314).

gations to hold moots and deliver lectures for the benefit of students, whose conduct was in any case unsatisfactory; so that, as far as the sons of nobility and gentry were concerned, "it would have been virtually impossible . . . for such a student to acquire 'in a year's residence after Oxford and Cambridge enough law to settle the disputes of tenants of the family estate or act as Justice of the Peace in his home county' ".[1] Nonetheless, it seems a reasonable claim that attendance at these centres of learning "provided these young men with at least an exposure to the civilizing, humanizing influences of the liberal arts, and with such familiarity with practical and contemporary ideas as they or their tutors might from time to time find necessary or desirable".[2]

If the chief functions of the Universities in this period were "to produce clerics for the state Church, and to give a veneer of polite learning to young gentlemen",[3] they seem to have had some effect upon certain individuals from south-west Wales.[4] Hugh Lloyd, gentleman, of Cardiganshire and Jesus, became archdeacon of Worcester; Evan Owen of Jesus, third son of George Owen of Henllys, was later chancellor of St. David's; Thomas Lloyd, esquire, of Cardiganshire, a chorister of Christ Church, was later chancellor of St. David's and the father of Sir Marmaduke Lloyd, a Great Sessions Justice in the county palatine of Chester.[5] Another of George Owen's sons overcame the stigma of bastardy with the distinction of appointment as Norroy King of Arms.[6] The knights Thomas Canon, James Perrot, John Vaughan and William Vaughan, all of Jesus, and Thomas Stepney of St. John's, all earned some credit in the worlds of affairs, of books, or both, even if Stepney's was the ambiguous description of "a great courtier" and the second Vaughan's was dearly bought at Cambriol. Sir Roger Lort had some pretensions to be called a poet; William Voyle, gentleman, to be a medical man; and John White, esquire, a political polemicist.

(1) K. Charlton, *Education in Renaissance England*, p.194.
(2) Curtis, *op. cit.*, p.268. Matriculation, of course, was no guarantee of actual attendance.
(3) Hill, *op. cit.*, p.301.
(4) For the social status of those hereafter named I have followed the epithets ("*arm.*", "*gen.*", "*cler. fil.*", "*pleb.*") accorded them in the *Alumni*.
(5) Who delayed too long his proposals to reform the Council in the Marches in its time of crisis because, according to his colleagues, of his "fear to do anything in the court" (Penry Williams, "The Attack on the Council in the Marches", *op. cit.*, p.19).
(6) H. Stanford London, "George Owen, York Herald, 1633-1663", *T.H.C.S.*, (1943-1944), pp.79-80.

Others reciprocated what benefits they may have received at Oxford with service to the last college founded there under the Tudors.[1] Jesus College enjoyed its first benefaction after its foundation from its second Principal, Dr. Griffith Lloyd, second son of Hugh Lloyd of Llanllyr; its second letters patent through its third Principal, Dr. Francis Bevans of Carmarthen; its new buildings and draft statutes through the devoted energies of its fifth Principal, Griffith Powell of Carmarthenshire; and its outstanding personality of the period in the person of Dr. Francis Mansell, from Muddlescombe, Carmarthenshire, three times Principal, fervent royalist in the Civil War, and ardent promoter of the college's interests. If the benevolence of some, like Dr. John Williams, proved disappointing, others provided some compensation. From Sir Thomas Canon came a rent-charge to maintain a lecture and a sermon; from David Parry of Cardiganshire, an income to maintain a Fellow.

But, college patronage apart, the cultural achievements of such as these were at least equalled by others of less well-to-do parentage. Some were the sons of clergymen, like Thomas Howell of Bryn, Carmarthenshire, who rose to be chaplain to Charles I and ultimately Bishop of Bristol, and whom â Wood, a little ornately, described as "a man not only flourishing with the verdure and spring of wit and the summer of much learning and reading, but happy in the harvest of a mature understanding and judicious in matters political, both ecclesiastical and civil".[2] His namesake, James, cler. fil., "a pure cadet, a true cosmopolite, not born to land, lease, house or office, was in a manner put to it to seek his fortune", which he pursued after travel in many countries, being successively secretary to the Earl of Leicester, Ambassador Extraordinary at the Court of Denmark, and, after an interval in the Fleet Prison, Royal Historiographer. He was author of fifty-two publications, in which he disguised a good deal of plagiarism with "a singular command of his pen" and "a parabolical and allusive fancy".[3] Others were of lay origins: Robert Record, who combined the Controllership of the Royal Mint at Bristol and the Surveyorship of the Royal Mines in Ireland, with a polymath's familiarity with mathematics, rhetoric, philosophy, history, astrology, music, mineralogy and every branch of

(1) For the history of Jesus College in this period, vide E. G. Hardy, Jesus College pp.1-106; C. E. Mallet, A History of the University of Oxford, vol. ii, pp.195-211
(2) Â Wood, op. cit., p.656.
(3) Ibid., vol. ii, p.265.

natural history;[1] Robert Lougher, who died virtually in Record's nephew's arms,[2] son of an alderman of Tenby, rose to be Fellow of All Souls, Professor of Civil Law, Principal of New Inn Hall, and Vicar-General to the Archbishop of York; Thomas Phaer, doctor of medicine, who was a poet, translator of the *Aeneid*,[3] and solicitor in the Council in the Marches. Their views were as various as their origins, ranging from Constantine Jessoppe of Pembroke's professed Arminianism in his *Concerning the Nature of the Covenant of Grace*,[4] to the Puritanism of William Dolben, supporter of lecturers at Haverfordwest,[5] who was so beloved of his parishioners that during his last illness they ploughed and sowed his glebe at their own expense so that his widow might not be left destitute. These men, at least as much as the substantial gentry, reflect certain aspects of Burckhardt's "renaissance man", with his "life of excitement and vicissitude" and its "exhausting studies, tutorships, secretaryships, professorships, offices in princely households".[6]

Gentlemen participated in some attempts to found local grammar schools, though fewer of these were established in south-west Wales than in any other part of the country in the sixteenth century.[7] "The King's School of Carmarthen of Thomas Lloyd's foundation"

---

(1) His publications, including *The Grounde of Artes* (1543), *The Book of Physic* (1547), *The Pathway to Knowledge* (1551) and *The Whetstone of Wit* (1557), which last he dedicated to "the company of venturers unto Muscovia", promising that he would "for your commodity shortly set forth such a book of navigation as I daresay shall partly satisfy and content not only your expectation but also the desire of a great number beside" (B.M. Lansdowne 980, f.252), earned him the description of "the founder of the English school of mathematics" (*vide* Hill, *op. cit.*, p.17; F. R. Johnson, *Astronomical Thought in Renaissance England*, pp.120 *et seq.*).
(2) P.C.C. 29 Brudenell. For Robert Record's will and his legacy to his brother's son, *vide* P.C.C. 29 Noodes.
(3) For this, dedicated to Queen Mary, he was granted in 1558 a strict copyright under the royal seal and a hundred acres of land and ten acres of meadow in Cilgerran, Pembrokeshire, with the herbage of the Forest there. In 1555 he was addressed as resident there by William Baldwin who, with George Ferrers, whom Phaer remembered in his will, constituted three of the four main contributors to the original *Mirror for Magistrates*, including the "Tragedy of Owen Glendower". Phaer's *The Regiment of Lyfe* and his *The Boke of Precedentes* show his ability as a physician and a lawyer (*C.P.R.* (Philip and Mary), vol. iv, pp.309, 363; Lily B. Campbell (ed.), *The Mirror for Magistrates*, pp.32-34).
(4) A Wood, *op. cit.*, vol. ii, p.175.
(5) Dolben matriculated from Christ Church as a "*pleb.*" (*Alumni Oxonienses*, vol. i, p.412); though, according to the *Dictionary of Welsh National Biography*, his father, John, was a merchant of Haverfordwest who married Sir Hugh Myddelton's sister.
(6) J. Burckhardt, *The Civilisation of the Renaissance in Italy*, vol. i, p.274.
(7) *Vide* L. S. Knight, *Welsh Independent Grammar Schools to 1600*, p.x; George Owen, *The Description of Penbrokshire*, vol. i, pp.146-147.

received its letters patent for erection on the site of the late Friars Minors there,[1] its founder bequeathing twenty marks to be paid to the master and twenty nobles to the usher, together with instructions to the executors to continue with the work and to ensure the active participation of the scholars in saying extensive prayers for the founder's soul.[2] This foundation does not appear to have flourished for very long; in 1576 two local aldermen, both prominent men in the shire, and the merchant Robert Toy, supported the Earl of Essex's successful petition to the Queen for a charter for a free grammar school in the town.[3] Whether this throve thereafter is doubtful.[4] Some time before 1609 Sir John Vaughan explained to Thomas Phillips and Francis Lloyd, gentlemen, that his "enclosure of the marsh or meadow by Carmarthen . . . was intended to be employed for the maintenance of a free school in Carmarthen, which would do good both for the town and country".[5] In 1619 the mayor and corporation of Carmarthen were led by Thomas Parry to believe that Francis Mansell was withholding from them a sum of one hundred pounds, being part of the four hundred pounds raised for musters and re-directed towards "erecting a free school in the town". They pursued the matter in the Council in the Marches and in the Privy Council for three years until Mansell managed to show that he had first repeatedly offered the money to the corporation and had finally paid it to the mayor, whereupon he was honourably discharged and Parry ordered to refrain "from all further molestation" of him.[6] In 1613 Thomas Lloyd of Cilciffeth granted property to the borough of Haverfordwest to maintain a schoolmaster in that town; this foundation was still prosperous enough in 1633 to admit sixteen free scholars.[7] But the achievement of the region in this connection is not impressive in an era of exceptional

(1) *L.P.H.VIII*, vol. xviii, pt. i (1543), no. 226 (22).
(2) P.C.C. 51 Alen.
(3) *Trans. Carms. Antiq. Soc.*, vol. i, p.201. The two were Griffith Rice of Newton, high sheriff of the county in 1567, and Walter Vaughan of Golden Grove.
(4) For some indication of its encountering financial difficulties, *vide* Knight, *op. cit.*, p.17.
(5) P.R.O. D.L. 42/120/104-105.
(6) *C.S.P.Dom.* (1619-1623), vol. cx, no. 46; vol. cxxiv, no. 1; vol. cxxvii, no. 25; vol. cxxxii, no. 71; vol. cxxxiv, no. 73; *A.P.C.* (1619-1621), p.365; (1621-1623), pp.303, 369.
(7) N.L.W. Haverfordwest Corporation Records, 219, 236. The property was administered by twenty-two feoffees, drawn from the local aldermen, citizens and gentry. Examples of leases in this connection are N.L.W. Eaton Evans and Williams, 1115, 1140, 1146.

growth in educational foundations in England by laymen, catering
for the needs of laymen.

3. CULTURE.

Between the Conquest and the Union, despite political misfortune,
the Welsh people "produced for their consolation a corpus of elegant
literature unequalled either in quantity or in quality, as far as we
know, in the nation's history".[1] The chief ornaments of this
creative achievement were the *awdlau* and the *cywyddau*, being highly
sophisticated forms of poetry in strict metre. The *awdl*, essentially
a poem of praise, was generally addressed to a gentleman-patron;
the *cywydd* likewise, in its several forms of *cywydd mawl* (praise),
cywydd gofyn (request) or *cywydd marwnad* (lament). Geared to the
entertainment of the leaders of society, themselves capable both of
critical appreciation of the forms' nuances and complexities, and,
often, of composition, these works were largely produced by itinerant bards on the occasions of religious feasts or of particular fes-
tivities in the houses of their patrons. Dr. Thomas Parry has
emphasised the social nature of this poetry, "produced by bards who
loved the company of men rather than solitude".[2] In these circumstances, the role of a patron was different in kind from that of the
Johnsonian "wretch who supports with insolence and is paid with
flattery". Not all bards were dependent upon patronage for their
material sustenance: witness, for instance, the supposedly gentle
birth of Dafydd ap Gwilym in Cardiganshire. But if the standard of
this poetry was to be maintained the patron, or at least some members of his company, who furnished the indispensable audience,
would need to be themselves well-versed in the strict metres, in the
Welsh language, and generally in the elements of the bardic
tradition.

To that tradition south-west Wales had made a significant contribution.[3] In the fourteenth century, in addition to the genius of its
own sons, it had attracted itinerant bards from other regions, such
as Iolo Goch from Dyffryn Clwyd. Einion Offeiriad dedicated to
Sir Rhys ap Griffith his *Gramadeg*, a curious compilation of instruc-

---

(1) Thomas Parry, *Hanes Llenyddiaeth Gymraeg hyd 1900*, p.99. Translations from
   Welsh prose works are my own. For assistance with translations from contemporary Welsh poetry I am indebted to Mr. Elwyn Evans.
(2) *Ibid.*, p.100.
(3) For assistance with the following paragraph I am much indebted to Mr. D. J.
   Bowen.

tion, drawn from a variety of sources, thought necessary for the education of prospective poets. From Carmarthenshire in the fifteenth century came such important poets as Lewis Glyn Cothi and Ieuan Deulwyn, testimony to the persistence of a favourable literary climate in this region. To some extent these conditions survived the Union. In the first half of the sixteenth century Griffith Dwnn was the subject of the adulatory inspiration of a number of poets, recorded much of their work in his own hand,[1] and appears to have deserved the appreciation of Robert Fynglwyd:

"Pwy yw'r plas gwynias i'r gweiniaid—porth aur
Lle porthir pob gwanblaid".[2]

In Pembrokeshire, still later, George Owen of Henllys, William Warren of Trewern, William Bowen of Llwyngwair: these were praised in terms similar to those addressed to George William Griffith of Penybenglog:

"Y pur Gymro, pêr gynnydd,
Pen stôr, post o aur rhudd,
Pingal wyt, pan glyw'r iaith,
Pêr frau iôn, pur Fryttaniaeth".[3]

Several features of the old procedures—the festive season, the itinerant tradition, the praise of a great man—are apparent in Siôn Mawddwy's address to three fellow-poets who, at Christmas 1613, had travelled to Pembrokeshire for the benefit of Thomas Lloyd of Cilcifleth, sheriff of the county in that year.[4] In Cardiganshire, Richard Price of Gogerddan;[5] in Carmarthenshire, the Rices of Newton:[6] throughout this period poems in praise of such as these testify to the survival of long-established practices.

But it is important to distinguish between a sentimental retention of traditional exercises and a continued development of virile cultural forms. Recent opinion has held of the bards that, from the later sixteenth century, "their literary work, already inclined to be

---

(1) H.M.C. *Welsh MSS.*, vol. ii, pp.499-504 (Llanstephan MS. 40).
(2) N.L.W. Llanstephan 133/881. Whose is the mansion, warm for the weak—a golden gateway / Where all the needy are succoured.
(3) *Ibid.*, /794. Thou pure Welshman, of fair increase / Of the greatest wealth, a pillar of red gold / But thou art a pinnacle when the nation hears / The pure British language, sweet, tender lord.
(4) H.M.C. *Welsh MSS.*, vol. ii, p.494 (Llanstephan MS. 38). "Echdoe ym Mhowys ... Ddoe yng Ngwynedd ... A heddiw ... yn Neheubarth ... Clywed ... am Siryf Sir Benfro ... Thomas Llwyd ... Minnau'n / drwm ... heb allu i fynd y y bell fawr ... i gadw'r / Llwyd a geidw'r / holl iaith".
(5) N.L.W. Llanstephan 133/677: Ieuan Tew (1590).
(6) *Ibid.*, /950, 951: Edward Dafydd (1640).

stereotyped and deadened by tradition, lost its vigour and vitality. Their style and language, with few exceptions, became stultified and their *cywyddau* dull, uninspired and monotonous".[1] Several factors contributed to this decline. It has been suggested that "it is obvious that the bardic system was degenerating from within"; and for this contemporary humanists held the bards themselves responsible.[2] Again, the adulatory poetic forms described above had passed their maturity by the middle of the sixteenth century and, with their every potential already exploited, could die naturally of old age.[3] Further, this cultural system was essentially oral, depending upon a personal relationship between the bards and their patrons and unsuited to the new world of printed books, wherein a necessarily limited market could not provide an adequate livelihood for professional poets.[4] The bards' adjustment to these new circumstances took the form of their evolution of the *arwyddfardd* (herald-bard),[5] prepared to provide genealogical services for ancestor-conscious gentry whilst remaining reluctant to abandon traditional poetic forms—a combination of attitudes itself a sign of decadence. South-west Wales reflected several of these aspects:

> "Y cerddwyr, ble y cyhwrddwn,
> O Dduw hael, pa fyd yw hwn!
> Yr oedd unwaith, feirdd enyd,
> I ni barch, mwya'n y byd,
> Drwy raddio, tro i'r eiddwych,
> Dafod a thant, a fu daith wych,"[6]

wrote Siôn Mawddwy to George Owen, with a wistful glance at previous eras. At the wedding of Thomas Warren of Trewern, Dafydd Emlyn scheduled in verse his host's illustrious kindred:

---

(1) W. Ogwen Williams, "The Survival of the Welsh Language after the Union of England and Wales: the First Phase, 1536-1642", *Welsh History Review*, vol. ii (1964), p.87.
(2) D. J. Bowen, "Gruffydd Hiraethog ac Argyfwng Cerdd Dafod", *Llên Cymru*, vol. ii (1953), pp.149-150.
(3) T. Parry, *op. cit.*, p.126.
(4) Glanmor Williams, *Dadeni, Diwygiad a Diwylliant Cymru*, p.28.
(5) For a discussion of this, *vide* E. D. Jones, "Presidential Address", *Arch. Camb.*, vol. cxii (1963), pp.3 *et seq.*
(6) N.L.W. Llanstephan 133/765. Poets, where shall we meet / O generous God, what a world is this / There was once, bards, given / To us the greatest respect / By graduating [*i.e.*, into the bardic hierarchy] there was an opportunity for those of keenness / In recitation and song, of a great journey [*i.e.*, *cwrs clera*, the minstrels' itinerary around patrons' houses].

"Y Perods yw'r himp irwydd,
A chwyrn waed rhyw Lacharn wydd,
Annwyl dwf Sion Arnoldl wedd,
A dawn fwyn Pictwn fonedd..."[1]

On the one hand, an instinctive cultural conservatism; on the other, forces making for change and social disintegration: these influences had grave effects upon Welsh poetry in the sixteenth and early seventeenth centuries. The former inhibited the successful evolution of alternative poetic forms, such as the *canu rhydd* (free verse);[2] and however far, and in whatever form, there is to be recognised in the latter a betrayal of the bards by the gentry, the fact remains that the achievement of Welsh literature in this period lies in prose works, largely of religious and partly of antiquarian inspiration. If poets were welcomed to the Bishop of St. David's seat at Abergwili in the 1560s,[3] the main literary concern of that establishment remained the translating of the New Testament. The publication of that work was financially supported by the Carmarthen merchant Humphrey Toy, who, in further sponsoring the printing of "*the service book* in Welsh authorised by my lord of London" and "a book entitled *A plain and familiar introduction touching how to pronounce the letters in the British tongue*",[4] neatly exemplifies the main preoccupations of his day in the sphere of publishing. The absence of sufficiently enlightened patrons has recently been suggested in at least partial explanation of the non-fulfilment of the ambition of some contemporary visionaries for a new, humanistic literature in Welsh to enable the language to take its place in Renaissance Europe.[5] Certainly the positive cultural contribution

(1) *Ibid.*, /766. The Perrots are an evergreen branch / And the fierce blood of a Laugharne tree, *etc.*
(2) T. Parry, *op. cit.*, p.169.   (3) D. J. Bowen, *op. cit.*, p.151.
(4) W. Ll. Davies, "Welsh Books entered in the Stationers' Registers, 1554-1708", *Journal of the Welsh Bibliographical Society*, vol. ii, p.168.
(5) Glanmor Williams, *op. cit.*, p.27 and *passim. Vide*, for instance, the aspirations and strictures simultaneously expressed by Siôn Dafydd Rhys in introducing his *Cambrobrytannicae Cymraecaeve Linguae Institutiones et Rudimenta* . . . in 1592: "Ac wrthych chwitheu Genedl Gymry a'm Cyfladwyr y doydaf; ac yn enwêdic wrthych y Pendefigion a Boneddigion Cymry, ych bôd (mal y tybygwn) yn ddiphygiol aruthr o ranu cwpláu ych dylŷedic rwym parth ac at eych Hiaith a'ch Prydyddion, a'ch Gwlad; yn amgênach môdd nog y gnotáynt y Cenhedloedd eraill tu ac at ei Hiaith, ae Gwlad, ae Hawdurieid, ae syberwyd . . . A pha Genhedloedd (meddwch chwi) a wnáent y cyfryw betheu ardderchawc hynny? Y Cenhedloedd arbennicaf o'r byd, sêf yr Arabieit, y Groecieit, y Lladinieit; ac yn eu hôl hwynteu yr Italieit, yr Hyspanieit, y Phrancot, yr Alemanieit, y Saeson, y Scotieit; ac ereill Genhedloedd yn rhy hîr eu cyrbwyll ae hadrodd". I have here retained the interesting orthography of the original, as printed in G. H. Hughes, *Rhagymadroddion, 1547-1659*, pp.73-74.

of the gentry of south-west Wales was less one of enlightened leadership than one of sporadic individual activity.

From the *nouveaux venus*, the Barlows, came Roger's *Brief Sum of Geography*[1] and George's *Garden of Pleasure*. Sir James Perrot, with his *Chronicle of Ireland* and other publications,[2] and William Vaughan, with the *Golden-grove*[3] and *Golden Fleece* chief amongst his several writings, added their works to those of George Owen. It has been suggested that the country gentlemen of south Wales were the founders of a "New School" in genealogical research, to which they brought a wider learning and a more scientific approach that saved much of the old learning and laid the foundations of the modern school;[4] though this is not easily reconciled with the standards of George Owen Harry's *Genealogy of the High and Mighty Monarch James*, in which heraldic accuracy fell victim to the whims of a loyal imagination. The vicar of Llanddowror, Robert Holland, translator of the *Basilikon Doron* and author of a work intended to unmask the art of "men of magic",[5] did express gratitude to Sir James Perrot, "that good knight", John Phillips of Picton and George Owen of Henllys, for their patronage, and possibly, together with George Owen Harry, collaborated with the last of these in his major work.[6] But Robert Record, who retained some connection with the region if only by his continued association with Robert Lougher, who lived there and was member of parliament for Pembroke borough in 1572,[7] had found from here little relief of his ultimate penury. South-west Wales nevertheless recruited a gentleman scientist of lively views in Sir William Lower, a Cornishman who married Sir Thomas Perrot's heiress, and who, with his assistant John Prydderch of Hawksbrook, Carmarthenshire,[8] gazed, through

---

(1) For a discussion of Barlow, who had accompanied Sebastian Cabot's expedition to La Plata in 1526, as author of this work, actually a translation of Martin Fernandes de Enciso's *Suma de Geographia*, vide E. G. R. Taylor, *Tudor Geography, 1485-1583*, pp.45-58.

(2) Notably his *Discovery of Discontented Minds* (1596); *Considerations of Humane Conditions* (1600); *Meditations . . . on the Lord's Prayer* (1630).

(3) Recommended, *inter alia*, by John Brinsley, in his *Ludus Literarius*, as a source of material for theme-writing and likely to improve pupils' English (Foster Watson, *The English Grammar Schools to 1660*, p.427).

(4) *Vide* F. Jones, "An Approach to Welsh Genealogy", *T.H.C.S.* (1948), p.378. Lewis Dwnn, at any rate, owed very little to financial support from the Welsh gentry (*ibid.*, p.377).

(5) Charles Edwards, *Y Ffydd Ddiffuant* (1677), p.205.

(6) J. Conway Davies, "Letters of Admission", *N.L.W.Journal*, vol. iv (1945-1946), p.86.

(7) *Vide supra*, pp.73, 198.

(8) *Vide* F. Jones, "The Squires of Hawksbrook", *T.H.C.S.* (1937), pp.343-344.

a small Dutch telescope from his house at Treventy, at the moon, noted amongst other things "the Dichotomy, that spot which represents unto me the Man in the Moon (but without a head)", and, marvelling at the acuteness of his associate's vision, communicated his discoveries to the Englishman Thomas Hariot.[1]

Hariot, one of the outstanding astronomers and mathematicians of his day, was an associate of Sir Walter Ralegh and Sir Philip Sidney and his circle.[2] In such individuals and groups English civilisation in this period found a focal point and a means to its great flowering. None is to be found who performed like service for the culture of Wales. In the south-west, at least, unenlightened persistence in familiar ways and forms was relieved only by individual efforts of little relevance to the cultural needs of this community.

4. LIFE AND LOYALTIES.

Attempts have been made to portray the way of life of sixteenth and seventeenth-century gentlemen.[3] Three points here need emphasis. First, the character of society in south-west Wales was introspective and closed. The aggrieved Lamentation Chapman, who claimed in 1592 that John Morgan Wolfe of Whitland had enticed him from Kent to become his tenant in Carmarthenshire, hesitated to attribute his misfortunes there to the fact of his being a stranger and an Englishman.[4] But Robert Craven, formerly of Lincolnshire, alleged that when living in Llanelli in 1559 he encountered bitter prejudice from several local men, including the gentleman David Philip ab Owen and the constable William Morgan. These, "being all Welshmen, and having without any just cause conceived great malice against your said subject", with thirty or forty others, by his account, besieged him and his family in his house and caused it damage before breaking in and assaulting him; and, on his appealing to the constable, he was himself, with his wife, put in the stocks.[5] An important objection by the tenants concerned to the appointment of William Lloyd of Clifford's Inn as beadle and collector of Crown

---

(1) *Carmarthen Journal*, 7 August 1936. For some account of Lower's correspondence with Hariot, *vide* F. R. Palmer, *op. cit.*, pp.227-228.

(2) C. Hill, *op. cit.*, p.139

(3) For Wales, for instance, A. H. Dodd, "The Social Order", *Studies in Stuart Wales*, pp.1-48; W. Ogwen Williams, *Calendar of the Caernarvonshire Quarter Sessions Records*, pp.lix-lxxxv.

(4) P.R.O. E112/59/23(ii).

(5) P.R.O. St. Ch. 5/C2/29.

rents and fines in three Cardiganshire commotes was that the "plaintiff is a north Wales man and never had any dwelling or abiding within the county of Cardigan".[1] In 1583 Bishop Marmaduke Middleton reported that "concerning the collection for Geneva I have dealt with some of the best of my diocese, whom I find not greatly willing because it is in another country".[2]

Secondly, in a poor society the gentry were themselves poor, and their standard of living modest. The eight so-called mansions rebuilt in Pembrokeshire in Elizabeth's reign[3] cannot have differed very greatly from the old Welsh long-house, or, at best, the Pembroke-shire stone farmhouse. Edmund Harries of High Freystrop, sheriff of Haverfordwest at the time of the Stepney-Garnons dispute and husband of John Voyle's daughter, slept in a decrepit bed "with a dormic coverlet made of an old carpet" in his sparsely-furnished four-roomed house, where only the hall contained a fireplace.[4] The manor-house of Abermarlais, seat of one of Carmarthenshire's leading families, was, though an improvement upon Harries's circumstances, by no means elaborate. The main living quarters consisted of a hall, two low chambers with two chambers over them, a study or closet next to the hall, a pantry and larder with a chamber over them, a kitchen and a bakehouse; another large chamber with a smaller one over it completed these appointments. A prison-house lodged in a tower on the east side, a brewhouse and a cornchamber over it, constituted the remainder of the buildings.[5] Within such structures there was no great luxury. A comparison between the goods and chattels of Sir Gelly Meyrick[6] and those of James Bowen of Llwyngwair, esquire, who died in 1629,[7] is instructive. The Earl of Essex's household steward possessed twenty feather beds; Bowen owned four. Meyrick had nineteen bolsters to Bowen's five. Compared with Meyrick's quilts and mattresses, silk curtains, hangings of carpet work and other

(1) P.R.O. E112/145/33.
(2) P.R.O. S.P.12/162/29.
(3) B. G. Charles (ed.), "The Second Book of George Owen's Description of Pembrokeshire", *N.L.W.Journal*, vol. v (1948), pp. 265-285.
(4) N.L.W. Probate Records: Diocese of St. David's (Archdeaconry of St. David's), 1608; partly printed in B. E. Howells, "The Elizabethan Squirearchy of Pembrokeshire", *op. cit.*, pp.37-39.
(5) *Trans. Carms. Antiq. Soc.*, vol. iii, p.110.
(6) *Arch. Camb.*, ser. 3, vol. x (1864), p.201.
(7) E. D. Jones, "A Pembrokeshire Squire's Chattels", *N.L.W.Journal*, vol. viii, pp.22 *et seq.*

bed-furnishings, valued at £24 4s., Bowen, nearly thirty years later, had coarse sheets and some Holland sheets, with some other equipment, the whole being worth £9 14s. Bowen had nine pewter dishes or platters; Meyrick possessed nine dozen. To match Meyrick's seventeen candlesticks, Bowen could have mustered four. In general, Meyrick's household effects were valued[1] at £38 0s. 8d., whereas Bowen's were worth £27 18s. 9d. Bowen's livestock, on the other hand, was estimated in value at £43 5s., Meyrick's at £37 15s. 8d. Further comparison of this with some of Sir John Perrot's payments to London merchants between 1567 and 1581 goes far to explain his social dominance: £49 4s. 3d. to a merchant-tailor, £400 to a saddler, £128 to a goldsmith,[2] amongst others.

Thirdly, patronage as exercised by the central government or by a courtier who, "by reason of his influence in obtaining favours from the Crown, soon found himself besieged by eager clients anxious for his protection",[3] should be distinguished from the circumstances by which local gentlemen were assured of a following for private ends. The distinction is not absolute. Place-soliciting on grounds of ties of blood and kinship is exemplified in letters such as Jenkin Gwynne's to Burghley, requesting a favour for one who "is of your blood and is heir to Philip Vaughan of Tyleglas, whose daughter was married to your honour's ancestor, and though he be a poor man, yet most of the best sort of men in south Wales do come out of his house".[4] Again, Thomas Jones of Fountaingate wrote to Salisbury, praying, on account of their descent from a mutual great-grandfather, that an action brought against him in the Exchequer might be transferred to the local courts.[5] But in this community, a form of dependence and allegiance different from that arising out of ability to bestow substantial favours is suggested by references in lawsuits to "servants" and "retainers". Specifically, Maurice Phillips of Llanbadarn Fawr was indicted before the Cardigan Great Sessions

---

(1) Meyrick's most valuable possessions had been taken elsewhere (*vide supra*, p.117) and are not included in this inquisition. From the following totals I have therefore omitted Bowen's silverware, of much inferior value.
(2) P.R.O. E210/D.9809, 9819, 9836.
(3) L. Stone, *op. cit.*, p.446.
(4) B.M. Lansdowne 12, f.10. The letter was presumably written on behalf of John Vaughan, who was later given the position of customer of Milford and wrote to Burghley to thank him for his favours on behalf of himself and of the whole house (P.R.O. S.P.12/154/7).
(5) P.R.O. S.P.14/69/16. This may have been the notorious horse-thief, Twm Sion Catti.

in 1583 for "maintenance of thieves and robbers".[1] Five men were charged at Haverfordwest in 1605 because they were "retained" by Alban Stepney "in defiance of the statute".[2] It is unlikely that such a relationship between a leader and his followers required reinforcement through "any writing, oath, promise, livery, sign, badge, token, or in any other manner wise".[3] Whilst the Earl of Essex might have employed men "in livery" or "wearing his cloth", local potentates would have found little difficulty when the need arose in raising a following from among their tenants or kinsfolk, through exploiting a feeling of natural loyalty. In common with so many others, the term "retainer" is loosely employed in actions at law as regards its reflection of social actualities. For all their shortcomings, the gentry still led their communities and could expect acceptance of their leadership.

(1) N.L.W. Wales 7/7.
(2) N.L.W. Wales 7/10.
(3) 19 Henry VII, c.14: Statute of Liveries, 1504.

Conclusion

To attempt, with Collingwood, to discover the relationship to known historical events of "the thought in the mind of the person by whose agency that event came about"[1] is difficult enough when the "agent" is a single individual. A corresponding study of a section of society is far more hazardous. It is further complicated by the nature of the reliable evidence most readily available, which tends to throw light upon the exceptional individual rather than upon the group as a whole. To ignore the existence or the prominence of such men as John Lewis of Glasgrug, John White of Tenby, William Vaughan, Sir John Meyrick, John Vaughan of Trawsgoed and others, would be as foolish as to regard them as necessarily representative of their community. In themselves they present great variations in ability and in behaviour. The author of *Contemplations upon these Times*, describing himself as "a cordial well-wisher of his country's happiness", supported his arguments on behalf of the Parliament with appropriate classical and scriptural learning, and, expressing the whole with cogency and restraint, revealed a genuine concern for Wales and Welshmen in a pamphlet[2] not inferior to the best contemporary publications of its kind. The author of *The First Century of Scandalous Malignant Priests* preferred less dignified means to what he considered a worthy end;[3] and his parliamentary speeches concerning episcopacy, though more methodically developed and less scurrilous in tone, resorted frequently to an extraordinary logic more consistent with puritan militancy than with intellectual discipline.[4] William Vaughan's project at Cambriol was, again, notable rather for an eccentric originality than for pioneer good sense. But to express these criticisms is to indicate how far modern preconceptions must stand in the way of a true appreciation of contemporary attitudes. Whatever their virtues and weaknesses, all these men, like Meyrick and John Vaughan, may be

---

(1) R. G. Collingwood, *The Idea of History*, pp.214-215.
(2) John Lewis, *Contemplations upon these times, or, the Parliament Explained to Wales* (1646: B.M. Thomason Tracts, E.349.19), *passim*.
(3) John White, *The First Century of Scandalous Malignant Priests* (1643: *ibid.*, E.76.21). The volume consists of an array of allegations of immorality and unclean living on the part of clergymen.
(4) *Id.*, *Concerning the Trial of the Twelve Bishops* (1642: *ibid.*, E.200.12); *Concerning Episcopacy* (1641: *ibid.*, E.198.18).

considered outstanding personalities.

It is for this reason that their opinions and activities may not be considered with those of the rank and file. As Professor Hoggart has said, in another connection, "They would be exceptional people in any class: they reveal less about their class than about themselves".[1] Sir James Perrot, for example, participated not only in parliamentary business but also in significant economic enterprises, by leasing the royal mines of Pembrokeshire in 1624 and by membership of the Virginia Company.[2] Pembrokeshire men, such as lieutenants John Butler and John Lloyd, and ensigns William Owen and Gelly Meyrick, saw active service in Sir John Meyrick's regiment in the Civil War,[3] whilst others, such as Sir George Vaughan of Penbre Court in Carmarthenshire, gave their service, if sometimes unceremoniously,[4] for the King. Others, like Sir Erasmus Phillips and Walter Cuny, acted as local administrators and surveyors in the time of the Commonwealth;[5] and the Committee for Compounding found some agents to carry out its business in south-west Wales.[6] But to trace and record aspects of the conduct of such individuals is not to discover the collective attitudes of social groups.

The evidence available for any single aspect of the activities of the gentry of south-west Wales is disappointingly weak and unsatisfactory. It has not been possible in this study to present convincing proof of any one point made along the way. Rather, the argument turns upon an accumulation of impressions based upon evaluation of evidence drawn from a wide range and illustrative of many different aspects, interpreted in the context both of contemporary developments elsewhere and of the historical environment of this region. Moreover, these gentry have been studied as an integral part of their local community rather than as a distinctive element within it. It is for south-west Wales alone that evidence has been

(1) Richard Hoggart, *The Uses of Literacy*, p.2.
(2) *Dictionary of Welsh Biography*, *sub* Perrot.
(3) Edward Peacock (ed.), *The Army Lists of the Roundheads and Cavaliers*, p.81. Many of the names in these lists defy identification, as their editor recognised. Thus "Captain Coney" of Glenham's regiment may as likely have been Walter Cuny of Pembrokeshire as a member of a Lincolnshire family (*ibid.*, p.12, note 57).
(4) *Ibid.*, p.11, note 55. Vaughan was severely wounded at Lansdowne in 1643 by a blow on the head from a pole-axe.
(5) Lambeth MS. 915, f.82.
(6) For instance, *Cal. Comm. Comp.*, vol. i, p.618: the Pembrokeshire committee asks that Walter Cuny and John Prydderch be added to its number.

cited; it is to this locality that the following conclusions apply. The only general observation to be admitted is that the characteristics of the gentry as here portrayed are not consistent either with the aspirations or with the impact attributed to rising or declining "generalised gentry" in England as a whole. This is a comment not upon the likely characteristics of gentry elsewhere, studied in accordance with the terms of this analysis, but upon the doubtful admissibility, for purposes other than that of academic stimulus, of broad hypotheses taking insufficient account of the variations within that agglomeration of localities which in this period made up the kingdom of England.

In south-west Wales the gentry, for historical, political, social and economic reasons, occupied a position of leadership. It was to them that people were inclined to turn for settlement of their disputes and differences. It was upon them that the duties, together with the privileges, of local administration were conferred by the central authority. It was they who represented the community in Parliament. To them men prompted by creative talents turned. Without their co-operation spiritual leaders declared that they could achieve little. Their example and influence had an important bearing upon economic developments within the community as a whole. By their social position and the material means at their disposal, together with their claims of blood and descent, they exercised a significant measure of control over the fortunes of those who ranked beneath them and the condition of generations to come.

In none of these connections was dynamic development achieved in this period. The growth of individual estates represented the continuation of a process of gradual accumulation and consolidation conditioned both by limited availability of capital and by social inhibitions. The use of land and natural resources developed, under mild pressures, along unsophisticated and non-innovatory lines, further illustrated in an omission fully to exploit good facilities for maritime commercial activity. Political activity in this region suggests a minimal grasp of significant political principles, and a dogged introspectiveness unshaken either by Essex's feudal fling or by the constitutional conflict at the centre. The duties of local administration, increasing in complexity in this period, were understood and performed by the local gentry in a manner showing awareness neither of the nature of their role in the overall structure of government nor of a recent emancipation. In spiritual matters, the condition of this region suggests no hearty allegiance either to Rome, or to the Church of England, or to "Puritan" reform. Cultural activity was characterised less by positive "anglicisation" than by decadence relieved only by some individual works.

It would appear, then, that the gentry of south-west Wales were characterised in this period by a general lassitude. But in view of the nature of the evidence examined, even so tentative a judgement cannot be pronounced without serious reservations. Questions concerning the nature of society in this period are more easily formulated and more conveniently answered on the basis of sociological and deterministic hypothesis and of assessment of plausibilities than, often, on the basis of detailed historical analysis. But the latter approach, equipped to recognise what may not, as well as what may, be known, is likely in the long term to prove less misleading than the former.

If the gentry and their community were indeed characterised by inertia, two explanations may be offered. First, the gentry were the leaders of their society and conditioned its attitudes and development. Those among them who were capable of appreciating, responding to and acting upon, the changing circumstances of their time, were incapable of communicating their awareness to those whom they might have led to effect. Those who remained in social, spiritual and intellectual communication with their community at large, lacked such awareness.

Secondly, the condition of south-west Wales in this period was the legacy of that region's historical background. The arresting of the evolution of native Welsh society might conceivably have resulted in the positive discarding of the forms of that society, in a process highlighted by the events of 1284 and ratified by the Union. This might have been accompanied by eagerness to participate in English politics; by a readiness to conform and co-operate with the forms of English administration and to litigate in accordance with the forms of still-evolving English law; by economic expansion and development along capitalist lines; by cultural "anglicisation". These would have been the characteristics of a lively society, positive in its outlook. They are not the characteristics of the community which has here been described. That community was conditioned by a heritage of disharmony and conflicting forces. Its leaders were able neither sufficiently to abandon old ways for new opportunities, nor effectively to seek development and adjustment of native forms to meet new circumstances. With the old order crumbling and the new world unexplored, south-west Wales lingered in limbo.

APPENDIX A

SHIP-MONEY COLLECTIONS[1]

	Writ of 1635	Un-collected	%	Writ of 1636	Un-collected	%	Writ of 1637	Un-collected	%	Writ of 1638	Un-collected	%	Writ of 1639	Un-collected	%
Cardiganshire	£654	—	—	£654	—	—	£654	—	—	£248	£12 8s.	5	£654	£654	100
Carmarthenshire	£760	£160	21	£760	—	—	£790[2]	—	—	£301	£300	99.7	£790	£690	87.5
Pembrokeshire	£713 6s. 8d.	£43 10s.	6	£712 6s. 8d.	£90	12.6	£683[2] 10s.	—	—	£260	—	—	£683 10s.	£233 10s.	34
Total	£2127 6s. 8d.	£203 10s.	10	£2126 6s. 8d.	£90	4	£2127 10s.	—	—	£809	£312 8s.	38.5	£2127 10s.	£1577 10s.	74

(1) Amounts from M. D. Gordon, "The Collection of Ship-Money in the Reign of Charles I", *T.R.H.S.*, ser. 3, vol. iv (1910), p. 162. Percentages calculated independently. Professor T. G. Barnes (*op. cit.*, p. 207) has checked Miss Gordon's figures for Somerset against the accounts in P.R.O. and has found no discrepancies.

(2) Note the transference in 1637 of £30 assessment from Pembrokeshire to Carmarthenshire.

APPENDIX B

DISTRIBUTION BY DECADES OF STUDENTS AT OXFORD, 1540-1640[1]

	GENTRY	PLEBS.	CLER. FIL.	INDE-TERMINATE	TOTAL
1540-1550				2	2
1551-1560				5	5
1561-1570	3			6	9
1571-1580	4	12	2	5	23
1581-1590	30	21	3	1	55
1591-1600	39	19	5	5	68
1601-1610	17	29	8	2	56
1611-1620	8	17	6	2	33
1621-1630	16	26	9	1	52
1631-1640	15	19	6		40
Total	132	143	39	29	343

APPENDIX C

DISTRIBUTION OF STUDENTS AT THE INNS OF COURT, 1540-1640[1]

	INNER TEMPLE	MIDDLE TEMPLE	GRAYS INN	LINCOLNS INN	TOTAL
1541-1550	2				2
1551-1560	2				2
1561-1570	1	1			2
1571-1580	1	1	1		3
1581-1590	4	2	2	1	9
1591-1600	3	5		6	14
1601-1610	1	14	2	5	22
1611-1620	5	6	3	1	15
1621-1630	1	2	6	2	11
1631-1640	4	3	12	3	22
Total	24	34	26	18	102

[1] For sources, *vide supra*, p.194, note 6. For important criticism of these sources, and some suggestions for adjusting statistics compiled from them, *vide* L Stone, "The Educational Revolution in England, 1560-1640", *Past and Present*, no. 28 (1964), pp. 41-80.

Bibliography

1. MANUSCRIPT SOURCES.

(a). BRITISH MUSEUM, CARMARTHEN RECORD OFFICE, LAMBETH PALACE LIBRARY, PUBLIC RECORD OFFICE, SOMERSET HOUSE. The classes of manuscripts kept in these repositories to which reference has been made are to be found in the table of Abbreviations.

(b). NATIONAL LIBRARY OF WALES. Material from the following collections of deeds and documents has been incorporated into this study:

Brawdy, Bronwydd, Crosswood, Cwmgwili, Derwydd, Dynevor, Eaton Evans and Williams, Haverfordwest Corporation Records, Llanstephan Manuscripts (particularly nos. 120, 133, 145), Llwyngwair, Maesgwynne, Maesnewydd, Milborne, Muddlescombe, Orielton, Poyston, Probate Records (Diocese of St. David's), Probyn, Slebech.

2. PRINTED WORKS.

(a). DOCUMENTS AND REGISTERS. (Volumes to which reference has been made in abbreviated form are included in the table of Abbreviations.)

Anon., *The Order and Manner of the Sitting of the Lords and . . . also the names of the . . . House of Commons*, London, 1628.

Birch, T., *Memoirs of the Reign of Queen Elizabeth from the year 1581 till her death . . .* , 2 vols., London, 1754.

Cobbett's Parliamentary History of England, vol. ii (1625-1642), London, 1807.

Dwnn, Lewis, *Heraldic Visitations of Wales and Monmouthshire*, ed. S. R. Meyrick, 2 vols., Llandovery, 1846.

Edwards, I. ab Owen, *A Catalogue of Star Chamber Proceedings relating to Wales* (University of Wales: Board of Celtic Studies, History and Law Series, no. 1), Cardiff, 1929.

Elton, G. R., *The Tudor Constitution: Documents and Commentary*, Cambridge, 1960.

Flenley, R., *A Calendar of the Register of the Queen's Majesty's Council in the Dominion and Principality of Wales and the Marches of the same* (Cymmrodorion Record Series, no. 8), London, 1916.

Foster, J., *Alumni Oxonienses . . .*, Early Series (1500-1714), 4 vols., Oxford, 1891.

Id., *Index Ecclesiasticus*, Oxford, 1890.

Id., *Register of Admissions to Gray's Inn, 1581-1889*, London, 1889.

Hargrave, F. (ed.), *State Trials . . .* , vol. ii, London, 1776.

Jones, E. G., *Exchequer Proceedings (Equity) concerning Wales, Henry VIII to Elizabeth* (University of Wales: Board of Celtic Studies, History and Law Series, no. 4), Cardiff, 1939.

Jones, T. I. J., *Exchequer Proceedings concerning Wales in tempore James I* (University of Wales: Board of Celtic Studies, History and Law Series, no. 15), Cardiff, 1955.

Lewis, E. A., *An Inventory of Early Chancery Proceedings concerning Wales* (University of Wales: Board of Celtic Studies, History and Law Series, no. 3), Cardiff, 1937.

Id., *The Welsh Port Books, 1550-1603* (Cymmrodorion Record Series, no. 12), London, 1927.

Id., and Davies, J. C., *Records of the Court of Augmentations relating to Wales and Monmouthshire* (University of Wales: Board of Celtic Studies, History and Law Series, no. 13), Cardiff, 1954.

Lloyd, D. M. and E. M., *A Book of Wales*, London, 1953.

Owen, E., *A Catalogue of the Manuscripts relating to Wales in the British Museum* (Cymmrodorion Record Series, no. 4), 4 vols., London, 1900-1922.

Owen, H., *A Calendar of the Public Records relating to Pembrokeshire* (Cymmrodorion Record Series, no. 7), 3 vols., London, 1914-1918.

Peacock, E., *The Army Lists of the Roundheads and Cavaliers*, London, 1874.

Pierce, T. Jones, *Clenennau Letters and Papers in the Brogyntyn Collection*, Aberystwyth, 1947.

Records of the Honourable Society of Lincoln's Inn: Admissions (1429-1893), 2 vols., London, 1896.

Register of Admissions to the Honourable Society of the Middle Temple, vol. i (1501-1781), London, 1949.

Rushworth, J., *Historical Collections of Private Passages of State*, 4 parts in 7 vols., London, 1659-1701.

Students admitted to the Inner Temple, 1547-1560, London, 1887.

Venn, John and J. A., *Alumni Cantabrigienses*, part i (to 1751), Cambridge, 1922.

Wood, Anthony à, *Athenae Oxonienses*, 2 vols., London, 1691.

(b). CONTEMPORARY WRITINGS. (The dates of editions only once referred to are included in the appropriate footnotes.)

Camden, W., *Britannia* (1607 edition translated, with "Additions", by Richard Gough), 3 vols, London, 1789.

Coke, Sir Edward, *A Commentary upon Littleton* (15th. edition by F. Hargrave and C. Butler), London, 1794.

Id., *The Fourth Part of the Institutes of the Laws of England: Concerning the Jurisdiction of Courts*, London, 1644.

Doderidge, Sir John, *The History of the Ancient and Modern Estate of the Principality of Wales*, London, 1630.

Harrington, James, *The Commonwealth of Oceana*, ed. H. Morley, London, 1887.

Harrison, W., *A Description of England*, ed. L. Withington, London, n.d.

Hughes, G. H. (ed.), *Rhagymadroddion, 1547-1659*, Cardiff, 1951.

Lambarde, William, *Eirenarcha, or the Office of Justices of Peace*, London, 1602.

Leland, John, *The Itinerary in Wales in or about the years 1536-1539*, ed. L. Toulmin Smith, London, 1906.

Morley, H. (ed.), *Ireland under Elizabeth and James I*, London, 1890.

Ogilby, John, *Britannia*, London, 1675.

Owen, George, *The Description of Penbrokshire*, ed. Henry Owen (Cymmrodorion Record Series, no. 1), 4 vols., London, 1902-1936.

Id., *The Taylors Cussion* (facsimile, ed. E. M. Pritchard), London, 1906.

Perrot, Sir James, *The Chronicle of Ireland, 1584-1608*, ed. Herbert Wood, Dublin, 1933.

Phaer, Thomas, "Anglia Walliae" (1562-1563), printed in *Arch. Camb.*, ser. 6, vol. xi (1911), pp. 421-432.

Smith, Sir Thomas, *De Republica Anglorum*, ed. L. Alston, Cambridge, 1906.

Townshend, Heywood, *Historical Collections: an Exact Account of the Proceedings of the four last Parliaments of Queen Elizabeth*, London, 1680.

Vaughan, William, *The Golden Fleece*, London, 1626.

Id., *The Golden-grove*, London, 1608.

Willson, D. H. (ed.), *The Parliamentary Diary of Robert Bowyer, 1606-1607*, Minneapolis, 1931.

(c). SECONDARY WORKS. (Full references to articles in periodicals, to unpublished theses, and, in most instances, to works forming volumes in series, are given in the footnotes and need not be repeated. This bibliographical list is limited to books specifically mentioned in the footnotes, with one or two additions. A review of all the literature consulted would be impracticable here. *The Bibliography of the History of Wales* (2nd edition, Cardiff, 1962), and the lists of "Articles relating to the History of Wales" published in *The Welsh History Review*, are indispensable guides to further inquiry.)

Allen, J., *Notes on the Sheriffs of Pembrokeshire*, Tenby, 1900.

Barnes, T. G., *Somerset, 1625-1640: a County's Government during the "Personal Rule"*, London, 1961.

Beales, A. C. F., *Education under Penalty: English Catholic Education from the Reformation to the fall of James II, 1547-1689*, London, 1963.

Beard, C. A., *The Office of Justice of the Peace in England in its Origin and Development*, New York, 1904.

Bell, H. E., *An Introduction to the History of the Court of Wards and Liveries*, Cambridge, 1953.

Brailsford, H. N., *The Levellers and the English Revolution*, London, 1961.

Brunton, D., and Pennington, D. H., *Members of the Long Parliament*, London, 1954.

Campbell, Lily B. (ed.), *The Mirror for Magistrates*, New York, 1960.

Charlton, K., *Education in Renaissance England*, London, 1965.

Cokayne, G. E., *The Complete Baronetage*, London, 1900.

Collingwood, R. G., *The Idea of History*, Oxford, 1946.

Collinson, P., *The Elizabethan Puritan Movement*, London, 1967.

Cruickshank, C. G., *Elizabeth's Army*, 2nd edition, Oxford, 1966.

Curtis, M. H., *Oxford and Cambridge in Transition, 1558-1642*, Oxford, 1959.

Davies, D. J., *The Economic History of South Wales prior to 1800*, Cardiff, 1933.

Dawson, J. P., *A History of Lay Judges*, Cambridge (Mass.), 1960.

Devereux, W. B., *Lives of the Devereux Earls of Essex*, 2 vols., London, 1853.

Digby, Kenelm, *An Introduction to the History of the Law of Real Property*, 5th edition, London, 1897.

Dodd, A. H., *Studies in Stuart Wales*, Cardiff, 1953.

Elton, G. R., *Star Chamber Stories*, London, 1958.

Finch, M. E., *The Wealth of Five Northamptonshire Families* (Northamptonshire Record Society Publications, vol. 19), Lamport, 1956.

Fisher, H. A. L. (ed.), *Collected Papers of F. W. Maitland*, 2 vols., Cambridge, 1911.

Flatrès, P., *Géographie Rurale de quatre contrées Celtiques: Irlande, Galles, Cornwall et Man*, Rennes, 1957.

Foxe, John, *The Acts and Monuments*, vol. vii, London, 1847.

Fussell, G. E., *The Old English Farming Books from Fitzherbert to Tull, 1523 to 1730*, London, 1947.

Gonner, E. C. K., *Common Land and Inclosure*, London, 1912.

Hardy, E. G., *Jesus College, Oxford*, London, 1899.

Harrison, G. B., *The Life and Death of Robert Devereux Earl of Essex*, London, 1937.

Hart, A. Tindal, *The Country Clergy, 1558-1660*, London, 1958.

Hexter, J. H., *Reappraisals in History*, London, 1961.

Hill, J. E. Christopher, *Economic Problems of the Church: from Archbishop Whitgift to the Long Parliament*, Oxford, 1956.

Id., *Intellectual Origins of the English Revolution*, Oxford, 1965.

Id., *Puritanism and Revolution*, London, 1958.

Hoggart, R., *The Uses of Literacy*, London, 1957.

Holdsworth, W. S., *A History of English Law*, vol. iv, London, 1924.

Howells, B. E., "Pembrokeshire Farming, *circa* 1580-1620", *N.L.W. Journal*, vol. ix (1955-1956), pp.239 et seq., 313 et seq., 413 et seq.

Hurstfield, J., *The Queen's Wards: Wardship and Marriage under Elizabeth I*, London, 1958.

Johnson, F. R., *Astronomical Thought in Renaissance England: a Study of English scientific writings from 1500 to 1645*, Baltimore, 1937.

Jones, E. G., *Cymru a'r Hen Ffydd*, Cardiff, 1951.

Jones, T. I. J., "A Study of Rents and Fines in South Wales in the Sixteenth and Seventeenth Centuries", *Harlech Studies* (ed. B. B. Thomas), Cardiff, 1938.

Jowitt, Earl, *The Dictionary of English Law*, 2 vols., London, 1959.

Keeler, M. F., *The Long Parliament, 1640-1641*, Philadelphia, 1954.

Kelso, R., *The Doctrine of the English Gentleman in the Sixteenth Century*, Illinois, 1929.

Knight, L. S., *Welsh Independent Grammar Schools to 1600*, Newtown, 1926.

Knowles, D., *The Religious Orders in England*, vol. iii (*The Tudor Age*), Cambridge, 1959.

Laws, E., *The History of Little England beyond Wales*, London, 1888.

Leach, A. L., *The History of the Civil War, 1642-1649, in Pembrokeshire and on its Borders*, London, 1937.

Lloyd, Sir J. E. (ed.), *A History of Carmarthenshire*, 2 vols., 1935-1939.

Id., *A History of Wales from the earliest times to the Edwardian Conquest*, 2 vols., London, 1911.

Mallet, C. E., *A History of the University of Oxford*, vol. ii (*The Sixteenth and Seventeenth Centuries*), London, 1924.

Mathew, David, *The Celtic Peoples and Renaissance Europe*, London, 1933

Mendenhall, T. C., *The Shrewsbury Drapers and the Welsh Wool Trade in the XVI and XVII Centuries*, London, 1953.

Mitchell, W. M., *The Rise of the Revolutionary Party in the English House of Commons, 1603-1629*, New York, 1957.

Moir, T. L., *The Addled Parliament of 1614*, Oxford, 1958.

Mollat, M. (ed.), *Les Sources de l'Histoire Maritime en Europe du Moyen Age au XVIIIe siècle*, Paris, 1962.

Neale, J. E., *Elizabeth I and her Parliaments*, 2 vols., London, 1953-1957.

Id., *The Elizabethan House of Commons*, London, 1949.

Owen, G. Dyfnallt, *Elizabethan Wales: The Social Scene*, Cardiff, 1962.

Parry, Thomas, *Hanes Llenyddiaeth Gymraeg hyd 1900*, Cardiff, 1944.

Phillips, J., *The History of Pembrokeshire*, London, 1909.

Phillips, J. R., *The Memoirs of the Civil War in Wales and the Marches*, 2 vols., London, 1874.

Putnam, B. H., *Proceedings before the Justices of the Peace in the Fourteenth and Fifteenth Centuries*, London, 1938.

Ramsbotham, R. L. (ed.), *Coote's Treatise on the Law of Mortgages*, 9th edition, London, 1927.

Read, Conyers, *Mr. Secretary Cecil and Queen Elizabeth*, London, 1954.

Rees, Sir J. F., *Studies in Welsh History*, 2nd edition, Cardiff, 1965.

Rees, William, *South Wales and the March, 1284-1415: a Social and Agrarian Study*, Oxford, 1924.

Richards, T., *Cymru a'r Uchel Gomisiwn, 1633-1640*, Liverpool, 1930.

Id., *A History of the Puritan Movement in Wales, 1639-1653*, London, 1920.

Roderick, A. J. (ed.), *Wales through the Ages*, vol. ii, London, 1960.

Rowse, A. L., *The England of Elizabeth*, London, 1950.

Id., *The Expansion of Elizabethan England*, London, 1955.

Id., *Tudor Cornwall*, London, 1941.

Shillington, V. M., and Chapman, A. B. W., *The Commercial Relations of England and Portugal*, London, n.d.

Spurrell, W., *Carmarthen and its Neighbourhood*, Carmarthen, 1879.

Stebbing, W., *Sir Walter Ralegh*, Oxford, 1899.

Stewart-Brown, R., *The Serjeants of the Peace in Medieval England and Wales*, Manchester, 1936.

Stone, L., "The Anatomy of the Elizabethan Aristocracy", *Econ. H.R.*, vol. xviii (1948), pp. 1-53.

Id., *The Crisis of the Aristocracy, 1558-1641*, Oxford, 1965.

Id., "The Elizabethan Aristocracy: A Restatement", *Econ. H.R.*, ser. 2, vol. iv (1952), pp. 302-321.

Id., *Social Change and Revolution in England, 1540-1640*, London, 1965.

Tawney, R. H., *The Agrarian Problem in the Sixteenth Century*, London, 1912.

Id., "The Rise of the Gentry, 1558-1640", *Econ. H. R.*, vol. xi (1941), pp.1-38.

Id., "The Rise of the Gentry: a Postscript", *Econ. H. R.*, ser. 2, vol. vii (1954), pp.91-97.

Taylor, E. G. R., *Tudor Geography, 1485-1583*, London, 1930.

Thomas, B. B., *Braslun o Hanes Economaidd Cymru*, Cardiff, 1941.

Thompson, E. P., *The Making of the English Working Class*, London, 1963.

Tout, T. F., *Collected Papers*, 2 vols., Manchester, 1932-1934.

Trevor-Roper, H. R., "The Elizabethan Aristocracy: An Anatomy Anatomised", *Econ. H. R.*, ser. 2, vol. iii (1951), pp.279-298.

Id., *The Gentry, 1540-1640*, Economic History Review Supplement, 1 (1953).

Trimble, W. R., *The Catholic Laity in Elizabethan England, 1558-1603*, Cambridge (Mass.), 1964.

Trow-Smith, R., *English Husbandry*, London, 1951.

Turner, R. W., *The Equity of Redemption*, Cambridge, 1931.

Usher, R. G., *The Rise and Fall of the High Commission*, Oxford, 1913.

Van Bath, B. H. Slicher, *The Agrarian History of Western Europe, A.D. 500-1850*, London, 1963.

Wagner, A. R., *English Genealogy*, Oxford, 1960.

Watson, Foster, *The English Grammar Schools to 1660: their curriculum and practice*, Cambridge, 1908.

Willan, T. S., *The English Coasting Trade, 1600-1750*, Manchester, 1938.

Id., *Studies in Elizabethan Foreign Trade*, Manchester, 1959.

Willcox, W. B., *Gloucestershire: a Study in Local Government, 1590-1640*, New Haven (Conn.), 1940.

Williams, David, *A History of Modern Wales*, London, 1950.

Williams, Glanmor, *Bywyd ac Amserau'r Esgob Richard Davies*, Cardiff, 1953.

Id., *Dadeni, Diwygiad a Diwylliant Cymru*, Cardiff, 1964.

Id., *The Welsh Church from Conquest to Reformation*, Cardiff, 1962.

Williams, Jonathan, *A History of Radnorshire*, Brecon, 1905.

Williams, Penry, *The Council in the Marches of Wales under Elizabeth I*, Cardiff, 1959.

Williams, W. Ogwen, *Calendar of the Caernarvonshire Quarter Sessions Records*, vol. i (1541-1558), Caernarvon, 1956.

Williams, W. R., *The Parliamentary History of Wales, 1536-1895*, Brecon, 1895.

Willis, Browne, *Notitia Parliamentaria*, 3 vols., London, 1716-1750.

Wilson, C., *England's Apprenticeship, 1603-1763*, London, 1965.

Index

NOTE. (a) *Personal names* have been modernised and made uniform throughout. Titles (gent., esq., *etc.*) are given as found in contemporary records, with the highest recorded rank favoured in cases of variation; otherwise, no such descriptions have been attempted. Members of families are grouped together in order of generation.

(b) *Place-names* have been made uniform throughout, and modernised by reference to B. G. Charles, *Non-Celtic Place-Names in Wales* (London, 1938), and Elwyn Davies (ed.), *Rhestr o Enwau Lleoedd* (Cardiff, 2nd edition, 1958). In a few doubtful cases contemporary forms have been given in the text with suggested modern equivalents in the Index. Places mentioned in the text are either shown on the Map or associated in the Index with a parish or district pinpointed there; lordships, commotes, granges, *etc.*, not there represented are described as such in the Index. Cross-references are given to all named persons associated with each place listed.
?=possible but uncertain identification.

Okeley, George, alderman, of Carmarthen, 124
Olde, John, cleric, 175(6)
Orielton, Hundleton, Pembs., *vide* Owen, Wyrriott
Owen, family, of Henllys, 43, 131
——, William, esq., of Cemais, 23, 43, 73, 131(5), 177(2)
——, George, esq., 14, 15, 23, 24, 28, 29, 43, 53, 55-57, 60, 67, 70, 71, 73, 76,
        78-80, 81(2) (4), 82, 85, 99, 120(5), 132, 133(4), 135, 137(9),
        140, 148-149, 160, 169, 182-183, 196, 201, 202, 204
——, Elizabeth, *née* Phillips, 99
——, Alban, esq., 46, 140
——, Evan, esq., 166(7), 196
——, George, York Herald, *etc.*, 196
Owen, Sir Hugh, of Orielton, 87, 155(5)
——, Sir Hugh, 111, 123, 125(5), 128
Owen, William, ensign, ? of Orielton, 210
Owen, G. D., historian, 32, 33
Owen, Leonard, historian, 53
Oxford, University of, 144, 194-197, 216

PADDY, George, of Leith, 165
Palatinate, Electorate of the Rhine, 106
Palmer, John, merchant of Laugharne, 88
Palmer, John, yeoman, of Laugharne, 73
Palmer, John, gent., of Tenby, 88
Papacy, the, 106, 110
Parckhurst, Robert, of London, 46
Parkington, *alias* Packington, John, Justice of Assize, south-east Wales circuit, 33
Parliament, 25, 93-112, 118, 121, 123-128, 169, 170, 183, 193(3), 209, 211
——, members of, 16, 41, 93-112, 116, 169, 204
Parry, David, esq., of Cards., 197
Parry, David William, esq., of Carms., 117(2)
Parry, Richard, gent., of Llanfallteg, 193
Parry, Thomas, of Carmarthen, 199
Parry, Thomas, historian of literature, 200
Paterchurch, Pembroke, *vide* Adams
patronage, 111-112, 115-118, 130-133, 138, 192(5), 200-205, 207-208
——, ecclesiastical, *vide* impropriations
Pembroke, *alias* Penfro, 12-15, 43, 90, 94, 97(3), 101, 104, 109, 118(2), 152, 160(4),
        162, 204; *vide* Jessoppe, Phillip, Powell, Poyer, William,
        Wilson
——, county of, *passim*
——, Earls of, *vide* Herbert
——, sheriff of (1630), *vide* Wogan
Penally, Pembs., 59, 64
Penardd, grange of, Cards., 37, 41
Penbre, Carms., 75, 185; *vide* Vaughan
Pencothi, grange of, Carms., 33
Penfro, *vide* Pembroke

Rice (Rhys) ap Griffith, Sir, of Dynevor, 26, 35, 36, 38, 113
——, Griffith, esq., 132-133, 186, 199(3)
——, Sir Walter, 45, 66, 101, 138
——, Henry, esq., 45, 62
Richard, Philip Fychan ap Philip, of Bayvil, 43
Richards, Thomas, historian, 194
Robert Fynglwyd, poet, 201
Robeston (Robeston Wathen), Pembs., 24(3), 59, 69, 71, 76, 185; vide Bowen
Roch, Pembs., vide Morgan, Walter
Rochelle, France, 159
Rosemarket, Pembs., 39, 74
Rowghane, Denis, cleric, of Ireland, 131(6)
Rowse, A. L., historian, 54
Rudd, Anthony, Bishop of St. David's, 184, 188
——, Sir Richard, alias Rice, of Aberglasney, 18(6), 124
Rudhale, William, of co. Hereford, 95(4)
Rushmoor, Carms., vide Phillips
Rutland, county of, 19

SACKVILLE, Sir Richard, Chancellor of Augmentations, 34
Sackville, Thomas, M.P. for Aylesbury, co. Buckingham, 95
Sackville, William, esq., of the Household, 34
St. Asaph, diocese of, 158
St. Botolph's, nr. Milford Haven, 35
St. Bride's, Pembs., 25, 82; vide Laugharne
St. Clears, Carms,, 64
St. David's, Pembs., archdeacon of, vide Pratt
——————, Bishops of, vide Barlow, Davies, Ferrar, Field, Middleton, Rudd
——————, cathedral of, 175
——————, chancellors of, vide Gwynne, Lloyd
——————, chantor of, 161; vide Lloyd
—————— Day, 175
——————, diocese of, 53, 158, 174-176, 178-183
——————, parish of, 183
——————, precentor of, vide Young
St. Dogmael's, Pembs., vide David, Sandhowe
St. Edward's Hall, Oxford, 38(10)
St. Florence, Pembs., 64; vide Gibbon
St. George the Martyr, chapel of, Berkshire, 32
St. Issell's, Pembs., vide Vaughan
St. Ives, Cornwall, 86
St. John's College, Oxford, 196
St. John of Jerusalem, Commandery of (Knights Hospitallers), 34, 35
St. Martin of Haverford, 38
St. Paul's, London, 161(2)
St. Peter's, Carmarthen, 124
Salisbury, Earl of, vide Cecil
Salop, county of, vide Shropshire

Printed in Great Britain
by
Crown Printers (Jones and Son), Morriston, Swansea.